MW01295697

Doing Disability Justice

DOING DISABILITY JUSTICE

75 Years of Family Advocacy

Larry A. Jones

Published 2010 by www.lulu.com

Copyright 2010 by Larry A. Jones

ISBN 978-0-557-55238-2

An earlier version of parts of this book was privately published in 1987 by The Association for Retarded Citizens of Washington under the title *Doing Justice: A History of the Association for Retarded Citizens of Washington.*

In memory of Wendy

TABLE OF CONTENTS

ACKNOWLEDGEMENTS

The author is indebted to the following persons and organizations, among others, for providing valuable information and assistance.

Individuals. Special thanks are due to Phyllis A. Barnes, who assisted in the earlier version of this book, and whose loyal and careful attention to detail led to a much improved text. Second, my late uncle Harley Jones, whose careful reading of the text led to many improvements. I owe another special debt to former Washington Secretary of State Ralph Munro for his work commissioning interviews of early leaders in the field, as part of his efforts to preserve the general history of the state, along with his special interest in persons with developmental disabilities. I also thank the following persons, several of them now deceased and a few of them my antagonists in battles about whether to institutionalize persons with intellectual disabilities: Margaret (Oakley) Alder; W. E. Auerswald; Charlene Behrns; Elizabeth Boggs; Evelyn Chapman; H. N. Clifton; John Delanty; Bean Driscoll; Mrs. Arthur Dunn; Gunnar Dybwad; Sue Elliott; Richard E. Fowler; Erik Froberg; Ila Gangnes; Grace and Jim Gould; Frank Hamilton; Patricia Hamilton; Van R. Hinkle; Kevin Isherwood; Allan Jones; Robert Leavitt; Cecile Lindquist; Leopold Lippman; Kathleen (Oakley) Maestri; Anna Magnuson; Gladys Mandley; Susan McKeehan; James McClurg; Judith Moore; Mrs. E. H. Riviere; June Robinson; Alan Sampson; R.C. Scheerenberger; Trudy Schmidt; Orlando and Jean Thomas;

Joseph Weingold; Colleen Wieck; and Katharyn Wright. In preparing this version, in addition to those listed above, I am indebted to Charlie Lakin, and David Braddock for their kind cooperation. Thanks to Susan D. Jones and Melanie Shaffer for editorial assistance, Erin M. Page for assistance in publication, and Paul Songer for overcoming technical obstacles.

Organizations. Thanks are due to the Arcs of Clark County, King County, Kitsap County, Pierce County, Snohomish County, and Spokane County, Washington, of Cuyahoga County, Ohio, and of the U.S.; the American Association on Intellectual and Developmental Disabilities; the Boyer Children's Clinic and Pre-school; Hoquiam School District; Lakeland Village; New York State Association for Retarded Children; Rainier School; United Blind of Washington State; United Cerebral Palsy of Seattle-King County; Washington Education Association. Special mention is due for the large quantity of materials posted online by the Minnesota Governor's Council on Developmental Disabilities, particularly focused on that state's history.

Libraries and Archives. The Washington State Library, Olympia; the Washington State Archives, Olympia; Seattle Public Library; Suzzalo Library and the Archives of the University of Washington, Seattle; Seattle School District Archives; Northwest Museum of Arts and Culture, Spokane; Spokane Public Library; the Tacoma Public Library for the photo of "chuck wagon" volunteers in the 1950s; the archives of the Coleman Institute for Cognitive Disabilities, the University of Colorado; the Archives of Northwest history at Washington State University, Pullman, and the Braddock Library on Disability, Coleman Institute, University of Colorado.

A NOTE ON NAMES AND LABELS

A popular poster in the disability rights movement in the late 1970s declared "Labels Jars, Not People!" But that understandable sentiment cannot be all-encompassing when one writes a history of past practices and ideas. Here are some names used in this history with suggestive, but not definitive, dates, since there are many variations.

NAMES USED FOR PERSONS WITH THE DISABILITY

1920	Feeble-minded
1930	Mentally deficient
1940	Mentally retarded
1970	Developmentally disabled
1975	People with developmental disabilities
2005	People with intellectual disabilities

NAMES OF THE STATE AND NATIONAL ORGANIZATIONS

1935	Children's Benevolent League of Washington (CBL)
1952	National Association for Retarded Children (NARC)
1952	Washington Association for Retarded Children (WARC)
1973	National Association for Retarded Citizens

1974	Washington Association for Retarded Citizens
1981	Association for Retarded Citizens of the US
1982	Association for Retarded Citizens of Washington (ARC of Washington, pronounced A-R-C)
1992	The Arc of the United States (pronounced "arc")
1992	The Arc of Washington State

INTRODUCTION

> Americans of all ages, all stations in life, and all types
> of disposition are forever forming associations. There are
> not only commercial and industrial associations in which
> all take part, but others of a thousand different types —
> religious, moral, serious, futile, very general and very
> limited, immensely large and very minute....In every
> case, at the head of any new undertaking, where in
> France you would find the government or in England
> some territorial magnate, in the United States you are
> sure to find an association.
> —Alexis de Tocqueville, *Democracy in America*,
> 1835

It took American families a century after de Tocqueville's famous observation before they began forming organizations to improve the lives of their sons and daughters and of others with intellectual disabilities. The Children's Benevolent League of Washington was the first large association of this type. It played a leading role in the emergence of the national families group, now known as The Arc and formerly as the Association for Retarded Citizens. Through this organization, advocates have won dramatic enhancements in rights and services for the millions of American citizens whose disability is lower intelligence.

If forming organizations in America is like baking apple pie, why did it take so long before these parents first began to organize? Because of the enormous stigma which our society places on diminished cognitive functioning, only a brave few were willing to acknowledge that a family member was affected in the beginning. Indeed, this book might be titled *More Profiles in Courage*, both to convey the obstacles which families had to face and to suggest the connection with John F. Kennedy, who, after prodding from his sister, finally made it clear that there was "mental retardation" even in Camelot.[1] Before the recent era of increased public acceptance, of which the Kennedys were both beneficiaries and promoters, parents faced aspersions of family degeneracy, rejection, and the exclusion of their children from schools, with a cloak of secrecy thrown over it all. Parents finally turned to each other, built an organization, and set about making the changes they wanted for their family members. Although their goals were modest at first, families quickly grew more visionary and devised previously-unimagined support services. Eventually professionals employed in the field began to lead in innovation, so that parents were not the only pathfinders. Today, joined by their sons and daughters, parents remain the advocates, the lobbyists, the interest group, that politicians expect and respect the most.

The times have changed so much that it takes a special effort to do justice to the leaders in the first few decades and their limited visions. Yet there persist themes common to all such family groups, due in part to the nature of disability itself and in part to inherited cultural traditions that tie the parents of 75 years ago to those today.

Justice Demanded from the Beginning

Family advocacy has been mischaracterized as one that evolved from a movement making a claim on public charity into one now motivated by a demand for justice that seeks to enforce the "rights" of persons with developmental disabilities. That is too restrictive. One of the meanings of justice is fairness. It turns out that families made political appeals on the grounds of justice from the 1930s.

It is true that the movement has made fewer direct appeals to charity and more to justice in recent times. In this change The Arc reflects the larger society, in which the demands of racial minorities and of women for justice led advocates for persons with cognitive disabilities to call for analogous rights to recognition, opportunity, and, when needed, support.

The obligation which parents felt (and continue to feel) to do justice is deeply imbedded in our common tradition. As the prophet

Micah put it 2,500 years ago: "What does the Lord require of you? To do justice, to love kindness, and to walk humbly before God." This familiar verse makes doing justice a religious obligation. Such ideas continue to percolate through our culture and motivate the actions of secular, as well as consciously religious, families. But the contemporary idea of justice is not a static theological or philosophical formula; rather, the process of "doing" disability justice implies continuing actions by human beings to bring into being their evolving conceptions of fairness, decency, and wholeness. Thus, it is not simply the earliest ideas which have been superseded. More recent terms have evolved along with the ideas they express. The terms "mainstreaming," "deinstitutionalization" and "normalization" quickly became outmoded. This ongoing national evolution of understanding and practice is revealed throughout the advocacy movement as it developed.

Chapter One portrays the first Washington parents and their attempts to support each other and to improve institutional care for their sons and daughters, while striving to minimize the familial separation which they believed to be necessary to gain access to needed programs.

Chapter Two describes how some parents came to a broader dream of the possibilities and how they forged ahead with plans for a national organization and for education of the public, in spite of the conflict their efforts caused.

Chapter Three tells the story of the glorious decade of the 1950s when children with cognitive disabilities finally came out of the shadows, out of the closet, and gained national official status as a normal part of humanity, acknowledged by celebrities, politicians, and the public.

In **Chapter Four** one of the central topics in mental retardation policy is addressed: institutions and how some families fought to advance them and to control them.

Chapter Five describes the gradual replacement of institutions by special education in local schools, as parents won that right for their children with severe disabilities. The new public acceptance of mental retardation was vigorously promoted by the parent groups, which grew strong and legitimate.

This growth resulted in new alliances with professionals and service providers, who assisted families in constructing that comprehensive system of services which persons with disabilities seemed to need (**Chapter Six**).

During the 1970s the Association for Retarded Citizens again re-calibrated its interests, adopting the ideology of normalization and demanding that persons with mental retardation be accorded equal treatment on the basis of newly-articulated rights (**Chapter Seven**). Younger parent activists again confronted school districts about the treatment of their children, while battling older parents and state officials over the continued existence of segregated programming and facilities. With the achievement of many of its goals and with the decline of new funding and programmatic initiatives during the Reagan years, the family advocacy movement struggled. One major bright spot was the development of self-advocacy by persons with disabilities themselves.

Chapter Eight describes a revitalization of The Arc, in part due to new leaders with a mastery of public grants. It also traces the development of new private sector achievements, particularly welcome in a time of a declining public service system.

Chapter Nine analyzes the Arc in the new millennium, its battles, and note that how it stands today shows striking similarities to where families stood at the beginning.

The **Postscript** makes suggestions about how activists can be more effective by learning from their predecessors.

The past seventy-five years have seen substantial, though incomplete, gains in justice by racial minorities, women, persons with disabilities, and other subordinated populations. One part of the achievements of these groups has been a re-writing of their history, re-told in their own way. In the case of persons with intellectual disabilities, especially those with severe disabilities, the lessons to be learned cannot be gained solely from first person accounts. In order to recover their history, this book expresses the voices of their parents and siblings, united in the association which they shaped to get job done—The Arc.

CHAPTER ONE:
CONSOLATION, CHARITY—AND POLITICS

About five years ago, Mrs. Oakley and I had to go through that terrible ordeal which so many of you have experienced, and I made up my mind at that time that if ever I could do anything to alleviate the heartbreaking strain and mental anguish of any person who was about to part with a loved one, I was going to do it. After two or three visits to the school I became acquainted with a number of the inmates and I began to wonder if there was not something I could do to make life a little brighter for them.

Time and circumstances did not permit my doing anything about it for a long time, but the thought was ever uppermost in my mind. That thought was that an organization of the parents and relatives be formed to promote the welfare and happiness of the inmates by sending them books, magazines, toys, tools and any other articles not furnished by the state.

With these words James F. Oakley began to explain his dream to a group of fellow parents who gathered at the County-City Building in Seattle, Washington, on October 21, 1935. His goals were modest, but when Oakley stood up and reached out to other parents, he helped set in motion events of great importance.

The families he addressed added their hopes to his. Together, they founded the first statewide family organization serving the needs of persons with intellectual disabilities, the Children's Benevolent League (CBL) of Washington. A dozen years later the League became a major contributor to the founding of a national organization, now The Arc of the United States, and which has 800 units and 140,000 members across the country.[2]

Today the Arc has the fifth largest annual revenue of any nonprofit charity in the country, over $3 billion, trailing only the YMCA, United Way, Salvation Army and Catholic Charities.[3]

Over the years the national Arc has promoted the development of organizations of families and others concerned with mental retardation in countries around the world through the International League of Societies for the Mentally Handicapped and its successor organizations.[4] But in the mid-thirties, according to leaders of the International Association for the Scientific Study of Intellectual Disabilities, there was no large group of families advocating for such children anywhere in the world except the Children's Benevolent League. Beginning as a club to offer gifts to children and to provide parent-to-parent support, within months the League became involved in political campaigns and quickly added functions as it grew. Its success as an organization has much to do with the fact that there are now hundreds of parent and consumer disability groups in Washington State alone and innumerable ones across the nation and globe.

What is the meaning and significance of these groups of parents and relatives? How does the reader decide whether all the efforts of the Arc and its members over the years are worthy of praise? That is a big question, but part of the answer is contained in the very first sentence of the very first recorded parental speech ever, when James Oakley said he had once resolved "...if ever I could do anything to alleviate the heartbreaking strain and mental anguish of any person who was about to part with a loved one, I was going to do it." So the first need identified was a parental need.

Why have parents' needs been so integral to the Arc? To begin with, it has always been the case that the birth of a child who clearly will have severe deficiencies dealing with the demands of his or her environment has devastated parental hopes for a healthy child who can meet the norms of society. Many families have found parents organizations can provide that solace, as well as providing information. In an achievement-oriented society like ours, the pressure to successfully compete is at its highest. And in the early days of institutionalization it may have been the best parents,—at least those who tried the hardest to do what professionals said was the best for their children,—who placed their children in institutions. Of course, there will always have been the families who were just "dumping" their children on the state, but there were other parents, who seem to have been common among early Arc parents, who had more noble motives. They made a *sacrifice* when they chose to institutionalize their child because they were told and came to believe that was best for their son or daughter. That painful sacrifice cried out to be acknowledged, a need that was supplied by the other parents in the Arc. Although implicit in Oakley's dream to help parents by helping their children and others at the Custodial School, it was not long before parent leaders like Newland Reilly explicitly stated that giving parents work to be done was the way to overcome the feeling of being utterly crushed. For the first fifteen years of parent organizations, as Alan Sampson and other early national parent leaders recognized, it is not too much to say that the main motive power energizing the Arc was to fight the assertion commonly encountered in the mouths of physicians, "There is nothing that can be done for your child." Families learned that there were important things they could do and often healed themselves in the process.

From the beginning, therefore, the Arc has been a self-help organization for parents. In the 1970s self-advocacy was added when Washingtonians quickly followed the lead of People First in Oregon, the first advocacy organization of persons with intellectual disabilities themselves, and organized a similar group. Often the contrast was between "self-advocate" persons with disabilities versus the actual or implied control of those parents who wished to exercise too much control over their children. Now, after the experience of a generation of parents and others committed to self-advocacy, it has become apparent that the Arc has always been a self-advocacy organization, one that addressed parental needs in addition to those of their family members with disabilities.

Vincent Oakley

James and Annie Oakley had seven children. The 1930 census records that their children all could read and write and all attended school – all except Vincent, a son who had Down syndrome. The Seattle Public Schools did not allow children like Vincent to go to school. In about 1930, when he was fourteen years old, Vincent

Oakley was sent by his parents from his family home to live at the State Custodial School (now Lakeland Village Residential Habilitation Center) at Medical Lake near Spokane. It was 300 miles away from home, but it was the only specialized facility, the only public program, for persons with mental retardation in the entire state. "Knowledgeable" persons convinced the Oakley family that sending Vincent there was the right thing to do.

In the summer of 1935 James Oakley, who had been a salesman, was an unemployed laborer, like many others during the Great Depression. He had time on his hands, and in July he began a correspondence with Charles Parker, the superintendent of the State Custodial School about the possibility of forming a parents' group.[5] Parker replied that he thought a "Parents and Relatives Welfare Association" for the state school would indeed be beneficial to all concerned and encouraged Oakley to proceed with his plans.

Locating parents and relatives of the residents at the state school was difficult, due to the school's policy of not revealing names of "inmates." But families Oakley knew supplied him with the names of other parents of state school residents. By the time the final arrangements for an organizing meeting were completed, about forty parents and relatives had been recruited. A Seattle newspaper announced the meeting.[6]

STATE CUSTODIAL SCHOOL FRIENDS WILL
ORGANIZE

For the purpose of organizing a group of citizens who will cooperate with the officials of the State Custodial School for the mentally deficient at Medical Lake, Washington, a meeting will be held at 8 p.m., next Monday, in room 210, County-City Building, Seattle. James F. Oakley, who is taking a leading part in forming the organization, is a member of the Knights of Columbus and C. O. F.[7]

Parents, relatives and others interested in the 1,500 mentally deficient children at Medical Lake School are invited to attend the meeting. Officials of the school, headed by C. A. Parker, superintendent, will be at room 810 County-City Building at 9:30 a.m. next Monday to interview parents and relatives of inmates on any matter regarding the school. Six hundred of the children in the Medical Lake institution are from King County. The institution has fifteen modern buildings on beautifully landscaped grounds.

The object of the organization to be formed here next

8

Monday is to cooperate with officials of the school and
to send toys, books and other little gifts to the children.
The St. Vincent de Paul Salvage Bureau here has contributed a quantity of toys for the children.

The assembled parents were receptive and resolved to band together to help their children and each other. Since the group was so
dependent upon the assistance of the superintendent, they accepted
his decision that the organization would not be allowed to collect
dues from members because this would "violate school policy."

Oakley acknowledged that the organization would need funds
to operate, "since we cannot go along on air," but he felt that the
money problem could be resolved once the organization was established.

Seattle in King county was not the only place that families
were mobilizing. Thirty miles south in Tacoma, Ada Percival, the
founding mother of the organization, was contacted by Superintendent Parker. Ada and Monty Percival had a son Robert, who was a
State Custodial School resident, and they probably attended the first
meeting in Seattle. In addition, Parker seems to have known the
Percivals when he was the principal of Sherman School "experimental branch in opportunity work for subnormal children" in
Tacoma a few years earlier. In any case Ada Percival later contended that Parker was concerned that no follow-up to the October
21st Seattle meeting had been called for some time and asked her to
help out. She rose to the occasion.

On December 9, 1935 at the Olympus Hotel in Tacoma, Mrs.
Percival chaired a meeting, which was attended by Parker, other
state school employees, and a dozen interested parents and friends.
After hearing from several state school employees, the minutes
record that two Tacoma school district teachers added their praise
for the State Custodial School, approving the parental decisions to
institutionalize their children.

Mrs. Mae Williams, a very dear friend and teacher of
slow type children, gave us such a grand talk on why our
children should be in the school at Medical Lake. In her
sweet way any one of us could understand that through
experiences with these children she was talking for their
good.
Mrs. Flagg, another very interested teacher in this type
child, gave us a nice talk on how she found the conditions
of the school at a recent visit there. Everything was very
favorable to her. Mrs. Flagg praised Mr. Parker very

9

highly, not forgetting Mrs. [Alice] Parker who takes the responsibility of our children in his absence.

Superintendent Parker spoke last, sharing his plans for the school. The minutes recorded the parents' impression: "As we see it, he is trying to make it a happy little world of their own."

After discussion, the families decided to organize and appointed a committee to draw up plans. More meetings were held in Seattle and Tacoma in early 1936 with the leaders commuting between the two cities to share ideas, encouragement, and cake. Late hours were the rule, but no one complained. As one theorist of voluntary associations has put it, "History in a democracy is made by those who take the time to go to important committee meetings and stay till the end."[8]

Organizing for Action

Among the questions which the founders of organizations must address are: Who are we? What is our name? What are our goals? Who shall lead our group? How shall the rules for the organization be drawn? What specific projects shall we undertake? and What methods shall we employ to obtain our objectives? The Founding Families resolved all these issues by June 1936.

A Name. James Oakley first proposed the name "The Order of the Purple Cross," on an analogy he saw to Red Cross, White Cross, and Blue Cross health groups. He used the "Purple Cross Association" stationery for a few months, imprinted with a founding date of August 11, 1935. The purple cross logo had a circular border inscribed with the motto "For the welfare and happiness of children." This name suggests a vision of the group as essentially one concerned with mental retardation as a medical or health problem. According to Oakley's daughter, the Purple Cross name was rejected primarily as being too Catholic in tone. Other suggestions included Parker's reference to a "Parents and Relatives Welfare Association," while the group in Clark county across the river from Portland, Oregon, referred to it as the "P.T.A." for the Custodial School, as did some Pierce county members.

Finally, a committee presented two names for the group to the Tacoma parents: "Star of Hope" and "Children's Benevolent League." The Pierce county parents chose the latter name, in agreement with the King county parents, and the name was shortly thereafter adopted by the state organization. The absence of any word indicating mental deficiency in all of the names considered probably reflects that sentiment, still strong today, which seeks to avoid the associated stigma. The word "Children" in the name chosen certainly reflected a notion of prolonged dependency associated with disability, since only about one third of Custodial School residents were under 18 years old in 1936. However, a second definition of "child" is son or daughter, and some of the residents of the school were certainly the children of the founders.

Incorporation and election of officers. Families from across the state met at the State Custodial School on April 4, 1936, and elected temporary state officers. James Oakley, who had declined formal leadership from the beginning, was not among them. The Seattle group's president G.N. Johnson was elected temporary leader, and Mrs. E.G. Auerswald was elected temporary state secretary. Charles Clark, E.G. Auerswald, Monty Percival, and Ray Hatfield drew up the by-laws. They told each Unit to review the by-laws, adopt or reject them, and return them to the state committee.[5]

On April 15, 1936, the Articles of Incorporation were signed in Tacoma by six men, with equal representation of the Seattle and Tacoma groups. They were Ray Hatfield, Otto Nelson, and Monty Percival of Tacoma, and Charles L. Clark, E.G. Auerswald, and G.N. Johnson, Sr., of Seattle. The papers, filed on May 29, provided for a board of trustees, with a president, vice president and secretary-treasurer elected annually by the board. The first officers of the organization were Monty Percival, a prosperous automobile garage owner, President; Charles L. Clark, unemployed, Vice President; and E.G. Auerswald, an accountant who the same year opened Seattle's premiere business college, Secretary-Treasurer.

Goals. The hopes expressed by James Oakley at the first meeting in October 1935 had been two-fold: parent-to-parent support for those undergoing the trauma of institutionalizing their sons and daughters, and improvements in the standard of living for the Custodial School residents. Six months later the founders reported their goals in Article III of the incorporation papers:

> The object and purpose of this association shall be to arouse public interest in all mentally and physically handicapped individuals in the State of Washington and the raising of the standard of care which they receive.

"All mentally and physically handicapped individuals" is a broad phrase, which welcomed parents whose resident child might have cerebral palsy or epilepsy, and not mental retardation. "Arousing public interest" suggests a willingness to come out of the closet and honestly admit the problem facing one's family—fifteen years

11

before parents are commonly supposed by scholars to have been so courageous, as we shall see.

Presumably reducing the associated stigma by creating more public understanding would make it easier for parents to deal with the unwelcome fact in their lives, but that is the only way in which the original organizational goals address the issue of parent-to-parent support. James Oakley had focused on helping parents through the trauma of institutionalization. Today, on the other hand, support is often focused especially on parents at the moment of diagnosis ("new parents"), although it may continue for years thereafter as families come to cope with transitions.

Projects and Methods. Wolf Wolfensberger, who played an important role in the national developmental disability movement in the 1970s, argued that there are three historical stages in the evolution of parent groups.[10] First, parents directly *provide* services for their devalued daughters and sons, since no one else is willing to do so. Second, parents try to *obtain* public funds for services, thus relieving themselves of the continuing, often crushing, responsibility for directly providing most services. Third, when the goal of the second stage has been significantly achieved, parent groups begin to *monitor* the quality of the services provided. How do the activities undertaken by the League in its first year fit Wolfensberger's framework?

Families collected toys, a direct service, from the very beginning. It was suggested at one meeting that each unit should have a committee assigned the task of finding merchants and producers who would donate their surplus to the school. In addition, Superintendent Parker urged units to adopt "orphan" children at the custodial school. If a unit did choose to adopt a child, the unit would be responsible for supplying the child with clothing, gifts and Christmas boxes, and for writing the child "cheerful letters from time to time."[11] CBL units immediately took up the task of being surrogate parents for at least some of those "forgotten" by their families. (Amazingly, at Fernald School, a nationally-famous institution in Massachusetts, it took until 1961 for the administration to begin a substitute parents program.[12])

However, some early CBL activities involved elements of Wolfensberger's later stages. For example, the custodial school's location in the northeastern corner of Washington State was inconvenient for the large majority of families who lived on the west side of the Cascade Mountains, especially for those "of little means." Thus, the CBL adopted as its next major objective the construction of a second west side state school. The public announcement was made at the first state convention, which was held in Yakima on June 27, 1936.[13]

The fifty delegates listened to a concert by the "boys and girls" of the State Custodial School marching band, who were dressed "in fresh gay blue and white uniforms."[14] After the concert, the delegates assembled in the Chamber of Commerce Building and adopted the platform. Delegates assembled there represented units in Seattle, Tacoma, and Spokane, as well as in the towns of Colfax, Walla Walla, Yakima, Aberdeen, Wenatchee and Bellingham—scattered across the state, they were truly statewide.

At the October 1935 organizing meeting months earlier, James Oakley had suggested that west side parents charter buses to travel from the Puget Sound area to the school and that they arrange for motion pictures of the residents to share with families unable to afford the trip. Now that other Western Washington families had become involved, and the potential power of united parents was better understood, the West Side families decided that they would have their own school, which the CBL would fight for. If the children had to live away from home, at least they would be closer to home. More families could visit more often.

Who Lived at the Custodial School?

We know that the new organization focused on the welfare of the sons and daughters of the concerned parents, but what else do we know about the "inmates" of the State Custodial School? The fact that a marching band could perform demonstrates that they had higher skills than might be imagined when thinking of today's residents.[15] In 1930 40% of the residents could read and write. Eighteen of the 468 girls and women were married.[16]

As it happens, that very year a parent had complained about a son being sent home from the school without his crutches and the Walla Walla county prosecutor asked the state for permission to send its own county public health nurse to do a formal investigation of conditions there. She reported:

> Inmates of this institution are segregated in separate buildings according to type of case, such as morons, criminally inclined, feebleminded, hopeless idiots, etc. Separate buildings are provided for boys and girls, or men and women.
>
> In the first building the higher type of cases are cared for. Instruction in reading is given in the recreations

13

room, a pleasant, well ventilated, well heated room. A dormitory with clean white beds (single) clothes closets, showers, etc., in this building, as in all others. The Christensen and Gregg boys were classed in this first group.

Older boys are taught gardening etc. The girls learn sewing and various housekeeping duties, and assist with these duties about the institution.

A hospital & drug room are provided for the ill. The ward was full of patients. Two doctors are provided to give medical care. 30 teachers are employed, or so the Dr. told us.

There are 1800 inmates in this institution at the present time.

One is impressed with the kindly and sympathetic attitude of all officials and attendants.

The wards, kitchens, dormitories, dining rooms were all spotlessly clean. The patients' clothing was clean, and they seemed healthy and well nourished.

When I asked the doctor about the crutches for the Christensen boy, he said the boy was "getting along without them when he left there."

My impression of the institution is most favorable.
Eva L. Crowell, R.N.
City School Nurse, Walla Walla[17]

Intense Political Action the First Year

CBL members made politics a primary avenue to achieve their aims. In its first year the CBL records show *six* different political actions that the CBL and its leaders were involved in.

In March 1936, some local parent units were involved in politics even before the CBL was officially incorporated. At their local meetings, they distributed petitions for a citizens' proposal, Initiative 101, which would have changed the state institutional superintendent's appointed position.[18] It would have bestowed civil service protection on the superintendent, as well as on a wide range of local, county, and state officials, changing the standard practice in Washington and most other states, which allowed an incoming governor to fire many former officials and replace them with personal friends. Washington has a strong tradition of passing legislation by citizen initiative citizenry, so the measure was no oddity. Nevertheless, this one did not pass, losing about 60% to 40%.

At the same time that CBL chapters were circulating Initiative 101, they were also supporting the candidacy of Monty Percival in his campaign for the state senate from the 28th Legislative District. Supported by CBL members across the state, he successfully obtained the Democratic nomination in the September primary – and went on to be easily elected in November with 72% of the vote. Percival would be able to lead the legislative efforts, a clear political triumph for the League.

The third political activity occurred when E.G. Auerswald, CBL state secretary, wrote a letter to each local unit, urging members to meet with their legislators. If necessary, they should recontact them.

> The date for the general election is drawing near, in which the legislators will be elected to represent you from your district. These self-same legislators should be familiarized with the aims and purposes of the Children's Benevolent League of Washington, and given an opportunity to express themselves.
>
> We do not want anyone in Olympia who is not sympathetic to the work of the Children's Benevolent League, and we also want to impress upon them the necessity for a school on the West side of the mountains.
>
> If you have not already done so, we urge you to have your next meeting attended by the candidates that are running for office, both Democratic and Republican. If you have a Democratic and Republican Headquarters in your district, you can supply them with a copy of the aims and purposes of this organization so that the candidates may be informed on our activities when they arrive at the meeting.
>
> Begin your program by emphasizing the aims and purposes of our organization, and then give everyone present an opportunity to state their position in behalf of the school and its activities, if elected.
>
> If you have had your October meeting prior to this date, it is essential that you call a special meeting for this purpose.

Fourth, the CBL's first political flyer appeared sometime in 1936. A copy survives from the Chelan County unit in the small town of Wenatchee, but it appears to have been based on a statewide model. It sought increased appropriations for the State Custodial School, which naturally was the emphasis for the parents closer to Medical Lake, in contrast with the families living west of the mountains who had decided the main issue was building a new, more convenient institution on the West side.

The Custodial School had its problems and the handout provided background facts local members would need to talk to their legislators. It also reveals CBL perceptions at the time: the children needed better food, more living space, and play equipment; the school should be as homelike as possible; and the children were being treated shabbily when compared to inmates of prisons, asylums, and other institutions.

One notable feature of the political flyer is its appeal to justice, not charity. Increasing the appropriations for the Custodial School will not raise taxes, it says, but merely require taking funds from other institutions. The per capita cost of each of the eight state institutions is then set out. The Custodial School is at the bottom, at 30 cents per day, while the State Training School for delinquent teenagers received four times that much at $1.24 per day per capita. The parents backed the proposal of Superintendent Parker to more than double the appropriation to 70 cents per capita ($11 in 2010 values).

Two other desires in the flyer have been a constant in lobbying from that day till present: first, let everything be as homelike as possible and second, look for further opportunities to develop abilities.

Interestingly, of the nine leaders of "the Chelan County group working for the betterment of Custodial School conditions" not one can be identified as having had a child at Medical Lake. This may rank as the first clear outreach to the community and people of good will. [19]

Auerswald's letter and the Chelan county flyer show that the CBL used fairly sophisticated political methods. The documents also demonstrate that the CBL did not view itself as an organization devoted only to a second school. The CBL strongly supported the efforts of Superintendent Parker at the existing school—after all, with the requested increase in its operating budget, a lot could be accomplished.

The first CBL political triumph was surely the election of CBL President Monty Percival as state senator from the 28th Legislative District in November, 1936. His victory assured the CBL that it would have a friend on the inside, when the Washington state legislature convened for its sixty day biennial session in January 1937. In an auspicious beginning, Senator Percival was elected chairman of State Charitable Institutions Committee by the Democratic caucus.

On January 15, Percival and his fellow Pierce County Democrat Harry H. Brown introduced Senate Bill No. 34, authorizing a new state custodial school in western Washington to provide "for the care, confinement, training and employment of defective and feeble-minded persons." The objective of the school was the "care, training, and employment" of its residents in order to render them "more useful and happy" and to "tend to make them as nearly self-supporting as their level of intelligence may permit."

The fifth identified political action of the families was that the CBL had clearly been hard at work collecting support from allies. On the same day SB34 was introduced, news stories appeared in the *Seattle Times*, which indicated the support of the Washington State Federation of Business and Professional Women and the Washington Congress of Parents and Teachers for a new custodial school. When Governor Clarence Martin unveiled his budget a few days later, the news there was also favorable, with a $350,000 item for construction expenses.[20]

The sixth and last CBL political activity in its first year was the actual lobbying in the 1937 state legislature. Led by CBL president Monty Percival, the effort succeeded, but with all the activity leading up to the session, it is obvious that other CBL members must have been among the citizen lobbyists in Olympia.

Because Percival chaired the committee which heard the bill, and because its co-sponsor H. H. Brown was on the Senate Rules committee, the bill moved smoothly, passing the Senate on January 28 and being sent on to the House. According to a tradition handed down in the Arc of Kitsap County, Lulu Haddon of Bremerton, who chaired the Senate Education Committee, played a critical role in securing passage of the bill by holding up other legislation till it was acted upon. But it does not seem to have been a bill that required much arm-twisting. The bill was passed by the House on February 10 and signed by the Governor on the 16th. Of 231 laws enacted in the 1937 legislature, it was the tenth; its relatively quick passage was due to a combination of strong support and a lack of serious opposition. Perhaps it was fortunate that the bill was introduced during the Depression when spending for public works was a popular undertaking, at least in Washington. Thus was created the second state institution for persons with mental retardation, first called the Western State Custodial School, and later Rainier School, named for the beautiful mountain looming over the campus.

The CBL got the new West Side school, but they did not gain any other powers in respect to services. Admission of feeble-minded children over age 6 could be initiated by parents, but it could also be initiated by each county superintendent of schools, in theory at least, over parental objections. It was duty of the parent to send the child to the school, if a referral had been made and if the Custodial School superintendent had accepted the referral. Parents were responsible for paying the child's transportation to the Custodial School and for the cost of suitable clothing provided by the state.

The other part of the CBL platform for the 1937 legislative session was increased funding at the State Custodial School. Its funding was the particular concern of East Side parents centered around Spokane whose children would not be moving, but it was also important to West Side parents, since all of their children would be living there till the second school was built. CBL parents had obtained a statement from the state PTA indicating its support for "adequate funds for the Medical Lake institution," along with the second school. The appropriations for the State Custodial School did increase, but not by the 75% which Parker told the League he wanted. The 30% addition in the biennial amount for 1937-39, to a total of $584,555, was the second largest percentage increase among the budgets for the various state institutions, but it was not much larger than the increase that most of them received.

Building the West Side School

After the legislative victory on the new school, CBL members became anxious observers of the progress of each phase in its construction, as chapter meeting minutes indicate. To begin with, the statute had established a committee to select a site for the new institution, made up of one senator (Percival), one representative (Carl Devenish from eastern Washington), and the director of the State Department of Finance, Budget and Business (Olaf L. Olsen), representing the Governor. A rural location was dictated by the legislation, which specified a site of at least 400 acres and expected that the school would raise most of its own produce. The committee considered fifty potential locations and on May 24, 1937, they chose a site at Buckley, thirty miles from Tacoma.

Naturally, the location of the new school was not a matter of indifference and Percival had lobbied hard to win the school for his area.[21] As a member of the Tacoma Chamber of Commerce, he convinced businessmen to pledge $10,000 to be used for the acquisition and improvement of the site, as an inducement to the state. As a further incentive, Pierce County agreed to give the state 160 acres at no cost. The school was also a beneficiary of the first federal funds available for mental retardation programs[22]: the Public Works Administration granted $265,000 to aid in the construction of the new school.

The Children's Benevolent League members originally got their information on the school's progress from a newsletter, "The Accelerator," written by Secretary Auerswald.[23] After a few issues, it was dropped in favor of a new Buckley newspaper, *The News.* Monty Percival was one of the founders of the paper, although he was not actively engaged in its publication. Percival encouraged CBL members to send in news items they wished to share, and many gifts made by CBL chapters to the school were acknowledged in the paper.

On August 7, 1937 the CBL held a combination victory party, convention, and picnic at the site of the new school. About 140 persons attended the event; among them were reported to be several CBL members who lived in other states. Although there was no official program for the meeting, the members toured the site, and Percival and Auerswald were re-elected for their second terms as CBL officers.

On September 1, 1939, as the war began in Europe, Frederick M. Lash, Ph.D., was appointed to the Superintendent's position.[24] The following month the first nineteen residents arrived at the new school by transfer from the Medical Lake School. The residents chosen for the new school were in a drawing from among the names of the individuals whose parents wished to have them transferred. The residents were transferred according to the order in which their names were drawn "providing they fit in at the new school."[25]

Anticipating flagging efforts as early as 1938, Secretary-Treasurer Auerswald wrote to the local units, praising the members for their successful efforts in helping to establish a new school and urging continued support once the school was completed: "Just because the foundation for the new school has been laid is not an indication that our work is done—to be exact—it has just begun."

President Percival toured the state, showing motion pictures of persons and events at Eastern State Custodial School and describing construction progress on the new school to one chapter after another. His photography implemented Oakley's early idea of taking movies at the custodial school to keep families in closer touch with their children. Superintendent Parker also visited chapter meetings, sharing photographs and answering parent questions; when he did not attend, a member of his staff frequently substituted.

The CBL recognized the importance of shared experiences and

encouraged families to turn to each other for support. Percival promoted parent-to-parent ties as an important outgrowth of local meetings.[26]

> These units, bringing together as they do, parents who
> having suffered the same affliction and met with the
> same rebuffs and misunderstandings from outsiders, are
> peculiarly fitted to be bound together by stronger ties
> than that of mere friendship.

The support these families gave each other resulted in lifelong friendships; they became like extended families. When the son or daughter of one family died, other CBL families often shared their sadness at the funeral.

Parents also shared joyful experiences. Fundraising was a CBL activity that gave members the feeling of accomplishment and raised their spirits. One of the first fundraisers was a jubilee in Tacoma on November 11, 1938. The CBL spent the proceeds of the event to purchase equipment for the new school, in this case, six radios League members also provided funds for special treats for residents of both schools on birthdays, Christmas, Easter, and other holidays. Although almost all of the money collected went to buy supplies for the schools and gifts for the residents, some units began to forward funds to the CBL officers for "state work." State work meant that, after only two years, wise leaders realized that to be an effective advocate, the CBL would have expenses beyond the direct gifts to the residents and the schools. For example, the Kitsap unit voted to send the state $12.00 in October 1938 and in the following May, made it permanent, by passing a motion to send the state secretary one dollar a month, payable quarterly.

During these early years a big part of membership was participating in the annual conventions. At the third convention in Seattle on August 27, 1938, unit presidents each cast one vote (Kitsap, 1938) and re-elected Monty Percival president. The fourth annual meeting was held in Tacoma on August 26, 1939, with a picnic at the Buckley construction site the next day. Officers elected at the state convention in Tacoma were Senator Percival, president, for his fourth and last term; Mrs. Charles Clark, vice president; and Otto Nelson, secretary-treasurer.[27]

The new school was also the focus of families' organizational attention in this period. The Buckley *News*, used as the state CBL paper, reinforced this emphasis, and may have led to the neglect of the interests of families whose children remained in the existing school in the eastern part of the state. But a controversy soon arose

20

which redirected CBL attention back to the older school.

The Ouster of Superintendent Parker

The new school at Buckley had been justified to the legislature as necessary to relieve overcrowding at the State Custodial School at Medical Lake. Despite the overcrowding, visitors reported that conditions at the school were better than in the past under Superintendent Parker – aided by the watchfulness of the League. Senator Lulu Haddon of Bremerton inspected the State Custodial School in 1938, deplored the overcrowding, but reported that "wonderful work was being done there," and quoted Parker's boss in Olympia, Olaf Olsen, to the effect that there was only one vital element missing:[28]

> The children in these schools and the inmates of the
> institutions for the mentally defective need love—the sad
> part being that there are not enough arms to go around.

Another 1938 visitor to the State Custodial School provided the most dramatic testimony by listing the changes from conditions ten years earlier.[29]

> Low death rate
> No straight [sic] jackets used
> No goose step but children march two by two
> Apathy and inactivity have been replaced by some-
> thing that the children can do
> Better attendants, certified teachers and registered
> nurses
> Better class arrangement
> Fine receiving hospital
> A building, Suncrest, for tuberculosis patients
> New ward for boys
> Segregation of groups
> Specialized training and nursery groups

Superintendent Parker was given credit for bringing about many of the changes at the school; and surviving correspondence suggests that he was a concerned advocate for resident interests. In a letter to his superior, Olaf Olsen, Director of the Department of Finance, Budget and Business, Parker expressed his deep concern over recent state budget cuts eliminating cosmetics and tobacco.[30]

> I am sorry that you found it necessary to strike the ar-

ticles lipstick and rouge as these are a necessary part of every girl's make-up. If they can't get them in the regular way, they have to beg, borrow, and get them in some other way from the other girls who are furnished these items from home.

As far as I am able to find out many of the older men have been furnished tobacco ever since the institution has existed. To stop them now would be nothing short of a catastrophe in the minds of those who have used it so long.

Smoking tobacco and chewing tobacco is one of the few pleasures that these older men at the Institution have, and they look for it each time it is issued almost in the same way as the food they get. Since this was a habit of so long standing, and since it was established so long before we came to the Institution, I sincerely hope you will reconsider.

Many of the older men at the Institution that sit around on the ward in the afternoon listening to the radio would be lost without their corncob pipe and a pipe full of George Washington Tobacco. I understand that tobacco is furnished the state patients at all other Institutions.

Parker's use of the phrase "since it was established long before we came," suggests that he and Olsen were already in conflict over spending practices.[31]

But the dispute was more complex than simple fiscal constraints. Chapter 53 of the Washington Laws of 1921 directed county school superintendents to report the names of

...all feeble-minded, insane, epileptic, habitual criminals, moral degenerates and sexual perverts, who are persons potential to producing offspring who, because of inheritance of inferior or anti-social traits, would probably become a social menace or wards of the State.

The State Institutional Board of Health received such reports and had the power to authorize sterilizations in cases they thought appropriate. In letters during June and July, 1939, Olaf Olsen expressed his concern that Parker was erroneously interpreting this eugenics legislation in such a fashion as to make sterilization a condition of release to the community. Citing two previous letters and a complaint from the State Director of Health, Olsen directed Parker to comply with his order not to make release contingent on sterilization. Parker responded with a denial of the charge, but he failed to convince Olsen of his compliance.[32]

In a letter dated January 17, 1940, Parker quietly tendered his resignation, to be effective March 1, citing a desire to re-enter the field of education. On February 3, the *Spokane Review* reported with banner headlines—"Vice rampant in Spokane"—a grand jury had named the county sheriff, auditor, and treasurer in a public report on corruption, but without returning indictments. Although Parker was not named in the public account, two days later the February 5 banner headline in the *Spokane Daily Chronicle* read "Custodial School Head Quits." The story reported that Olaf Olsen and several school employees had been witnesses before the grand jury; there were allegations of mistreatment of children at the institutions.

The battle to save Parker was led by two fathers, Newland Reilly, an assistant editor at the *Spokane Chronicle*, and A. G. Naundorf, a Spokane lumberman whose brother-in-law Harold Cassill was city editor at the *Chronicle.*[33] Clearly the CBL would receive favorable media coverage from at least one source!

On February 3, 1940, as "Chairman of the Legislative Committee" of the Spokane Unit of the CBL, Newland Reilly wrote a lively letter to Governor Clarence D. Martin asking him to reverse the decision.[34]

> Information has come to me from three unrelated political sources that Charles A. Parker, superintendent of the State Custodial School at Medical Lake, is to be made the "goat" of the Spokane grand jury investigation, just closed. The story in each case is that Olaf Olson had made "an agreement with the grand jury" that Parker would be sacrificed, if the jury would not criticize various incidents at school.

But writing as "the father of a boy, who, through an unexplained mystery of nature, is...in the school," that would be "an unfortunate mistake and a blot on your administration."

> Prior to Parker's arrival at the school, it was necessary for me to maintain supplies of sugar, butter, fruits and breakfast foods for my boy...That condition has vanished.

And there were other improvements:

> He changed it from an asylum, where children were required to sit for hours in long rows of chairs, to one of the best institutions of the type in the nation. We here in Spokane have made a comparative study of other institu-

23

tions, and have found little in the great endowed, private schools, such as Vineland in New Jersey, that Parker was not offering at Medical Lake.[35]

It was not that there had been no incidents (what institution is without them, Reilly wrote), but they were against Parker's orders. In fact, Reilly said that his son was a victim of an incident:

> My own son suffered a broken arm two years ago. It was my impression that the "accident" was the work of an attendant, and I told the man I'd shoot him, if I could prove deliberate intent on his part. He left the school soon afterward.

Admitting to the Governor that he had threatened a state employee with death may not have been the most politic point to make in Naundorf's letter and it has not been a tactic frequently used by parent-advocates in subsequent decades.

On February 4, as President of the Spokane Unit of the CBL, Naundorf telegraphed Governor Martin that

> Parents, Relatives and Friends of children at Eastern State Custodial School[36] herewith enter a most vigorous protest against contemplated changes in the management of the school and demand as taxpayers and citizens that no change be made until a public hearing shall be held on charges allegedly presented by supposed disgruntled employees of the school before the Spokane grand jury.

Naundorf asserted that the CBL was happy to accept whatever outcome a complete investigation might demand, but alleged that the grand jury testimony was misleading and that the many improvements made under Parker would be put at risk by a change of superintendents.

The CBL did obtain a meeting with Olsen in Spokane on February 8. Besides Reilly and Naundorf, state CBL officers Charles L. Clark and E. G. Auerswald of Seattle, and other parents, attended the meeting. According to the *Chronicle* the following day, petitions from "all but one" employee and from "several hundred older girls" were presented on Parker's behalf, but the parents were unable to persuade Olsen to retain the superintendent. Letters from CBL members and units around the state also failed to sway the Governor, and the "resignation" stood. However, Olsen did promise that the parents could nominate individuals from whom the Governor would select a few to act in a purely advisory fashion to the management of the school; they would be given "access to all records and activities and would consult with the superintendents on management problems." Thus, the families lost the battle, but began to win the war: they began to achieve official status as advocates for their sons and daughters over whom they had lost all rights, when they gave them up to state custody.

So Parker may have been fired for his spending policies, for his sterilization practices, for both of these, or for another reason. (A later superintendent recalled hearing stories of kickbacks from contracts given to Spokane physicians.) In regard to sterilization, correspondence indicates that Parker's successor was equally unclear as to the procedure and Olsen had to respond at length in April, 1940. Nor, it should be noted in passing, was Parker being accused of abridging the civil liberties of the residents (although the state Supreme Court ruled sterilizations unconstitutional in 1942 after hundreds of operations had been performed).[37]

Having failed in its 1936 effort to have the superintendent covered by civil service, the League was unable to prevent Parker's demise four years later.

Depending upon the true facts of the case, which remain obscure, even civil service protection may not have prevented Parker's departure. Perhaps because he did have something to hide, Parker had not informed his supporters in the CBL of his impending resignation. After it became public, however, Parker played the good soldier, traveling the state to local CBL units and reassuring them about conditions at the school and the qualifications of his successor, Lester F. Mason.

The CBL's Next Battle – With Each Other

The last of the pre-war political battles that the CBL fought in the press was between the leaders of the Seattle unit of the CBL and the Percivals, who were the center of the Tacoma unit. The occasion was Superintendent Lash's firing of Dr. Chisholm as resident physician at Rainier. State Senator Monty Percival, head of the Tacoma CBL, charged that Lash had fired Dr. Chisholm without cause and solely because of his testimony before the Senate Committee on Charitable Institutions, which Percival chaired. According to Percival, the Committee asked the doctor to testify about the deaths of two "inmates. One was a boy "who had been given too much opiate" and the other was a child who was unable to assimilate food."[38] Rainier Superintendent Lash denied that the firing had anything to do with Chisholm's testimony, but refused to give another reason.

Then a news story appeared, reporting that that members of the

Seattle unit of the CBL had met with Dr. Lash and backed him fully, including the dismissal of Dr. Chisholm.

> Harold Isanhath [*sic*], president of the King County unit of the Children's Benevolent League, said that Percival's statements "had excited scores of parents throughout the state whose children are in eleemosynary institutions." "Parents and relatives of inmates of such institutions have been hearing about children starving, being whipped, and suffering all kinds of punishment," Isanhath said, "whereas the true situation, especially at the custodial school under Dr. Lash, is that conditions for inmates are ideal."[39]
>
> A special committee of the society has been investigating conditions at state custodial schools, Isenhath said, and has found the Buckley school "the best managed and most modern in the United States."

In an apparent aside the story continued

> Mr. Isanhath, a Seattle automobile salesman, said the league is not criticizing Mrs. Percival as a social worker at the school, but is convinced that she is doing fine work at the institution.[40]

But the following day the paper reported. "Social Worker at School Quits.".[41]

> Mrs. Monte [*sic*] Percival of Tacoma, a pioneer worker for the establishment of the Western State Custodial School at Buckley, said today that she will not return "under these circumstances" as a social worker for the institution.
>
> The King County unit of the Children's Benevolent League, an organization of about 2,000 persons interested in handicapped children, last week indorsed Dr. Lash's action and declared it was satisfied with the work of Mrs. Percival at the school.
>
> Mrs. Percival estimated that she has worked for the interest of the school the past sixteen years but said her actual employment at the institution covered about thirteen months. She has not been at the school since last month, when she obtained a leave of absence to be with her husband at the Legislature.

This is the public story in its entirety and there is no account in the Arc records. It is interesting that the Pierce county CBL unit is not mentioned, but perhaps the other roles of the Percivals seemed to be enough to speak their minds. Monty Percival died soon thereafter, but Ada Percival remained president of the Tacoma unit for another five years.

Why Did the West Side Parents Succeed?

From 1916 till 1925 Nellie A. Goodhue, Seattle's first director of special education programs, and director of the school district's Child Study Laboratory, led an unsuccessful campaign for a Western Washington Institution for the Feeble-minded[42]. She enlisted the support of legislative leaders and in 1916 formed a lobbying committee that included representatives of "the Chamber of Commerce, the King County Medical Association, Social Welfare League, State Board of Health, Juvenile Court, University of Washington, Women's Federated Clubs, and Public Schools."

As part of her campaign in 1924 Goodhue co-authored a Red Cross survey of all school district superintendents, judges, social workers, and the superintendents of the state's institutions – that is, not only the State Custodial School, but also the institutions for male and female juvenile delinquents.[43] The reason for the survey was stated:

> Although Washington has for a number of years been
> making provision for its feebleminded, the facilities for
> their care have not kept pace with the needs. Perhaps the
> chief reason for this is that the actual needs have not
> been recognized. It is hoped that a study of the actual
> problem will throw light on the number and condition of
> the feebleminded and arouse the public to the responsi-
> bility it must assume toward them.

The report estimated that there were 6,000 "feebleminded persons" in Washington. Of these, most were "at large," which is language normally used to refer to criminal suspects. And indeed, the report states that "[e]ach of the 2107 [identified] feebleminded is a potential criminal." Naturally, the committee reported with alarm the need to address the threat posed by the remaining 4,000 feebleminded who were neither monitored nor controlled.[44]

Those were the decades in America when Darwinian ideas, infused with a little understanding of genetics, led many to worry about genetically inferior stock, especially immigrants from dissimilar cultures dragging down the achievements of a country that had been founded – as it was then thought —by white Anglo-Saxon Protestants. This fear was usually linked (as it was here) with the idea that feebleminded persons did and would inevitably have larger families.[45] Such ideas led to calls for programs to promote persons of good genetic makeup.[46]

Even trying to imagine the mind-set before the painful lesson taught by the Nazis was taught, it is difficult to understand what Goodhue must have been thinking as the head of special education for the largest school district in the state when she signed the report that included the following paragraph:

> *The Feeble-Minded in the Schools*
> Many teachers comment on the difficulties experi-
> enced in the association of the feeble-minded with the
> normal pupils in their classes. They hamper the work of
> the class. Their presence is a real detriment to the others.
> In addition they themselves do not receive the proper
> training and after repeating the same grades year after
> year they finally pass out of the schools, unfitted to do
> anything towards their own self support. **Money thus
> expended is wasted.**[47]

The report argued that there were three categories of the feeble-minded:

> **...Needing Institutional Care**
> Class 1. The delinquent, degenerate, uncontrolled who
> are a menace to the home, school and community.
> **These will bring an unbearable burden on the tax
> payers if not segregated and given proper training
> now.**
> Class 2. The feebleminded who are now cared for in
> corrective institutions, for example, the Girls' School at
> Grand Mound and the Boys' School at Chehalis.
> **Their presence reduces the efficiency of these insti-
> tutions.**
> Class 3. The feebleminded whose families cannot give
> them the necessary care, protection, and control.
> **These unprotected, uncontrolled and untrained, at
> large will recruit the ranks of criminals and repro-
> duce their kind.**

The report concluded by identifying a menace.

Western Washington, with its many feeble-minded
adults and children at large, and many others reported in
schools, represents a menace to the state that needs immediate attention. That Western Washington needs an
institution for its feebleminded is so obvious that there
can be no question as to the wisdom of its provision. The
idea of such an institution is not punishment, but care
and training. To send children from Western Washington
across the mountains to Medical Lake is little short of
punishment, both to them and to their parents. Next to
the humanitarian point of view, which requires us to take
care of these unfortunates, the element of public protection is the most important, since these defectives are so
easily led into crime and misdemeanor. Experience
proves that even in extreme cases, judges, jurors, or
commissioners, hesitate to send a child, who so obvi-
ously needs care, to an institution that is so far away.
Many troublesome cases could easily be provided for
with parental consent, if the institution were fairly handy
so that the parents would not feel that their child was being banished.[48]

But even though Nellie Goodhue put in years of work trying to
justify an institution in Western Washington, her work was to no
avail. Why were Goodhue's efforts unsuccessful, when the Children's Benevolent League accomplished the goal within a year of
getting organized? Was it because there were no parents on her
committee? Was it because a parents' organization worked harder
or had more credibility in the legislature?

In the earlier period parents were not viewed as allies of teachers in the struggle for better conditions for persons with disabilities;
indeed, the opposite was true. The sense of parents as problems is
apparent, for example, in an address by Stevenson Smith of the
University of Washington Psychology Department. Speaking to the
Section for the Study of Special Children of the Washington Educational Association on the need for a second institution, Smith
argued that

Even now such an institution is greatly needed in the
western part of the state where there are hundreds of children whose parents are unwilling to send them so great a
distance as Medical Lake. It may be objected that these
parents should not be humored in this matter and should
be obliged to sacrifice their feeling and to accept with

29

gratitude the provision which the state makes for their children. This, however, does not work out in practice.[49]

In his address to the teachers' group, Smith flattered and encouraged them when he concluded, "Probably no people in this state are as well able to further this matter as those who are teaching in the public schools." But when the bill was finally enacted in 1937, parents, not teachers, led the effort.

Not only did the selfish parents not wish to be separated by hundreds of miles from their children, many also persisted in their belief that their children could be educated in regular classrooms, in defiance of teachers' professional judgments.[50] Other parents were likely to protest when their children were "debarred" from school as uneducable, when their intelligence scores fell below 50.[51] In still other cases involving Seattle schools, the Superintendent decided that "(i)t may be necessary to debar a child from the Special Classes in order to force the parents to place that child in a State Institution."[52]

Prof. Stevenson Smith was the only person who was part of both the early failure and the later successful effort to build a west side institution. Perhaps he could have explained the difference. It may be that Smith put the idea of a west side school in the minds of the parents, when he addressed a February 14, 1936, CBL meeting in Seattle. Before that date, all surviving records assume the group would be a parents' club for the school at Medical Lake. But as early as March, the idea of a second school is being discussed by League leaders and members, as shown in the minutes of the Clark county unit.

It is possible that part of the change was that the CBL parents did not arrive in 1936 lobbying about a social threat, as had Goodhue. One can imagine a legislator thinking "Lots of things are potential threats, but no one voted me into office to deal with potential problems. We have enough problems already facing us. On the other hand, when a group of parents comes to see me in Olympia who say this is their number one priority, I take note."

It would be naïve, however, to think that parent power made all the difference. The time must be right, and so must be the ideas. Nellie Goodhue served at the end of the Progressive Era in American history in the early 1920s and a subsequent conservative upswing, a circumstance reflected on the Seattle School Board[53] and in Washington state politics generally.[54]

By the middle of the Depression Washington politics had again taken a progressive turn, indeed so much so that a member of FDR's cabinet, James A. Farley, is said to have joked to the 1936 state Democratic convention that there were "47 states and the soviet of Washington."[55] The press and politicians spoke openly of "left-wing" and "right-wing" battles in the legislature. True, mental retardation programs remained a non-politicized issue, with no significant ideological component, but even so the general climate of change, of social welfare expansion, and of construction projects as providers of Depression-era employment, probably helped the Children's Benevolent League achieve its notable early success.

It would also be naive to minimize the importance of parent efforts, by claiming that obtaining a second state institution, particularly one long foreseen, was not a very creative act. The experience of this political victory taught these parents that they could be a significant force working on behalf of their sons and daughters as citizen lobbyists, a lesson they never forgot. In addition, now that families had come out of their isolation and found each other, they realized the value of mutual support, of the consolation and advice by another in a similar situation. Although the sense of affliction is less prevalent today—with a more understanding, less condemning, public,—it has not disappeared. The role of counselor and adviser, older parent to "new parent," continues. Also, much of the ordinary activity of the CBL members was devoted to charitable activities for the children at the schools, and this role has remained a common and accessible one for perhaps the largest fraction of families. The CBL had been founded and it proved to be what many parents needed, an opportunity to influence their destiny and that of their sons and daughters. But just where the parents were headed, they did not yet know themselves. The issue of defining their long-range objectives proved to be the next major task of the Children's Benevolent League of Washington.

James Oakley, organizer, first parent meeting, 1935

Vincent Oakley at home in Seattle

Purple Cross Association

Seattle, Washington
Feb 10th, 1936.

Mrs Percival
c/o Montys Garage
A St. Near Post Office
Tacoma, Wash.

Dear Mrs Percival:
      This letter is to inform you that the next
meeting of the Purple Cross Association will take place at the
Washington Room 4th floor, Chamber of Commerce Building, 215
Columbia St, Seattle, Wash. Friday Feb 14th at 8.p.m.

      Stevenson Smith, Director Child Welfare
Dept, University of Washington. And Mrs Loretta S.Slater
Executive Secretary,American Legion, Child Welfare Committee,
will address those present.

      Will you kindly spread the news amongst
the good people of your organization,and tell them that Seattle
extends a hearty and cordial invitation to come over and help
us dispose of the coffee and cake, which the entertainment
committee are going to furnish.

      By the way,Mr Johnson suggested that I tell
you,that if the cake you brought over two weeks ago is still in
existance you may bring it along.

      Hoping to see you and a big delegation from
Tacoma on Friday night.

      Sincerely yours.

      James F. Oakley

           Secretary

3336 36th Ave So,
Seattle, Wash.

Purple Cross letterhead

State Custodial School and staff, 1930

**Custodial School Supt. Woodruff allowed parents to remove
residents 1910**

**Nellie Goodhue, Seattle's first director of special education.
Argued feeble-minded were criminal menace, 1924**

Prof. Stevenson Smith ran diagnostic clinic. Frequent speaker at CBL conventions

Custodial School Supt. Charles A. Parker (R) and girls art teacher Grace Nelson, 1930s

Senator Monty Percival. First CBL president, 1936

ADA L. PERCIVAL

Ada Percival, longtime CBL leader and link to national professionals, 1940

E G Auerswald, CBL Secretary. Directed statewide legislative nights, 1936

Newland Reilly, WWII CBL leader. First parent speaker to AAMD, 1941

MEMBERSHIP CARD

Parents · Relatives · Friends

Children's Benevolent League of Washington
STATE CUSTODIAL SCHOOL

DEDICATED TO
HEALTH, HAPPINESS and SECURITY of CHILDREN

Member _____

Address _____

Phone _____

CHELAN COUNTY UNIT

CBL membership card, 1936

Rainier State School, aerial view

CHAPTER TWO:
FIRST STEPS TOWARD A
NATIONAL VOICE

> Yes, our ambitions are mighty, but our program is not for today, nor tomorrow, but for years to come.
>
> I submit to you that no other group, no matter how highly trained, can arouse the enthusiasm, the will-to-do, as can this group, nor adequately fund the financial outlay without some driving force, and they have that force. What is it? Their own mentally deficient children.
>
> —Alan Sampson, May 1947

In the 1930s the parents of the Children's Benevolent League had been, for the most part, well-intentioned, committed amateurs concerned about mental deficiency. Every member and supporter valued the League for what it was doing—providing mutual support among parents and working for better institutions for their sons and daughters. It achieved some success on both counts. Yet some leaders—Ada Percival, Newland Reilly, Alan Sampson, Bob Leavitt, and others—came to believe they had to learn more and do more. What they learned and what they came to believe launched them on a larger crusade. In the process, they alienated a significant fraction of their former constituency. But these visionary leaders were willing to accept the loss, because they were confident in their judgments. By the end of the 1940s they had succeeded: they won a new and larger constituency within the state and a national parents' group was within sight.

In the beginning the parent members of the League could not learn what they needed to know by talking to older, experienced parent advocates, since there were none. Their knowledge of mental retardation beyond their own children came from listening to the speeches of the superintendents and Professor Smith. But however well-informed these men were, they were only a few individuals. Thus the CBL families began to turn to the national organization of professionals in the field, then called the American Association on Mental Deficiency (AAMD).[56] Founded in 1876, the 644 members in 1940 included institutional staff, together with scattered educators and social workers.[57] The AAMD published a journal and held an annual convention. Although with its 1,500 members the CBL was already larger than the AAMD, the professional organization was the scene of national policy deliberations in mental retardation. If parents wished to begin to shape the future, they would have to learn what the AAMD knew and influence what it did. The parents were so enthusiastic about what they were learning from the AAMD that they were soon demanding that the superintendents of the state institutions be members. After the war, they tried to require that each local CBL unit become an affiliate of the AAMD and half did.

Parents Connect with the AAMD

It is commonly asserted that parents began to participate in the AAMD only at the end of the 1940s, when it became the platform for launching the national parents' movement,[58] but that is wrong. Ada Percival, a founder of the CBL, and long-time president of the Tacoma chapter, became a member in 1940.[59] In 1946 she was made a Fellow of the AAMD.[60]

At the time, she was apparently the AAMD's only parent member.[61] How did she come to join? Perhaps due to the influence of Mae Fisher Williams, the Tacoma special education teacher and "very dear friend" who spoke at the original Pierce county CBL meeting in December 1935. Williams had joined the AAMD in 1935, and for several years she was the sole active AAMD member from Washington state. For example, she served on the Resolutions Committee from 1940-45. But Williams was not the only Washingtonian at the AAMD meetings. In June 1941 several CBL leaders attended the national AAMD conference in Salt Lake City, among them Ada Percival and Newland Reilly. Two months later Reilly gave a detailed speech to the CBL convention enthusiastically telling all that he had learned in Salt Lake City.

First Parent Speech to the AAMD

In 1941 Newland Reilly spoke to the national AAMD meeting as president of the Spokane Unit of the CBL, a pre-war speech by a parent.[62] To the group of institutional superintendents and staff gathered from across the country, Reilly described the CBL and asked them to promote the formation of parent groups in their respective states. But he was a newspaperman, not a salesman, and, as Reilly acknowledged, "I'm hotheaded and I say things that I regret afterward." [63] Perhaps thinking of himself as a muck-raking, truth-telling reporter, he told it like he saw it, even if that was impolitic. Thus he not only told of several cases in which the CBL had defended superintendents and had successfully lobbied for increased appropriations, he also criticized other administrators. For example, five years earlier one had told the Reilly family when they placed their son, "if you are wise, you will go home, have other children, and forget him." Reilly proclaimed, "I helped spike his return to the school only this spring." And that, had he not made the offensive comment, "he might be superintendent."

Reilly argued that

> Whether you like us or not, we are fixed entities in
> your lives. We don't want to be part of your work, but
> nature, in its own wisdom, has said that we must be.
> There is one thought that I would like to leave with you,
> and that is that a group of rehabilitated parents – if they
> are for you,— can be real job insurance for you, but, if
> you are falling down on your job, they are equally com-
> petent to raise particular hell.

With words like those coming from an avowed hotheaded parent, how many superintendents in other states would feel that they wanted to start a parent group, too?[64] With friends like these, who needs enemies, they might have thought. Furthermore, how much help could a parents group provide, when Reilly had to admit that the CBL had failed to prevent the dismissal of Superintendent Parker and that it was in the midst of a unresolved battle over the replacement of Superintendent Mason?

But Reilly did conclude by urging the development of parents groups elsewhere:

> We in the state of Washington feel that we have pioneered a new field of work, which is of real benefit to the parents, to the children and to the school staffs, and my closing thought is an appeal to you to help spread in your own state the work that has been undertaken – more successfully than any of us dreamed – by the Children's Benevolent League in the state of Washington.[65]

Geography was certainly an important factor inhibiting the development of a national group. The state of Washington is way off center. In the days before the Internet, before faxes, before cheap and convenient long distance telephones, freeways, and airplanes, it was harder to lead the formation of a national organization from the upper left hand corner of the map.

The bombing of Pearl Harbor six months later and America's all-out war mobilization was the overwhelming factor why this speech did not galvanize a national movement of parents. With wartime gas rationing, parents could not travel to national meetings if they had wanted to. The CBL even had to cancel its state-level conventions during the war because of rationing.

There is one more reason why no parent movement started in 1941. Indeed, perhaps as important as any trepidation over parent power, was the fact that Reilly's speech from its title "Let the Parent Live Again" onward, stressed the value of the organization for the parents, not for the child with disabilities. Parent rehabilitation was not a priority task for a superintendent of a state school.

Parent to Parent

Because the value of The Arc has always been to the whole family, not just the child with disabilities, it is easy to see how constant the concerns have been over 60 years. But there have been differences as well. In the early part of the twentieth century, persons with intellectual disabilities were thought to be genetic throwbacks to an earlier state of humanity or of a genetically inferior fraction among us. The "eugenics" movement held that sterilization was the proper cure for the threat that persons with mental disabilities posed to society. Thus an image was created of a racially poorer, less intelligent class of persons, and this view did form part of Newland Reilly's mindset, as he admitted, when he was called upon in 1936 to form a Spokane unit of the emerging statewide families' organization.

[Superintendent] Parker urged me to take the lead in the organization of a group in Spokane. I refused. I might as well be honest and admit that I refused because I was so unsocial, due, largely to years of isolation with the boy, that I considered myself better than other parents of retarded children in the Spokane area. I felt that my wife and I were exceptions. No others had suffered as we had suffered. Other parents, I thought, were low-grade morons, who never should have been permitted to have children, whereas my wife was a college graduate and the holder of a life diploma as a high school teacher, and I had won some recognition as a newspaper man.

I was wrong, of course. I have learned since that all parents have suffered equally, and that a majority are fine people....

[When a unit was finally founded three years later] a little group of us faced sub-zero weather one January night, [at the instigation of one man] A.G. Naundorf, an executive of a large industrial plant, who has given of his time and money to promote the work of the league. Mr. Naundorf has taught me by his example that no man has a right to be too proud to associate with his fellow sufferers, no matter what their mental or social position....

[Later that year] the real upsurge in the social consciousness of the Spokane group became obvious when the first social meeting was held at a member's house after the members had been meeting about five months. The results took the leaders by surprise...

Finally, the facts became clear. We saw what our parents needed was a very simple thing – nothing more than a chance to talk, without explanation or apology, about our children. We could give that, and it cost us nothing.

Each parent had a normal, deep and earnest love for his child, and each had a rational desire to chatter lovingly about the thing closest to his heart. One can not talk freely to an "outsider" about a boy or girl whose mind is not normal. It is only when we meet others who have similar problems that we can open our hearts and express our innermost thoughts. And when our parents meet in the street, in the home or in the unit meeting, they talk gaily to each other – and I mean gaily – about mentally retarded Susie or Johnny, just as other parents discuss normal children...[66]

Reilly also provides hints as to how to organize parent groups and incorporate "new parents" and then adds:

> The organizer of a parent group must not lose sight of the fact that talking is not enough. Talking is merely a by-product, a sort of catalytic agent, which produces results. Before a group really gets down to talking, it must have work to do.[67]
>
> Above all, an organizer should not present a program for the social readjustment of the parents. None of us wants to be rehabilitated. Rehabilitation must come as a result and not as an aim.

Comparing these words to the experience of families today, it is hard to know whether to accent the many shared similarities or the differences. Today the experience of the shattering loss of being a "new parent" meeting other supportive, more experienced parents, is not typically at the date of institutionalization, but at the date of diagnosis. This is frequently when a mother is still holding an infant in her arms, as opposed to the inherently different experience 50 or 70 years ago, when at age 5 or 14 or 22 years, a son or daughter was then "committed to the state." But, there is the shared experience persists: the "coming out," and coming to terms with the fact that this child is different from any one a parent had anticipated, and by talking to other more experienced parents who have been through it before. And, for many parents across the country, joining hands to work for a better life for their own children soon developed into actions for others.

Report to the CBL Annual Meeting

In August 1941, in addition to the usual addresses by Prof. Stevenson Smith[68] and the superintendents, Governor Arthur B. Langlie spoke to the three hundred members and supporters gathered for the CBL annual meeting. While the governor was there, Newland Reilly delivered an address based upon what he had learned at the AAMD convention. After describing his new awareness of the magnitude of the problem of mental retardation, Reilly confidently outlined a comprehensive program that Washington could establish from experience elsewhere: identification and registration of mentally retarded persons (South Dakota); special public schools (New York City); outreach social workers (Connecticut); and avoiding a colony system (Rome, New York). From what he had learned, Reilly also suggested that increased sterilization might be warranted (although he recognized most parents sought to deny the sexual desires of their offspring). Also the construction of a facility might house "borderline" cases who were "sex-delinquents" or who committed petty crimes. Reilly called for "a competent, properly staffed and adequately financed research bureau" in order to develop methods and standards of "proper schooling" for mentally retarded students. Clearly, Reilly was now conscious of a wide breadth of issues on a national basis.

The issue of institutions versus family and community services was addressed by Reilly. He argued that the state of Washington had committed a great crime against a number of boys and girls in the state school at Medical Lake by keeping them in the school when they should have been released to take their place, even in a small way, in the world.

Reilly professed his belief that the problem of inadequate "parole" (as it was then termed) was being corrected, but he felt there was still much more to be done in this regard. Nevertheless, Reilly assumed a continuing need for custodial schools. Increased training and professionalism were urged for all school personnel from the "lowly attendant" to the superintendent, so that the ideals intended for the schools might be realized. The superintendents should be required to attend the national professionals' association, the AAMD, convention each year. The management of the schools should not simply be a patronage position for a friend of the Governor, Reilly declared in the Governor's presence. Rather,

> The tenure of the superintendent should be controlled by an independent board, appointed by the governor, and serving somewhat in the capacity of regents, such as the regents of the University of Washington.

Reilly's ideas on family support and foster care were perhaps his most advanced. Family support had always been a concern of the League, but Reilly developed a new vision based on his experience at the AAMD. The CBL's family support goal was limited to much the same idea as James Oakley had originally conceived it: parents should be available to offer consolation to other parents, as they too experienced the trauma of separation when they decided to institutionalize their sons and daughters. On behalf of the CBL, Reilly now appealed to the Governor and legislature to establish a program of family support. His appeal to the cost savings, as well as the inherent merit, of family care has been echoed repeatedly by later generations of parents.

> Washington appears to be leading in experiments with what is known as family care and foster homes. Our state social security department is placing a number of children in foster homes, where intelligent, high-minded foster parents are seeking to make the most of a child whose mind is not of the best. It is a grand step in the right direction, and one which this league...should study and develop.
>
> This program of family care and foster homes is greatly handicapped by a lack of sufficient trained social workers. Miss Sweeney, the social worker at the Medical Lake school, is doing a grand job in this direction, but she is only one little woman, and can be in only one home at a time, and the need for her services is great.
>
> Extension of this program on a sound basis gives promise of paying actual dividends to the state, instead of costing money. It has been found, especially in Connecticut, that a wise, able and thoroughly trained social worker can give home training to the parents of mentally retarded children to a point where requests for institutional care for the child are withdrawn. This means that the child can remain in society perhaps becoming an economic asset, and the state is saved the cost of institutional care for it.

Taken together, Reilly's proposals addressed many of the same needs identified by later generations, as they labored to put in place a comprehensive service system. At the very least, the speech shows that the CBL by 1941 was aware of the larger world of mental retardation policy and program design in the United States. These parents meant to be a part of the action.

The War Years

Progress toward every goal that Reilly had described ceased with the attack on Pearl Harbor four months later. The custodial schools lost employees to the war effort; the Western State Custodial School even lost its superintendent. At the Eastern State Custodial School Superintendent Mason reported that his staff was 32% below normal, with eleven residents employed six days a week as student or second attendants, and the daily per capita cost reduced to 78 cents. Governor Langlie froze all additional construction funds at the Buckley school; his 1944 successor Mon Wallgren continued the policy, leaving the school uncompleted till after the war.[69] It was not a time for new initiatives unrelated to the war effort. The CBL did manage to minimize some of the damage—increased wages for institutional workers were obtained, in order to stem the staff attrition due to high "war wages," and the League also solicited an increased number of volunteers at the schools to compensate for the staff shortages.[70]

Why Did a National Movement Emerge?

In 1952 Seattle area parent Janice Leavitt was celebrating the publication of the first issue of the national newsletter and remembering that its name *Children Limited*, had been invented in her living room. She remembered that they and their friends the Reillys had been talking about a national voice for eight years, that is, from 1944.With the coming of peace and the end of gas rationing, the time was ripe for CBL leaders to reach out again to families nationwide—and because Americans are always forming associations—there is no need for any special theory about why parent associations popped up across the country and a national union was accomplished.

However, some have offered special reasons about how the war had *caused* the formation of family advocacy groups, rather than delaying their emergence. These theories explain too much, because they assume that without the war and its special characteristics, parents groups would not naturally have formed.

Thus Bair, quoting Gunnar Dybwad and adding her own ideas, contends that post-war ideological humanitarianism (especially anti-eugenic feelings generalized from anti-Nazism) was a factor behind the growth of parent movements in America and Europe.[71] In addition, Bair argues that a redefinition of traditional roles, because of male military experience and female labor force participation, broke citizens free from habit and left them ready to tackle new tasks. Rosemary Dybwad, another informed observer, does not directly address the cause.[72] Pelka claims that the post-war efforts were "in large part due to the participation of returning veterans," but offers no proof or explanation for why this might be true.[73]

Farber contends that the post-war baby boom, coupled with improvements in medical technology, led to more severely retarded babies for middle-class parents. These couples then launched a post-war crusade for services, in order that their own drives for upward mobility could proceed unhindered.[74]

But whatever merit these hypotheses may have, they are inadequate. They ignore the fact that in several ways World War II interrupted the outreach which the CBL was already making beyond Washington state's borders. The war delayed the emergence of a national parents' movement by nearly a decade. To begin with, beyond Anna Percival and Newland Reilly, no more CBL parents joined the AAMD or attended its national conventions till the war was over, but immediately after the war, more Washington parents joined the AAMD and attended its conventions. The little they had participated in the AAMD had spread the idea of family advocacy quickly. Mildred Thomson, the president of the AAMD when the national parents' group was finally formed, had heard about the CBL early and tried to help a parents' group form in Minnesota. Writing about a Minnesota state agency committee during the war, she recalled:

> Several years earlier [that is, before the war] I had secured information about the accomplishments of a group of parents organized in the state of Washington in 1937 [sic]. At that time Mrs. Florence Greiner, who was with the Hennepin County Welfare Board, had spoken to a father who was a man of initiative but he had not thought it feasible to start such a group in Minnesota. Now in 1943 this committee, composed largely of social workers, discussed this possibility and agreed with the Hennepin County father. Nothing was done.[75]

So from about 1940 national AAMD leaders like Thomson knew of the CBL as a parents group worthy of imitation. Thomson goes on to argue that the mental health movement "had started before the war and been halted by it," by implication including mental retardation. Its postwar resurgence, she contends, was due in part to the leadership of highly principled conscientious objectors who served in the institutions during the war. Out of their shock at conditions there, she speculates, came the landmark 1947 National Mental Health Foundation publication about institutionalized children with mental disabilities titled, *Forgotten Children.* (CBL President Reilly was irritated by the presence of conscientious objectors at the schools and looked forward to their speedy dismissal when the war was over.[76])

That the League members believed they were the lone parents group, and that the League had become known nationally, are apparent in a CBL publicity pamphlet, probably printed in 1942: "It is a known fact that there is no other organization anywhere quite like ours, and its work has received the widest praise by national authorities on the subject of the retarded child."

Presumably other AAMD contacts made the League's existence known to other parents, but the suspension of ordinary activities during the war may help explain why the League's attempt to exchange information with "a somewhat similar group in New York City, being interested in one Custodial School" failed to produce an answer.[77] (This was probably the Welfare League at Letchworth Village in New York, founded in 1939.) The Vancouver chapter did successfully reach out to several families across the Columbia River in Oregon: indeed in 1940 the local unit sometimes met in the Portland home of one Oregonian who became an officer of the group. But that was all.

Last Separate Steps

Internally, the CBL continued to evolve, although more slowly, during the war. For the first time an organizational address was adopted, President Isenhath's home on Queen Anne Hill in Seattle. Over this address, a circular and a brochure were published in 1942-43, describing the goals and activities of the League. These early public awareness materials were aimed at describing the CBL to potential parent members.

Perhaps the most important claim that the brochure made was that the League had 1500 members, a strong claim on legitimacy. During the depths of the Great Depression, Superintendent Parker had asserted that there were 10,000 "registered members." Given the times, it is hard to criticize these claims of membership because the members paid "no fixed dues."[78]

The brochure described the nature of their monthly meetings. Every meeting included discussion of some aspect of the programs in the two state schools. In addition,

> Many parents have made new social contacts within
> the groups, and are finding that these contacts give them
> a firmer grip on themselves. All have found a new under-
> standing and sympathy, for each understands the other's
> problem.

This parent-to-parent support function was included within the two declared purposes of the League:

> To exercise watch-care over the children at our two

State Schools, and to add to their happiness, comfort, and well-being.

To unite parents in this work, to help them understand their mutual problems, and to assist them in re-establishing normal social relations.

The eighth annual CBL convention was held in Seattle on August 7, 1943. It was perhaps most notable for the emergence of Coast Guard Lieutenant Alan Sampson, a young insurance salesman. In 1943 he was the toastmaster, but Sampson was to become the standard-bearer of the progressive faction within the CBL. Four years later as president of the CBL, Sampson would give the second speech by a parent to the AAMD. Seven years later his leadership was recognized by his election as the first president of the national parents association, the National Association for Retarded Children.

Finding the Funds to Do Big Things

In his original speech in October 1935, James Oakley had foreseen potential problems, given Superintendent Parker's belief that dues could not be allowed for a parents' organization. Inadequate finances had indeed become a constraint that progressive forces had to overcome if they were to expand the scope of League activities. The minutes of the 1943 Annual Convention reveal the first serious effort to develop a financially stronger state organization that would be able to do more than simply send gifts to the schools. In the previous year, of $936.82 collected, $812.55 went for gifts, leaving $20 a month for expenses. In result of that, President Isenhath proposed a system of prorated assessments on local chapters to provide the state organization with a monthly budget of $25. Although the majority of the board favored the collection of dues, and A. G. Naundorf of Spokane argued that the total amount generated should be $100 a month, the proposal was opposed by past president Roy Fowler of Bellingham.

Fowler objected to these plans stating that the services of the members of the Children's Benevolent League could not be bought. He argued that the State officers had done all the work of the League without remuneration in the past, and that all funds raised by the Units should be used for the direct benefit of the children. After a general discussion it was moved, seconded and carried to table this matter and pass it on to the new officers.

Lack of success in fundraising continued at the following state convention in August 1944 at the Gowman Hotel in Seattle, when a motion to collect dues from local member units was defeated again, even though Secretary-Treasurer Cunningham reported that the budget for the past year had declined to $704.33. Newland Reilly of Spokane was elected president. Although he was the League's best publicist, and had provided a vision of new program possibilities in his 1941 speech to the AAMD, he had opposed the collection of dues as "unconstitutional." Fitfully, the convention took some steps toward a stronger, more unified organization. Most fundamentally, the convention authorized a by-laws committee to propose a revised constitution. Also, the first formal budget was adopted, although the delegates defeated Reilly's call for a presidential expense item. (This angered him "on principle" and led him as a self-confessed "hothead" to refuse to travel to local chapter meetings for a year.) At an Executive Committee meeting held a month after the state convention, a motion was passed to assess the seven local units their proportional shares of a total of $1,200, with $900 to go to state school residents. Reilly opposed a motion to collect dues of a dollar from each local member and the motion was defeated.

After Ten Years

The CBL held its tenth annual meeting was held in Seattle on August 5, 1945, the day before the Hiroshima bombing which sped the end of the war. Celebration of the League's anniversary was muted. General membership conventions were still prohibited by wartime gasoline restrictions.

In a sign of organizational vitality there was a contested election for president, in which Newland Reilly, the incumbent, defeated the younger challenger Alan Sampson, who then was re-elected vice president. At the convention Reilly presented a 37-page brochure about the League, in the guise of an annual report for the preceding year. It was titled *For the Happiness of Children: The Story of the Childrens Benevolent League of Washington.* In effect, it shows how strong and ready the organization was to seize the new possibilities that would come with peace.

In a foreword to the brochure, Superintendent Mason of the East Side school gave his approval, noting that the AAMD and "many other authorities on the care of mentally retarded children" were favorably impressed with this "unique" organization and its possibilities. As before, the organization's goals were described as promoting "the happiness of children" and providing parental support.

The brochure described the services to those whom it had become CBL practice to call "new parents" as follows:

> Another task undertaken by the League is the rehabili-
> tation of parents, whose hopes and dreams crumbled
> when first they learned a beloved infant never would ma-
> ture normally. Their sufferings reached a peak when at
> long last, usually after one or both has had a breakdown,
> they put their child in a school. Many, if not most, re-
> quire reorientation socially.
> To the parent, the League offers a unique service.
> Each League meeting is a forum where one parent may
> talk to another about a retarded child as though he were
> normal. Each has suffered and each understands. Parents
> of normal children never can know what it means to a
> parent of a deficient child to brag just a little about ac-
> complishments of a child, who never will accomplish
> anything—not ever.

Reilly knew, of course, that there were residents of the state
schools who were accomplishing many things: there were boys and
girls receiving training and, along with adult residents, raising most
of the food for the school. Nevertheless the pain experienced by the
parents of these children seemed just as great as those of the "pa-
thetic boys and girls, many with distorted bodies."

The League's benevolent activities during the previous year included two dozen major categories of gifts and services rendered to
the residents and the schools. Last, but "most important," however,
were its monitoring and advocacy functions.

> The State of Washington is very generous, but there
> are times when State officials entrusted with the care of
> the children need a little prodding—sometimes not too
> gentle prodding—and the League has demonstrated time
> and again that it is willing to go to bat with anyone and
> everyone from the governor on down to the mostly lowly
> hall attendant.

Reilly's combative style is apparent here, as it was in his easy
expression of irritation at those within the CBL who rejected a
presidential expense budget item. It also showed up in his account
of the origins of the CBL. According to his version, the League
"was created by courageous, far-seeing Puget Sound area parents,
who knew a militant organization was needed to coerce the State
into constructing a new Custodial School." The available evidence
from 1936-37 does not indicate much militancy or coercion, beyond

that normal in politics, as his brochure put it:

POLITICS OUR MEAT

The League definitely is a political organization, but it is NOT interested in partisan politics. It aspires to only one "ism" —happiness of children. League officers have had numerous clashes with members of State administrations, both Republican and Democratic, over affairs in the schools, and are ready for another.

What were the issues that Reilly was thinking of? A recent one certainly was the impounding of state funds for construction at the custodial schools over the previous four years. Reilly had aroused the interest of the new governor, Mon Wallgren in releasing the appropriated funds as soon as possible, in part by leading a legislative committee on a tour of the new school at Buckley the previous winter. The second issue was the familiar one of appointment and retention of superintendents. In 1936 the League had backed the unsuccessful civil service initiative, and in 1940 Newland Reilly had led the equally ineffective drive to retain Superintendent Parker. In his 1941 convention address Reilly had reiterated CBL support for civil service and in this 1945 report expressed his belief that "our campaign last winter prevented the dismissal of the superintendents of the two schools on political grounds." As long as programs for persons with mental retardation remained institutional in form, the CBL was certain to focus a significant amount of its attention on the superintendents; they had the power to make important differences in the lives of the residents.

Reilly reprinted the annual reports and financial statements for the local units in the state report, along with those answers to his question on what hopes for the future the members had. Their desires were for a more "business-like" organization (that is, financially and organizationally solid) and for expansion to more parent members. R. E. Hurlbert, secretary of the Bellingham chapter, put a particular emphasis on the latter point: "...to see it grow and expand into other States. Every state needs the League as much as Washington did."

Reilly who also strongly supported the goal of a national organization, included a page of instructions headlined,

It would not be difficult for parents in another state to
ORGANIZE A LEAGUE.

Beyond the page of advice on how to start, the League promised additional assistance to parents in any other state who requested it. As Reilly saw it,

> The time should come when every State in the Union
> will have a parents' organization similar to the League,
> and *when we can have a national over-all body.* [79]

These words reflected the natural desire of committed and sensitive parents scattered in isolated meetings across the nation. After gas rationing ended with peace in August 1945, it once again became possible to envision the formation of a national organization. Soon it happened.

Reorganizing the CBL for More Effective Action

In April 1947, after several years of preparation, the CBL's articles of incorporation were amended for the first time since its founding. The leaders in this effort looked forward to new possibilities as a result, but the departure from tradition looked more like a threat to others in the CBL.

The organizational goals were now declared to be

> (1) to arouse public interest in all physically and mentally handicapped individuals; (2) to aid and comfort
> such persons and the parents of subnormal children; (3) to
> arouse public interest in and to support reforms, legislation, and research in the State of Washington and
> elsewhere relative to support and care, and prevention of
> such subnormalities; (4) and to generally raise the standards of care.

This 1947 statement of purpose differed from the 1936 charter in several respects. By making the scope of operations "the state of Washington and elsewhere," the CBL declared its interest in forming a national organization. In addition, the CBL political goals of reforms and legislation were acknowledged as legitimate. Finally, it recognized research into the prevention of mental retardation and into methods of better care as a vital concern.

As important as the change in goals were the changes in organizational rules. The recurrent east and west side differences were addressed by the creation of a first and second vice-presidency, with the president and first vice-president required to live on different sides of the state. (Not surprisingly, this attempt to legislate unity failed.)

A more effective change was membership, which was divided

55

into two categories —non-voting "contributing members," and "active members," who must be guardians, relatives, or "others directly interested in the welfare of one or more mentally or physically handicapped individuals." The intention of this provision was to welcome the general public into League membership but to prevent the contributing members, the general public, from taking control. Actually, there had always been a small number of non-parent members in the League. For example, at the first convention in June 1936, the Aberdeen chapter was represented by a Miss Bess Daws, who was a probation officer and was presumably interested in the CBL for its potential value in her work. In a wartime brochure the League said it was "mainly" composed of "parents, relatives, and friends," but that membership was open to "anyone who has the interest of the mentally retarded child at heart and is willing to bring happiness into his life." Nonetheless, in 1947 the board demonstrated a new interest in non-familial members by adding that explicit provision to the by-laws.[80]

In an attempt to place the League on a firmer financial basis, it finally adopted a system of per capita assessments on chapters, and dues became a requirement for all members. Of the one dollar annual dues, a quarter was retained by the county chapter, and the remaining *75% sent on to the state*. This is an amazingly high percentage to the state organization. It has never been matched by any other known group of family advocates and shows how committed the new state leaders were to doing bigger things.

The new rules authorized the board to collect and spend funds as it saw fit, including acquiring real property; it could even incur debt up to 60% of liquid assets. With its new financial base, the League was no longer primarily a funneling agent for voluntary contributions to the schools; it could respond to whatever needs it identified.

The financial progress of the League and the shift in spending priorities took place rapidly. For example, in the fiscal year 1942-43, the state CBL budget had been $936, of which 87% was expended in direct gifts to the residents and schools. In 1944-45, the comparable figures were $1224 and 75%. In 1946-47, $2032 and 75%. But under the new system, the income for 1948-49 came in at $6,581, with direct gifts to residents comprising only 40% of the $4,243 actually expended. Now the League had a budget surplus which was larger than the entire budget two years earlier.

Further evidence of post-war organizational revival was apparent at the 1948 state convention. Representatives of chapters covering the eleven most populous Washington counties attended, and six committees were functioning—Convention, Legislative, New Chapter, News and Information, Finance (East and West), and Membership. The Membership Committee reported 1,115 active and 1,915 associate ("contributing") members. While this figure of 3,000 members was the same number claimed shortly after the CBL's creation a decade earlier, these members were contributing money, not just promising "support." And they were serious. When the membership chair believed the dues were too high at one dollar, and suggested that they be lowered to fifty cents per year "like the PTA and women's organizations," she was outvoted.

But along with new strength came conflict about how to use it. At the summer convention the delegates passed a resolution to recommend retention of both superintendents, regardless of the outcome of the election. However, after the November election restored Republican Arthur Langlie to the governor's office, the issue was reexamined at a special board of trustees meeting in Seattle in December. President Nolden noted that he had intentionally not invited the superintendents to this meeting, "so that we can openly express ourselves." Then Bob Leavitt of Seattle moved to repeal the League's August motion, arguing that it would be unfair to tie the hands of Governor Langlie, since he might make an outstanding appointment. The board passed Leavitt's motion, which included a provision that "this action was not meant as a condemnation of the Superintendents."

But that resolved only one issue. Prophetically, Nolden addressed the board as follows:

> I am not quite satisfied with the harmony and unified program of the CBL. We are now 12 distinct Chapters. We do have a common purpose, but at times we are selfish and jealous of each other. We are fearful that a strong chapter may usurp the powers of the smaller ones. But that is not right and certainly not just. Our Chapters became strong by reason of hard work, and it is only because of the population advantage that some are larger than others. A unification of program and activity is paramount in my mind and the faster we can return our thoughts to the fundamentals of our League, the faster we will grow into one healthy, strong State-wide organization.

In March 1949, signs of discord in the CBL continued to accumulate.Thus the Bellingham chapter on the west side of the mountains sent a letter protesting the board's repeal of support for the incumbent superintendents.

> We are well aware that both Superintendents have
> faults, have made mistakes, and will still make them. But
> in our judgment, their existence is invaluable, and has re-
> sulted in improved conditions at both schools. We realize
> there is some personal feeling against one or both men.
> This should be subordinated, as all of us realize that, dur-
> ing the existence of the CBL, personal feelings have
> caused a great deal of unnecessary trouble.

Bellingham's letter stated that political patronage would be the likely motive for any change, and stated their chapter's desire that no action against either superintendent be taken without local unit approval first. The fear of the state organization proceeding to make policy on its own is notable, for there was no memory of a large difference between the state and local chapters. The emerging discord shows the increasing distance that had developed with the evolution of a stronger state organization that could not rely on automatic acquiescence by the chapters.

At the annual meeting in August 1949 several resolutions were adopted in a clear Seattle-led West Side struggle with the East Side led by Spokane. The progressive West Side majority triumphed and authorized

- establishing a permanent state office
- hiring an executive secretary
- publishing a League newspaper
- creating a presidential advisory board of six prominent and interested non-parents
- creating a standing committee on legislation
- empowering the state CBL to take actions without ra-
tification by the local chapters
- and seeking an affiliation with the American Association on Mental Deficiency as soon as possible.

The League would never be the same.

In his convention address, outgoing President M. P. Nolden of Spokane argued for less emotion and more tolerance of differences that were exacerbated by geography. He hoped that all would agree that, if not the sole goal of the League and its members, at least "our first and foremost obligation is and always should be the immediate care of our own children in Washington's institutions." Further,

> it is my sincere hope and I pray that we may not be led

astray from this train of thought but rather that it be enlarged upon—and directed honestly and with full purpose so that the standard of care of these of our own flesh and blood may continue to rise, to the end that the State of Washington may be an example to the rest of the nation insofar as the necessity of institutionalizing the subnormal child is concerned.

Thus, a national role for the League was conceded, but it was solely as exemplar: the CBL was to be a beacon of hope, a model state program for others to emulate. It is safe to say that the postwar leaders, Alan Sampson, Bob Leavitt, and their allies, felt this was selling the organization short. There was more that could and should be done, not only for their own children, but for all handicapped children, and not only in Washington, but throughout the nation. As Bob Leavitt put it, "I always felt that we really started the organization and not those earlier people. All it was before us was a therapy group for parents."[81]

Significantly, except for the position of eastern vice president, the Seattle group swept the elections at the convention: H. N. "Cliff" Clifton became president, Bob Leavitt western vice president, Clyde Korth treasurer, and Phil Reilly secretary.[82] It would be fifteen years until the president of the association again lived east of the mountains.

At the end of the year, Earl Floyd, who had formerly been CBL secretary, announced the formation of a new Spokane-based organization, the Lakeland Village Associates (LVA), which has survived to this day as an institutional families group. LVA's goals were to "add to the happiness of children at Lakeland Village" and "to help parents understand their mutual problems"—the same two goals articulated in 1935 and now only one small part of a larger venture. Floyd hoped (in vain) to expand LVA beyond Spokane, with separate chapters in various population centers in the eastern half of the state. According to the publicity brochure,

THERE IS JUST ONE REASON for this new organization and that is a conviction, based upon experience, that our work can be more efficient when done for one school than when spread out over the needs of two separate schools.

OVERHEAD COSTS of the Associates will be nominal. There will be NO office and NO paid employees. Membership dues, amounting to $1 a year, plus funds raised by special projects, will meet operating costs. All other funds received will be spent for the happiness of children at Lakeland Village.[83]

Floyd and his successors in the LVA would ensure that East Side traditionalists had an organizational home. But what kind of dreams could be built on such a foundation?

Another Fight over Superintendents

The year 1949 ended with another acrimonious board meeting held November 20 in Ellensburg. The special meeting was called to confirm that the chapters had drafted the convention resolutions. East Side members disputed the legality of the procedure, while Bob Leavitt of Seattle vigorously defended it. Helen Betts, now eastern vice president, reported that an attorney had examined the record for them and declared all CBL actions before December 10, 1948 to be valid, but those afterward mostly invalid. In reply Alan Sampson argued that the 1947 constitution provided a clear legal basis for what they had done, and President Clifton decided it was so. Since the procedure was ruled valid, the resolutions stood.

At this point, "an acrimonious and disconcerting exchange between the East and West groups" broke out over a second issue that had been festering during the fall. In September, shortly after the League convention, Rainier School Superintendent Frederick Lash, an appointee of prior Democratic governor, had come under public criticism from a Tacoma physician, who attacked his placement of a resident in the community. In response, Lash offered to resign. In fact, Lash had fallen out of favor with Leavitt, Sampson, and others in the CBL, and they were inclined to let him go, except that they distrusted the governor. Earl Floyd, CBL officer and bookkeeper at the school, had worked for Langlie's reelection and hoped to be superintendent himself.[84] Governor Langlie considered the Lash appointment and consulted with League officers, who were opposed, insisting on a professionally qualified successor. After a wider search produced no acceptable candidate, the League began to press for a decision, which resulted in Lash's resignation. The governor's office released a statement that Rainier School "had been riddled with political manipulations and it must be cleared up."[85]

The League called a news conference and attacked the governor's allegations. President Clifton demanded a legislative investigation of the "incredible" charges against Lash (somewhat cynically, since the League officers knew of "dirty linen" at the school).[86] At this point the *Seattle Times* editorialized against the League, urging that continued controversy could only damage the chances of finding a good replacement—which turned out to be true.[87]

The League fought back and placed a large newspaper advertisement headlined "Why, Governor Langlie?" (*e.g., Seattle Times*, October 29, 1949). The ad had an appearance of objectivity, since it merely reprinted a pro-Lash editorial from a weekly newspaper, but the writer was Phil Reilly's father-in-law. As luck would have it, the leading candidate for the position—Rudolph Depner, M.D., of Worcester, Massachusetts—was traveling through the state when the pro-Lash ad appeared. Only hurried consultation with Clifton to obtain his approval and telegrams of support from county chapters persuaded Depner to accept.[88]

There was a similarity between this affair and a previous public controversy involving the League. In 1940 the League made an unsuccessful attempt to retain Superintendent Parker. Ten years later the issue was still the institutional superintendency, but this time the League was politically stronger. Although the officers did not manage to keep Lash, they did not really wish to, and the governor granted them a veto power over the replacement.

It was a dispute, however, on which the leadership could be criticized. East Siders at the League meeting in November demanded to know whether state CBL funds were used to purchase the ad; Phil Reilly replied that only King county funds were expended, but, through an oversight, the ad had not acknowledged this fact. President Clifton rose and gave his version of the procedure involved and defended his actions. He said he believed some units were planning to ask for his resignation, but he had done no wrong. The minutes then read: "There was no comment on this point, but the subject of the two schools and their administration continued with soaring tempers." Helen Betts declared that the ad and the surrounding publicity were unfavorable and damaging both to the schools and to the League.

Bob Leavitt then spoke vigorously in defense of President Clifton and the Executive Committee's conduct of the Rainier State School campaign. According to the minutes, Leavitt felt that

> more disturbing than the subjects of controversy at
> this meeting was the lack of cooperation received at all
> times, on all issues, from the East Side, due to the differ-
> ence of subjective and objective thinking; that is, the
> West Side is interested in the far-reaching ideal of re-
> search and pursuing a progressive course toward better

care and aid for <u>all</u> handicapped children, not only our own now in the schools. He went on to express disappointment in not having accomplished anything worthwhile as a state organization and said that "with or without you, we are going to accomplish our purposes as long as we have a prayer in our hearts and breath in our bodies to do so."

According to the minutes, "this brought spontaneous applause from most persons present." At this point, the meeting calmed down with a resolution offered by the newest board member, Mrs. Glen Sheeley of Aberdeen which passed unanimously. It expressed generally shared sentiments in regard to both schools, However, the damage had been done, and both Betts and Leavitt, eastern and western vice presidents, resigned in order to clear the air.

The effects of the division were still obvious two years later. The CBL had become substantially a West Side organization, as the eastern locals sent in letters of dissolution. For the first time in the history of the CBL, the superintendent from Lakeland Village did not deliver an address at its 1951 convention. And at the April 1951 board meeting, local chapters from King, Pierce, Clark, Whatcom, and Twin Harbors attended from he west, and only Chelan county came from the other side of the Cascades. The number of units represented—six—was the lowest in years.[89] The board discussed, but took no action, on the report of another competing group formed in the east at Walla Walla, which proposed to call itself the "Children's Benevolent *Club* of Washington."

On the other hand, there were some signs that the League could overcome the split in the state. During the summer Clifton indicated that there was a "distinct possibility of affiliation or a working agreement with the Spokane Council for Retarded Children." This was a newly-formed group composed of about eighty members, "mostly parents who have mentally retarded children at home." In fact, the Spokane Council had voted in February 1951 to affiliate with the newly formed national parents group, but it wasn't until August that they were comfortable enough with the more institutionally-focused CBL to join. The local history of the Spokane unit shows that, in order to gain the expertise they needed to get a school for children with mental retardation in their community, they did not contact the CBL. Instead, they corresponded with Sally Schmidt, director of the Cleveland, Ohio, Council for Retarded Children, and with Elizabeth Boggs, educational director of the New Jersey Council for the Retarded.[90] Parent groups were breaking out of their involuntary isolation.

62

Joining Hands

In the spring of 1947 Alan Sampson addressed the AAMD convention in St. Paul, Minnesota, on "Developing and maintaining good relations with parents of mentally deficient children." According to AAMD president Mildred Thomson, "This was an innovation—the first parent to attend a meeting and speak as a parent."[91] Newland Reilly's speech six years earlier had already been forgotten, even though it had been printed in the AAMD's journal. Like Reilly's, Sampson's talk was reprinted in the fall issue of the organization's quarterly, the *American Journal of Mental Deficiency*. For a second time, opinion leaders in the field of mental retardation heard the CBL story. Ultimately the idea of parents' organizations became the common coin of the land.

Sampson's speech had two major refrains. First, the League was not an untried and untested experiment, but had a proven record. It had "outgrown its swaddling clothes." Second, parents' groups were natural allies of the professional community involved in mental retardation programs. Sampson sought to overcome the opposition he perceived that professionals directed at "meddlesome parents." Thus he referred worried superintendents to their Washington brethren, who had more than ten years of experience with parents' groups, while failing to mention the League's periodic conflicts with superintendents and other state officials. In contrast to Reilly's address to the AAMD six years earlier, there was nothing in Sampson's words to alarm a superintendent over the potential downsides of parent power.[92]

Sampson claimed the CBL had 5,000 members and supporters and recalled how parents had lobbied for a second institution. In the recent 1947 session alone, the CBL had: persuaded the legislature to abandon the words "custodial schools" and rename the institutions according to parent wishes as "state schools"; defeated a proposal to assess parents a $500 fee for the care of their children; and successfully supported a retirement bill for employees. But most of all, parents had obtained increased appropriations for the state schools. Sampson told how the League contacted each legislator by mail and visited many of them personally at their homes prior to each session, in order to familiarize them with the problem and needs of handicapped persons. They introduced each member of the relevant legislative committees to the superintendents. Thus, "a league can be a great power for good, and is a strategic weapon for any superintendent to have at his beck and call."

So much for the proven benefits of parents groups—what of the future? Sampson urged his listeners to hear what Washington families were planning to do, and to ask themselves whether they also desired allies in the struggle for improvements. The League planned to expand, especially in gaining associate memberships from the public at large. With the funds resulting from these memberships, the CBL was committed to a "permanent and sustained" public education campaign that would circulate brochures and educational matter to physicians, county school superintendents, social workers, legislators and the general public. This material would contain the latest and most up-to-date scientific and professional information about mental deficiency, leading to the elimination of "age-old bogies." For example, Sampson said,

> If we have authentic proof that the incidence of mental
> deficiency is higher in children who had whooping
> cough prior to one year of age, or that it is higher in chil-
> dren born after [a mother reached] age forty, we will
> publicize these statements, and help to minimize such
> accidents in future generations. Yes, our ambitions are
> mighty, but our program is not for today, nor tomorrow,
> but for years to come.

Naturally, one could not have publicity efforts, unless there were solid findings, and thus the League was also committed to obtaining funding for research laboratories and medical facilities.

If nothing else, parents had the will and the credibility. Long before George Lucas and *Star Wars*, there was what Sampson called "the force."

> I submit to you that no other group, no matter how
> highly trained, can arouse the enthusiasm, the will-to-do,
> as can this group, nor adequately fund the financial out-
> lay without some driving force, and they have that force.
> What is it? Their own mentally deficient children.

Sampson also made a more debatable point on parent organizations and advocacy in his speech. He noted that it would be to the advantage of superintendents to have an official parents' organization to control otherwise troublesome parents. As parents joined with other parents, he believed, they would learn to adjust and appreciate the difficulties faced by institutional employees.

> I can make the positive statement, that from my ex-
> perience, the League does eliminate, by training, by
> explanation, and by regulation, much of the time that
> would otherwise be wasted by our superintendents, their

assistants and attendants in useless conversation and argument with disgruntled individuals. Our own members know better than to find fault with minor annoyances. Our method requires all reports to be made to a local unit President, or to a grievance committee, who in turn investigate in an official and straightforward manner, any complaints or accusations, and if unjustified, will drop the matter, after reporting to the complainant. These are channeled through unbiased officers, one person only contacts the Superintendent, or the State officials, and to the degree possible, we make stringent effort to quash all minor and intolerant complaints at origin. Result: appreciation by institution heads.

Although the procedure described by Sampson was not formalized as a policy by either the CBL or the superintendents, such a relationship had already developed gradually. There is a parallel in American labor union history. As unions obtained the New Deal legislative protection as advocates for workers, they in turn accepted the responsibility for eliminating wildcat strikes and other disruptive actions by unruly or militant employees. Already parent organizations in the disability field were accepting the role of managing and controlling the expression of discontent on the part of individual parents. This pattern, part co-optation and part inevitability, would reappear in new guises in later phases of advocacy efforts.

Back in Washington state, President Sampson proudly reported the national break-through by CBL at the state convention in Bremerton in August 1947. He was sure that a national parents' organization was now an obtainable goal: "To say that I was highly gratified, immensely pleased at our fine beginning, is putting it mildly."

At the AAMD convention he had shared a panel with the superintendents from Letchworth Village in New York and from the Epileptic School at Cambridge, Minnesota, who both were supportive of parents groups forming. Correspondence with additional, newly-discovered allies across the country continued in the wake of President Sampson's speech, as the CBL shared its story and offered advice. By mid-1948 thirteen different fledgling organizations, would-be organizers, and interested parties had written to the CBL. Later in the year a "Children's Benevolent League of Utah" was even started, after permission to use the name was granted (the Benevolent Societies formed at Willowbrook and other institutions in New York and in Iowa also borrowed their names from the CBL). The earliest contacts were listed by Sampson as follows:

1. The Association of Friends of the Mentally Retarded, Minneapolis
2. Crowley School (for the retarded) PTA, St. Paul
3. Dr. Arthur Rautman, head of Special Education, Michigan State Normal School at Ypsilanti
4. An unorganized group in Cleveland, Ohio[93,] as well as one in Columbus
5. A parents organization at Letchworth Village, Thiells, N.Y.
6. Human Betterment League of Iowa, Sioux City
7. Iowa Society for Crippled Children and the Disabled, Des Moines
8. Clarence Gramb, M.D., Milton, Mass.
9. Social Service Director, state institutions, State of Iowa
10. A group in Patterson, N.J., which has since organized along our pattern.
11. A social worker in London, England
12. Mrs. Edith Stern, a free lance writer, of Washington, D.C.
13. The Mentally Handicapped Children's Organization of Oakland, Calif.

Not surprisingly, some AAMD leaders began to see the potential of gaining many thousands of parents as members. At the 1948 AAMD convention in New Orleans, part of the agenda was devoted to parent group action. Speakers included Mr. Reuben T. Lindh of the Minneapolis Association of Parents and Friends of the Mentally Retarded, and Mrs. L.H. Riggs of the Hamilton County (Ohio) Council for Retarded Children.[94] That same year the AAMD Council recommended that a category of "affiliate" member be created for those "interested" but not "professionally engaged" in the field (Sloan and Stevens, 1976: 201). In fact, by 1948, in addition to Ada Percival, nine Washington parents from different units scattered across the state had already joined AAMD as individuals or as CBL chapter representatives.[95] 1948 was also the year that the first family members outside Washington state had joined the AAMD:[96] namely, the writer Edith Stern from Silver Springs, Maryland, and Mollie Riggs from a group in Cincinnati. An affiliate status would actually have dropped their standing in the AAMD. And on the other hand, one can imagine that some AAMD leaders might have supported the creation of a separate national organization for parents and their allies in order to prevent the AAMD being swamped with lay members who would out-vote the professionals.

In Washington state the CBL president M. P. Nolden distributed a letter to local units relaying the tentative AAMD offer of parent memberships with annual dues of three dollars. Like Sampson earlier, Nolden was impressed with the opportunity for keeping abreast of scientific and programmatic developments that AAMD affiliation could provide. The AAMD wanted to capitalize on parental support for research and some of its members wished parents to be members of a new AAMD research branch, to be called the National Foundation of Mental Deficiency.[97] Nolden recommended that parents strongly consider joining. But neither this gesture by the AAMD, nor its invitation for one delegate from each parent group to attend its 1950 convention to discuss the form of affiliation, eventually succeeded in capturing the mass of Washington parents as AAMD members.

In May 1950 Sampson and President H. N. "Cliff" Clifton were actively involved in promoting a national parents' organization at the AAMD convention in Columbus, Ohio. They distributed many copies of the CBL pamphlet "Children Limited" to those in attendance. Both CBL leaders also delivered multiple speeches. Sampson was named chairman of the five person steering committee, while Clifton captured the strategic nominating committee.

The report by Sampson and Clifton to the June CBL board meeting was upbeat.

> Very encouraging was the inquiry by professional
> people from many states as to how parent groups could be
> organized in their respective states and the rank and file
> membership of the AAMD expressed their interest in and
> the importance of the national movement of parents' or-
> ganizations now sweeping the land.

In August 1950 Sampson reported that those involved in the "national group" had not yet decided how the association would be structured "but it is evident that most state groups will wish to maintain their own identity and whatever affiliation decided upon will be in an advisory capacity."

Given the tasks a national organization faces, however, and the obstacles it must deal with, it is hard to see how a purely "advisory" or "affiliate" form of organization could have worked. Leaders of the CBL and other pre-existing organizations would naturally favor an "advisory" capacity, because they would not lose their separate identities and power bases. The eventual outcome was a federation, unlike other national top-down organizations, as far back as the March of Dimes.

This fragmentation of efforts has been endemic in the parents' movement. But since vices are often virtues considered in another light, the movement has been genuinely alive at the grass-roots level, unlike organizations with more centralized structure. One of the outcomes of the local character of much local parent activity has been to provide meaningful work for families—an expression of their desire to really parent their children with disabilities. As Woodhull "Bill" Hay, first secretary, and second president, of the national parents' group put it, there was the "need to challenge the validity of the finality in the words, *'Nothing can be done for your child.'*"[98]

Victory has a Hundred Fathers

Social conflict within groups is a mechanism for the adjustment of norms to new conditions.[99] Thus the Children's Benevolent League had to leave behind those parents who refused to change when the organization had, and the national parents group had to split with the American Association on Mental Deficiency as the latter was outgrown. On both the state and national levels, these progressive leaders conceived new possibilities and devised improved organizational structures which supported progress toward these goals. Among these leaders, those who are euphemistically termed "forceful personalities" were over-represented. These are the men and women who prophetically announce their visions of a New Age with new possibilities, and proceed to implement them. Washington state had its share.

The leaders also frequently claimed that theirs was the oldest parent advocacy organization and spearheaded the formation of a national association.[100] The claims of the CBL have been already been described, so the competing accounts should now be considered as well. Fortunately, in June 1950 Woodhull Hay mailed a survey to every identified parent group in the country. Hay subsequently reported that there were more than 125 groups with approximately 13,000 active members, of which the CBL was by far the largest.[101] A large part of his survey results survive.[102] The most important contenders are profiled below.

Ohio

In Ohio, the Council for the Retarded Child of Cleveland was incorporated September, 17, 1935, after some earlier activity related to the exclusion of children with mental retardation from the public schools.[103] In any event a couple brought a lawsuit that their daughter could not be lawfully excluded from public schools, because the state constitution guaranteed a public school education for all.[104]

The Exclusion of Beldene Goldman. In the fall of 1933 Beldene Goldman, aged about 8 years old, was denied admission to the public schools of Cleveland Heights, a suburb of Cleveland, Ohio. The school district had been offering an "Opportunity Class" for children with mental disabilities.[105] Beldene was among the children who had attended during the 1931-32 and 1932-33 school years. On November 14, 1932 the district board of education, like Seattle and many other districts across the country which were doing the same thing at approximately the same time, adopted a new regulation excluding children with IQs below 50 from education in the subsequent years. Such actions were partly due to "irrational" eugenicist fears, but they were also enabled by the new availability of intelligence testing which had only become widespread fifteen years earlier in screening World War I recruits. And the Great Depression likely brought an impetus to save scarce educational dollars by excluding some children.

Beldene's father Ben Goldman was a lawyer.[106] He and his wife Goldie filed suit over the exclusion, arguing that the laws of Ohio compelled attendance at school for all children between age 6 and 18. But the record also shows that they argued over the facts – their daughter had been tested multiple times, with IQ scores of 44, 61, 47, and 55. Beldene would have been admitted on half of the test results, so the parents clearly hoped that the evidence of the higher scores would be enough to win continued schooling for their daughter.[107] But the original trial court appears to have allowed the school district to use any rational basis for choosing which test results it would accept.

Winning but losing. The trial court did accept the parents' argument that, under the applicable law, only the state department of education had the right to adopt specific rules as to those who were uneducable, not local districts. The school district appealed. The Court of Appeals declared that

> Education for all youth is deemed of paramount importance.[108]

69

But, it added,

> As a matter of common sense it is apparent that a moron of a very low type, or an idiot or imbecile who is incapable of absorbing knowledge or making progress in the schools, ought to be excluded.

The court reconciled the two propositions by essentially adopting the position that there is no duty of school districts to educate children who cannot be educated. However, the Court of Appeals agreed with the trial court that only the state department of education could issue a rule, so, technically speaking, the Goldmans won. Beldene *had* been wrongly excluded from school during the 1933-34 school year.

However, all that would be required to exclude Beldene was the adoption of a state rule excluding children with IQs below 50 before the following September. Perhaps the board of education did adopt such a rule, because without that continuing exclusion why would the same Goldie and Ben B Goldman (along with Bessye Ruth Bassett) incorporate the Council for the Retarded Child two years later, which founded its own private school?

The stated purposes of the organization were

> to study and to assist the educational agencies now in existence for the general welfare of retarded children, and to provide additional educational facilities, and to promote the general welfare of such children.

Ohio in 1950. When Sally Schmidt returned the 1950 survey to NARC, she claimed that the Council for the Retarded Child had been organized in 1931 and had about 500 members. The Council has styled itself "the first corporate organization for retarded children in the United States." It has also claimed to be "the first organized group to work with the retarded child who was living at home, with its parents in the Community."[109]

Schmidt was not a parent of a child with mental retardation herself, but a longtime leader, editor of the Council's newsletter, and author of the Council's history. By at least 1950 she was President. On August 11, 1950 she replied to Woodhull Hay's further inquiry about other Ohio units that she had mentioned previously, and the Council letterhead indicates a strong and diversified organization, which was headquartered at the Cleveland Rehabilitation Center, 2239 East 55th Street, Cleveland. Besides the presidency of the Council, Schmidt also was one of the three persons on its Advisory Committee, which was accompanied by the names of the

70

persons on the Community Services Division, the Education Division, the Medical Division, and the Legislative Division. The bulletin of the Council ("The Forgotten Child") had its first issue in September 1950 and reported operating 13 classes for children with IQs below 50. (At the time, having the public school district operate the classes was not a listed purpose of the Council.)

Sally Schmidt also claimed that she founded the national association, by persuading the AAMD president-elect, Richard Hungerford, to call a parents meeting at the Columbus, Ohio, convention in May, 1950, and by there making the motion to form a national organization.[110] She claimed she did so under conditions she regarded as extreme. The parents' meeting in Columbus was "a true disaster," because of the New York leader Joseph T. "Jerry" Weingold. "In all of my living days I was never more perturbed at what was known as a man".[111]

New York

It was well known at least in New York that there was a parents' group at Letchworth Village, an institution, called the Welfare League for Retarded Children, which is said to have been founded in 1939 and incorporated April 10, 1940. But it is described as a small group of parents who contributed toys and other improvements to the institution and was entirely apolitical until the 1950s when other groups were formed.[112]

The leadership claims of the Empire State and its leader, Weingold, are similar to Schmidt's in Ohio to the extent that each involves self-promotion.[113] Weingold claimed that the New York State Association for the Help of Retarded Children (AHRC) was "the first attempt to form an organization for the retarded in the community as well as in institutions."[114] He also went on to credit himself as the one in Columbus who "called for the formation of a National organization." More concretely, the NYSARC restates his claims that he prepared a proposed constitution for the National ARC, as well as an agenda for its September 1950 meeting in Minnesota.[115]

Given AHRC's strategic location in New York City, these claims have often been accepted at face value. Thus, David and Sheila Rothman accepted the account of New York as "the leading force in organizing the national ARC,"[116] repeating earlier claims.[117]

The official 60th anniversary history of NYSARC contends that Ann Greenberg should get the credit for its very first beginnings.

On July 7-9, 1948 Greenberg placed a small ad in the *New York Post* reading "To mothers of retarded children, ages 4-8: Are you interested in helping to start a day nursery for your children?" and listing a telephone number where she could be contacted.[118] About ten people showed up for a meeting. They held another meeting where twenty appeared. Finally in December 300 people came to a larger organizing event with the result the Association for the Help of Retarded Children was incorporated on January 31, 1949. It was one of these later meetings that Jerry Weingold attended with his considerable talents and dedication. Soon thereafter he became President, then Executive Director, beginning a long career.

New Jersey

A New Jersey woman is given credit by Segal for first expressing the desire to help "all mentally handicapped children," not just their own, in 1946,[119] which of course shows ignorance of the CBL. A few years later New Jersey parent groups began developing fast, under the guiding hand of Lloyd Yepsen, AAMD president in 1948.[120] National leadership soon passed to New Jerseyan Elizabeth Boggs.

Minnesota

Minnesota's claim to priority also acknowledges the importance of sympathetic professionals. According to Clarence Lindstrom, past president of the PTA of the special education school, so-called "Beta classes" began in St Paul as a New Deal (WPA) project in 1934 at the Hill School. In 1935 there were three teachers and 36 kids. In 1937 it became a part of St. Paul Public Schools and the class was relocated to the Crowley School. "In 1937 the strongest little PTA was formed" said Clarence Lindstrom. "It is still one of the few in the country."[121]

A second example of professional involvement, and more important to founding the national organization, was the role of Minnesota's Mildred Thomson in the AAMD. Elizabeth Boggs, a New Jersey participant in the 1950 parent meeting, confirmed the important role played by Mildred Thomson. As president of the AAMD in 1950, Thomson told the parents that a separate organization would be a stronger one. As head of the newly formed AAMD Liaison Committee, she invited the parents to meet in Minnesota in the fall and supported their development.

Minnesota also had formed the Association of Friends of the Mentally Retarded in Minneapolis in 1946, claiming 61 paid members in 1950, and had as its goals the improvement of both institutions and community schooling. Its projects included lobbying and delivery of gifts to institutional residents and personal contact with their parents.

California

In the Golden State the Alta Vista Parent-Teachers Association claimed that it had been organized "9-10-19 Washington Grammar PTA; Reorganized 11-1936 as Alta Vista PTA." Reporting 67 paying members, it claimed its purposes were "Those of Nat'l & State PTA – Our Special Interest being that of the Retarded Child in School." Its projects similarly were parent-teacher mainstays, and "legislative activities through P.T.A. district organization." The Hay survey questionnaire was filled out by Rosemary French, vice-president. From the lack of attention given to this association's claims of origins in 1919, it seems that the NARC founders did not believe that it had been sufficiently separate from the regular PTA group that early.

Perhaps they asked other Californians such as George Bemis, Charles Griffith or Mrs. W.F. King, who were elected NARC directors in September 1950. They could have asked the San Leandro Mentally Handicapped Children's Association, who reported that they had organized in 1940 and had 60 members. Its purpose was to assist "in every possible way" and its projects included "education furnished by a School and parent classes."

The Exceptional Children's' Foundation of Los Angeles, founded in 1946, had 315 members. Its purposes were "to develop to the fullest extent possible the mentally retarded child by providing educational, recreational, and social adjustment facilities and to provide a permanent home for these children." Its projects included "clinical facilities through local hospital; parent education; educational classes for all ages; boy scout troop; girl scout troop; social activities, such as picnics, parties, etc." It also noted that another group existed (though they returned no survey to Hay): the Mentally Handicapped Children's Organization of Oakland.

Gathering at Last

Which efforts were first and whoever should get credit, all agree that, when called to order on Thursday, September 28, 1950, the first meeting of the National Association of Parents and Friends of Mentally Retarded Children at the Radisson Hotel in Minneapolis was an emotional experience for all who attended. Thomson later captured "the intense feeling of parents" by telling how she met in the hotel lobby a father who had been in Michigan when he heard of the first day's meeting from a press account and, in a day when flying was uncommon, immediately flew to Minneapolis to make the beginning of the second day.[122] The minutes record that delegates were recognized from New Jersey, Washington, California, Connecticut, Minnesota, Wisconsin, Ohio, Texas, Missouri, Vermont, New York, Illinois, Massachusetts, and Michigan. A total of 42 persons attended.

Washington's Alan Sampson addressed the group as head of the Steering Committee, elected by parents attending the AAMD meeting in Columbus four months earlier. He, too, emphasized the emotional essence of the organization, especially compared to service, labor, and professional organizations.

> To me, this is a thrilling and auspicious occasion; another milestone, carved from travail and tears, and indomitable purpose, in the progress against intolerance, for understanding.
>
> Each of us present are here because originally we were hurt, chagrined, and bitter, and in trying to solve our own individual problems, we have, quite without knowing it, contributed to our own growth, and sensible acknowledgment as well as broadening the community acceptance of mental subnormality....
>
> We propose to embark on a new venture for us. A new experience, but we have many patterns to copy, from which we can model. With but one exception, emotion. None of the other organizations mentioned have this tricky danger to guard against. We do, because we are parents, and because our problem is our children and at one time or another we have been emotionally disturbed, unsettled, and we will be again....I caution us all to check our emotions, our personal dislikes....It is only in this way that we can in the allotted time bring to a satisfactory formation this magnificent purpose of a national federation of parents' clubs.

In his speech Sampson asked "how old are we" and answered that 1931 was the year that the first local group (in Cleveland) claimed to have started. Sampson went on to state that from the single origin there were now at least 80 local groups organized, acknowledging a survey by Woodhull Hay. The growth had been so great, he said, that "History is already my talk at St. Paul in '47; New Orleans in '49 and the combined meeting [with the AAMD] at Columbus in '50."

Sampson went on to outline the proposed articles and by-laws, a name for the group, and standing committees. The issue of official affiliation with the AAMD was referred by the committee to the full body of delegates, because the committee had heard so many ideas and the topic was so important. Sampson reported that the Standing Committee felt there should be a Liaison Committee, so that the two organizations might jointly, for example, disseminate

> an approved list of private schools throughout the na-
> tion, or establishment of national standards for any and
> all schools for the mentally retarded, or effective pro-
> gram[s] for special classes in the public schools, or a
> system of licensing private schools.

Once the convention began, Sampson was elected chair of a "Name and Purposes" Committee. After the committee met overnight, three names were suggested for the organization: National Federation of Parent Associations for the Mentally Retarded; National Association of Parents of Mentally Retarded Children; and National Parents Council for the Mentally Retarded. After discussion, the delegates chose the second, adding "and Relatives" after Parents.

The Purposes of the organization were:

1. To promote the general welfare of mentally re-
    tarded children of all ages everywhere – at
    home, in the communities, in institutions, and in
    public, private and religious schools.
2. To further the advancement of all ameliorative
    and preventive study and research in the field of
    mental retardation and of therapy.
3. To develop a better understanding of the prob-
    lem of mental retardation by the public, and
    cooperate with all public, private and religious
    agencies, Federal, State and local departments
    of education, health and institutions.
4. To further the training and education of person-
    nel for work in the field of mental retardation.
5. To encourage the formation of parents' groups,

75

to advise and aid parents in the solution of their problems, and to coordinate the efforts and activities of these groups.

6. To further the implementation of existing legislation on behalf of the mentally retarded.

7. To serve as a clearing house for gathering and disseminating information regarding the mentally retarded, and to foster the development of integrated programs in their behalf.

8. To solicit and receive funds for the accomplishment of the above purposes.

The minutes show that the full delegate body had made only one substantive change from the committee report. In purpose number 6, a second clause was deleted that proposed to "encourage the enactment of legislation in behalf of the mentally retarded." Presumably the deletion, which was moved by Eugene Gramm, a journalist from New York, was out of concern that lobbying by non-profits might be prohibited; his successful motion also directed a referral of the issue to "our legal staff." Delegate Harry Bloom of New Jersey, the "legal staff," reported on Saturday that the phrase "relating to legislative pressure" should be deleted and the motion was carried.

Fifteen years earlier the Children's Benevolent League had declared its purpose to be "to arouse public interest in the welfare of all physically and mentally handicapped individuals," but public interest *had* been aroused and could be assumed by the delegates. By their very organization they were accomplishing the goal that the CBL had set forth.

The Name and Purpose Committee also urged the employment of an executive secretary who would coordinate facts, materials and news from local units "into a National Bulletin for all."

On Saturday, September 30, Alan Sampson was elected president and the convention decided to delete any reference to an executive director in the bylaws.[123] Four CBL leaders were elected as part of the original twenty-two directors of the national parents' organization: H. N. Clifton, Bob Leavitt, Harold Watkins, and Roy Fowler. No other state had as many directors. California was next at three and New York had two. In 1954 Washington state also helped place NARC on a solid footing by loaning its executive, Leo Lippman, to NARC for four months.

Minnesota Governor Luther Youngdahl gave the evening address.

The minutes of the Sunday board meeting record the words of

their strong supporter:

> Miss Mildred Thomson, immediate past president of
> the AAMD, expressed her appreciation of being able to
> be present at the sessions of the convention, stated her
> view that this association would be the association of the
> country that would do most for mentally retarded chil-
> dren, that it was wise to establish an association as one
> entirely independent of others, asserted that the AAMD
> would help in any way it could, and gave this association
> her best wishes for its increasing usefulness.

Next to the journal of the AAMD, the publication most widely
read by professionals in the field was the *Training School Bulletin*,
produced by the Vineland Training School in New Jersey. The
editors immediately approached Sampson for an article on the new
phenomenon represented by the NARC. In his article Sampson,
always the diplomat, asserted that "understanding professionals" in
New Jersey, in neighboring New York, and in Washington deserved
a lot of the credit, because they had "helped the parents realize that
much can be gained by unity and communication between them in
the interests of their children."[124]

The national media attention to the problem, the hundreds of
inquiries that the overworked national secretary was fielding, and
the rapid formation of over a hundred different organizations across
the country all testified to the fact that the time to address mental
disability had finally arrived.

> Amazingly enough, an exchange of ideas revealed that
> in widely divergent parts of the United States, local
> groups have sprung up, activated by the same desperate
> need as motivated others, elsewhere. Without knowledge
> of the other groups they have developed much the same
> program, the same fundraising methods, *the same de-
> mand for fair and needed legislation* as their sister
> groups on separated seaboards.[125]

At the end of the first year at the NARC's convention in Grand
Rapids, Michigan, Sampson's presidential address was full of
optimism, reporting increased publicity in national magazines,
successful legislative efforts in a number of states, and a flurry of
inquiries from other states where unorganized parents wanted to
start a chapter. From the very first year, the actions of Congress
were a focus. In a letter dated April 23, 1951 President Sampson
wrote to the new chapters across the nation to write their senators to

reverse the exclusion of children with *mental* disabilities from a bill that provided federal aid on training teachers to work with children with disabilities. This led to an immediate conflict between NARC and the National Society of Crippled Children and Adults ("the Easter Seal Society") which opposed the expansion of the legislation.[126]

The Promise

The formation of the national organization quickly began to reshape every state and local parents group through the exchange of information, inspiration, and, more gradually, through the establishment of federal programs and funding. It was exactly what the visionaries in Washington state had hoped for and what they expected. Their disappointments, as later recalled, seem to stem from an overly optimistic belief in what was possible. Neither society nor the fact of intellectual disability yielded as easily as they hoped. Yet the actions they took would have been impossible without the hope that sustained them. As the American Christian social ethicist Reinhold Niebuhr observed

> [T]he inertia of society is so stubborn that no one will move against it, if he cannot believe that it can be more easily overcome than is actually the case. And no one will suffer the perils and pains involved in the process of radical social change, if he cannot believe in the possibility of a purer and fairer society than will ever be established. These illusions are dangerous because they justify fanaticism; but their abandonment is perilous because it inclines to inertia.[127]

CBL annual dinner 1940s

One Out of Fifty, CBL brochure 1949

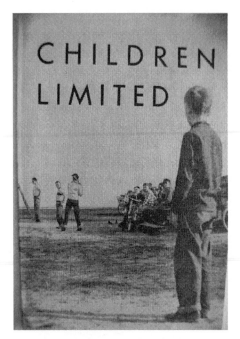

Children Limited, CBL brochure 1950

Alan Sampson, CBL president, first NARC president 1950

Children Limited

NO. 1, VOL. 1   AUGUST, 1951

State C. B. L. Convention Friday, Saturday

Gov. Arthur B. Langlie signs House Bill 310 while Mrs. Vincent F. Jones, representative from the 46th district, looks on. Mrs. Jones and Reuben V. Knoblauch, representative from the 25th district, (picture on page 3) were instrumental in passage of the bill, which provides that mentally retarded children may attend special classes in the public schools of Washington.

DOLL ADDRESS, BUCKLEY FILM TO CLIMAX SESSIONS HERE

An address by Dr. Edgar A. Doll, showing of the motion picture film taken at Buckley, and talks by leaders in the medical and legislative fields will highlight the Washington State Childrens Benevolent League convention to be held at the Winthrop Hotel in Tacoma, Friday and Saturday, August 10th and 11th.

The convention is under the direction of the Tacoma chapter of the league.

Program

Preliminary proceedings open Friday at 4 p.m. with registration in the Presidential Suite. Coffee hour will be held from 4.30 to 6.30, and committees will meet at 7.30 p.m., at which time procedures and programming will be organized.

Saturday, the convention opens in the Wedgwood Room at 9 a.m., after the trustees and committee breakfast is held at 7.30. After the invocation, reports will be given by Olaf Caskin, with presentation of the charter; new parents organization will be reported by Alan Sampson. Robert Leavitt will report on the C.B.L. trust fund, the state president's report and the American Association on mental deficiency report will be given by State President H. N. Clifton, and chapter reports will be given.

Dr. Ross Hamilton, director of education for handicapped children, office of the state superintendent of public instruction at Olympia, will speak at 11.00. Dr. Ross is well conversant with House Bill 310, which was passed by the legislature at the last session.

Barber To Speak

Dr. T. M. Barber, superintendent of the Mt. Rainier state school at Buckley, will give a report during the lunch hour in the Crystal ballroom. At 1.30 the convention will get under way again in the (Continued on page 2)

Hamilton Outlines HB 310, To Speak at CBL Convention

Dr. Ross Hamilton, director of education for handicapped children, state superintendent's office, Olympia, outlined House Bill 310 at a conference on the education of mentally handicapped children, held in Seattle recently.

House Bill 310, passed by the state legislature in its most recent session, provides funds and authority for training of exceptional children in the regular school system. Dr. Hamilton explained that this is optional with the local school boards.

Gives Background

In his talk, Dr. Hamilton outlined the background of mental retardation in relation to how it has been handled in the state of Washington. He briefly explained how the state, almost from the beginning, has made provision for various state schools, out of which came the State School for the Deaf, the State School for the Blind, State School for girls, the Boys Training School, Lakeland Village, and Rainier State School.

Dr. Hamilton told his listeners that in 1943, the legislature passed chapter 130, which extended special educational services to physically handicapped children. In 1947, chapter 240 was passed, which extended special medical and educational services to cerebral palsy children. In 1949, the legislature passed chapter 186, which extended basic state school apportionment to pre-school age physically handicapped children of three years of age and up.

(Continued on page 2)

Children Limited. First CBL/Arc Newspaper, 1951, shows Gov. Langlie signing law providing state funding for all special education students

1950s publicity illustration

CBL annual dinner 1951. From left, standing, Van Hinkle, Elinor Reilly, unknown, Alan Sampson, Olaf Caskin, Mrs. Caskin, priest, superintendent, Ross Hamilton, H. N. Clifton. Seated, Lela Mae Clifton, Supt. Les Mason, Edgar Doll, Mrs. Hinkle, E. H. Riviere, unknowns

MRS. EARL MAGNUSON
Perseverance Pays Off

**Anna Magnuson led a successful fight for state funding for
students with severe disabilities, 1951**

Ross Hamilton, state director of handicapped education, 1950s

Leo Lippman, CBL-ARC executive director, 1952

**Harold Watkins, president, and Eric Froberg, vice president for
Western Washington, elected 1953**

Mrs. John Epton

Katherine Epton, legislator 1957-69, led creation of developmental centers

Bus donated to Rainier School by Pierce County CBL-WARC 1954

**Tacoma CBL members publicize their annual carnival, 1952.
Prizes included 900 pounds of beef and a 13-foot home freezer.
Proceeds went to buy "supplies and gifts for the children" at
Rainier School and Lakeland Village**

**President Mae Wise accepts symbol of 1960 convention from
Grace Gould (obscured)**

CHAPTER THREE:
VISIBILITY AND VIABILITY

The paper we have dreamed of for the past eight years is now a reality....The name *Children Limited* was the brainchild of Phil Reilly as he lounged on our sofa one winter evening...and we all hoped it might be used nationally either as the name of the organization or for its voice.[128]

—Janice Leavitt,
on the first issue of NARC paper in 1952

Somewhere along the line, I think there should be a positive effort made to broaden the composition of this body, the Board of Trustees. You in this room are a wonderful group of people, but it seems to me the nature of the problems with which we deal has changed to the point where we must have new machinery to move the new mountains.

—Leo Lippman, 1960

When families united nationally, they found that they could educate the public far more effectively. They did so quickly, and Washington families soon found the ideas of the public and families in other states were now influencing them in return. No longer able to control their own destiny, the family advocates working together in a national organization at least had far more tools to work with.

Of course, public awareness did not come all at once. The early CBL leaders had laid the groundwork, and in the 1950s the organization, renamed the Washington Association for Retarded Children, continued to build on that foundation. As the parents' organization grew, the "plight" of children with mental retardation and their families gained broad public exposure. This visibility was no accident. The parents had built an organizational weapon to fight myths and misconceptions about retardation, the "bogies of the nineteenth century," as Alan Sampson had put it. As these families succeeded, others joined with them, and the public at large offered new levels of support. A strong organization and a high profile went hand in hand. Along with publicity, WARC attained a paid staff, a pool of talented leaders and members, an enlarged funding base, internal organizational specialization, supporters, and allies.

Stepping Out of the Shadows

The Children's Benevolent League had recognized the need for increased public awareness as early as its 1936 incorporation papers, and it had published small brochures during the war. But the by-law revisions of 1947 signaled new vigor in the CBL's approach to generating public support. Hiring a publicity director indicated a new optimism and hope in parental attitudes.

Irwin "Dutch" Blumenfeld became the organization's publicist and first employee or independent contractor.[129] *One Out of Fifty* was the twelve-page, two-color brochure which resulted from the six-month contract awarded to Blumenfeld.[130] Over 3,500 copies were mailed to legislators, health officials, and service and fraternal organizations. The 1948 text described the high frequency of the problem, termed "mental deficiency," and then offered a portrait of its victims. Most of them remained at home and even attended the public schools where they were "often the objects of ridicule and scorn and always a serious problem to parents and normal brothers and sisters." Other "mental-deficients" enjoyed the advantages of the state's two specialized schools, which unfortunately had waiting lists. The Road Ahead, as described by the brochure, lay in two areas of League activities: obtaining more and better institutions and promoting research into the "causes, treatment and prevention of mental deficiency." Wherever they were, these children stood "in the shadows of life, in a half-world of their own, apart from normal children."

The shadow imagery persisted for many years. One letterhead depicted a mother and father huddled together in shadows cast by dark clouds hanging overhead. From a small break in the darkness a (divine) ray of light streamed, betokening a new day. National, state, and local chapters attempted to portray a positive image of emergence from the shadows with logos of children whose faces were half in shadow and half in sunlight. It was an appropriate image for the time, since it conveyed the parents' real feelings that tragedy had struck.[131] Even though parental hopes are still crushed today, and tears still fall, it was a different era then. One Seattle member recalls asking for donations on a downtown street corner about 1950. She was approached by a woman, of eugenicist opinion, who said

> "You ought to be ashamed of yourself, having such a
> child in an advanced scientific age as ours!"

Spokane parent Kathryn Epton remembered when she and her children were pushing her cerebral palsied son Johnny in a wheelchair and a woman in a Pennsylvania hotel shrank up against the wall and said

> "Aren't you afraid your other children will catch
> it?"[132]

To combat such ideas, the CBL responded with publicity efforts aimed at the public and at parents of children with mental retardation. Thus, the pamphlet *Children Limited* was published in 1950. Over the next several years, 32,500 copies were distributed. And, after several abortive starts in the prior decades, the CBL began to publish a quarterly state newsletter in 1951, using the name *Children Limited.*[133] With a glossy four or six page format, the newspaper featured photos and articles on programmatic, legislative, and organizational events. Stories submitted by local chapters were a regular feature. The name of the state newsletter did not survive long, however. After the August and December 1951 issues were published, the CBL relinquished the name "Children Limited" to the national organization, where it was used as the national newsletter's title for over ten years.

WARC then adopted *HOPE for Retarded Children* as the title of its quarterly newsletter. *HOPE* continued the WARC tradition of high quality journalism, providing up to date medical information from national authorities, national programmatic developments, as well as announcements of events from around the state. Legislation proposed and enacted was always a focus of the newsletters.

At the national level, the first issue of NARC's *Children Limited* newspaper appeared in August 1952 with a resounding front-page headline:

> **At Last!**
> **One Voice To Speak For All America's Retarded!**
> As you read these words history is being made for the
> mentally retarded of America – and you, reading now,
> are a living, breathing, vital part of that history. For here,
> at last, is the first issue of the first national publication of
> parents and friends of the retarded!
>
> Who and what are the retarded? They are known by
> many names, mentally deficient, mentally defective, ex-
> ceptional. Charles Dickens called them "those who are
> forever children," and Pearl S. Buck wrote: "Of all of
> God's children, these are the most innocent."
>
> We know that they are with us everywhere and have
> always been with us. We know that they come to us re-
> gardless of race, creed, social station or level of parental
> intelligence. We know that they are terribly handicapped
> by an intellectual impairment, the conditions for which
> may occur before, during, or after birth. And most bitter
> knowledge of all: we know that by every cool calculation
> of society, they are "the least of these."
>
> Here in America, where the standards for our retarded
> are probably higher than anywhere else in the world, the
> over-all national level of care, treatment and opportunity
> for them is so woefully inadequate, that sometimes par-
> ents must wonder, in all honesty, "Does the constitution
> of the United States include these, too?

Hope for a Salk-like Cure

In Washington state public acceptance of persons with mental disabilities also reached a milestone in the autumn of 1953 when a full-page advertisement by WARC appeared in the *Seattle Sunday Times* and other newspapers. Adapted from an earlier ad in the *New York Times*, it used the successful image of another health campaign to elicit the support of the public. 1953 was the year of the dramatic breakthrough on polio: Jonas Salk had announced the development of a vaccine to prevent the crippling disease. NARC capitalized on that hope. WARC's ad showed a cute pre-school boy walking down the sidewalk. The photo was captioned, "This is a picture of a crippled child!" The copy read:

> No, you see no braces on his legs, no supporting
> crutch, no miracle of modern prosthetics to enable him to
> take his place in the world. Yet his affliction is all the
> more tragic...because, you see, it is his little brain that is
> crippled. He is mentally retarded.

The language of the advertisement provides a classic image of persons with mental retardation as "pitiful cases."[134] But the text was upbeat in telling the story of WARC, its achievements, current activities, and goals. The message ended with an appeal for understanding and for parents of mentally retarded persons to join WARC.

For the first time, the names of luminaries appeared in print supporting WARC's efforts. Governor Langlie was the first of fifty-six sponsors listed in the ad. He proclaimed:

> On behalf of the people of the State of Washington, I
> want to compliment the Washington Association for Re-
> tarded Children for their inspiring efforts devoted toward
> the welfare of the mentally retarded children in our state.
> The cooperation of this voluntary organization with the
> state's Division of Children and Youth Services can con-
> tribute immeasurably toward the beneficial care of these
> children. May I urge our people to give their support to
> this cause and program.

Other endorsements were offered by Seattle mayor Allan Pomeroy; Episcopal bishop Stephen F. Bayne; Norman Clein, president of the Seattle Pediatrics Society; Pearl Wanamaker, State Superintendent of Schools; Henry Broderick, prominent Seattle businessman; Raphael Levine, the city's most prominent rabbi; and University of Washington president Henry Schmitz.

The celebrities in WARC's advertisement symbolized its rise to public visibility in the 1950s. In earlier decades the organization's activities had rarely appeared in print except for annual stories about state conventions. The first general feature story on WARC part of a three-part series, appeared in the *Seattle Times* in October 1950. By contrast, a review of Washington newspapers shows that in the 1950s, between 600 and 1,000 articles a year mentioned the state or local WARC chapters! A rapid change had occurred.

The last form of print media which WARC pioneered during the early fifties was a speaker's manual. Originally distributed in

1954 as a 38-page volume for use in Washington, parent groups across the nation requested copies. The manual provided members with outlines for speeches, responses to typical questions, and tips on how to win invitations to speak before community groups. Periodic updates were provided through the state newsletter.

Movie. Parents took advantage of other media as well. In perhaps their boldest move, WARC unveiled a color and sound motion picture called *Children Limited* in 1951.

It was a 30 minute, color motion picture, produced by Starling Studios in Seattle.

The Library of Congress described the film:

> Summary. Presents the general problem of mental retardation. Portrays institutional care of various types of mentally retarded children and explains the need for other kinds of service at the community level. Describes the possibilities, importance, and advantages of occupational, physical, and recreational therapy, and of job training. Demonstrates the cooperation and activity of parent and child within their environment, and indicated the value of home care.

The film quickly became popular throughout the United States. *Children Limited* gained worldwide recognition when the U.S. Information Agency circulated the motion picture to Norway, Israel, New Zealand, Brazil and Iran, according to an article in the state newsletter.[135]

Radio stations occasionally granted interviews or provided public service announcements in support of WARC projects during this decade, but the novelty of the fifties was television. In just the first six months of 1953, WARC was featured in television interviews on mental retardation on Seattle stations KING, KOMO, and KIRO, which were the local network affiliates of NBC, ABC, and CBS, and Tacoma's KTNT. The most ambitious of these projects was a March 20, 953 half-hour broadcast on KING's "Community Workshop." The program featured parents, teachers, WARC leaders, and a representative of the state Division of Children and Youth Services.

Two National Celebrities Tell Their Stories

Events on the national scene influenced Washington publicity efforts and the thinking of its members more and more during the 1950s.

Members read about programs and events in the NARC paper that few of them had ever dreamed possible.

Pearl Buck. Pearl Buck was one of America's best known authors. Her novel *The Good Earth,* drawing on her life in China, was the best-selling book of the early 1930s. In 1938 Buck became the first American woman to be awarded the Nobel Prize for Literature.

But she wrote another book as well. *The Child Who Never Grew* (1950) described her thoughts about her daughter Carol to an amazed public, surprised to learn an unknown side of the author. The book painted a grim picture of the disability, so that even though she took note of a new parental movement which seemed to be growing across the country, her story reflected, and to some extent justified, abandonment as the right move.[136] She wrote, "Every retarded child means a stricken, heartsick family."[137]

Part of what we must learn is that even in 1950, Pearl Buck, a very well-educated woman, accepted the old stereotypes. One of the most shocking passages reads:

> The total number of retarded children is not large...and yet it is enough to cause trouble everywhere. Homes are unhappy, parents distraught, schoolrooms everywhere confused by the presence of these...As parents die or cannot care for them, as teachers give them up, these children drift helplessly into the world, creating havoc wherever they go. They become the tools of those more clever; they are the hopeless juvenile delinquents; they fall into criminal ways because they know not what they do.[138]

Buck decided that abandoning hope was the correct approach. This was quite contrary to what most parent advocates were saying. Their view was captured by the title of the state newsletter *HOPE.*

Buck's view was shaped by an incident at the famed Mayo Clinic in Rochester, Minnesota, where she had gone seeking treatment for her daughter. After the doctors left, a man with a German accent quietly moved in to talk to her about her child. Buck wrote, "Now comes the moment for which I will be grateful as long as I live." After asking whether the doctors held out hope, he said:

> Listen to what I tell you. I tell you, madame, that the child can never be normal. Do not deceive yourself. You will wear out your life and beggar your family unless you give up hope and face the truth...Americans are all too soft. I am not soft...This child will be a burden on you all your life....Prepare yourself, madame! Above all,

do not let her absorb you. Find a place where she can be happy and leave her there and live your own life. I tell you the truth for your own sake.[139]

No wonder Buck thought it best to institutionalize her daughter at Vineland School.

There is another paragraph of Buck's that shocks the conscience today.

...[I]n addition to the practical problem of how to protect the child's life, which may last beyond the parent's, there is the problem of one's own self in misery. All the brightness of life is gone, all the pride in parenthood. There is more than pride gone, there is an actual sense of one's life being cut off in the child. The stream of generations has been stopped. Death would be far easier to bear, for death is final. . . How often did I cry out in my heart that it would be better if my child died! If that shocks you who have not known, it will not shock those who do know. I would have welcomed death for my child, would still welcome it, for then she would finally be safe.[140]

One can hardly read *The Child Who Never Grew* as a self-help book for other families, even if Buck intended it as such. It painted a grim picture. And yet for many parents, the publication of her book was a sign that at least public discussion of their situation was occurring. As late as 1959, Washington WARC members were reading about her speech to the NARC convention in an article called "Pearl Buck Declares Research Key Task, Endorses NARC."[141]

Dale Evans. In 1950 the cowboy singing star of movies and television Roy Rogers and his wife Dale Evans had a daughter with Down syndrome. Robin Rogers died two years later of heart complications. Dale soon wrote the book *Angel Unaware*, which is a fictional conversation between the little angel Robin and God in heaven. The book's title is wrong. It was never the angel who was unaware. It was the people around her who, in their materialism, pride, and occasional hatred, misunderstood God's intentions. Handicapped children are angels sent to draw their parents and families closer to God. Dale writes that Robin succeeded in doing that for Roy and her.

In *Angel Unaware* Robin relates to God the words of the doctor who makes the initial diagnosis.

> "Take her home and love her. Love will help more
> than anything else in a situation like this – more than all
> the hospitals and all the medical science in the world."
> That's one thing that I learned Down There, Father – that
> the doctors are just beginning to discover how much help
> You are in any situation. They're beginning to talk seri-
> ously about "tender, loving care." You are getting
> through to the doctors.[142]

Other doctors advise them that putting Robin "in a home" is the best thing to do in cases like these, but Dale refuses. As she later realizes, if she had "put her away," Robin's divine role to teach them faith would have been frustrated.

The book does warn that there are prejudiced persons to be dealt with.

> Mommy heard once that some doctor had said that
> babies who came into the world in my condition should
> be lined up in a row and 'machine-gunned,' because they
> were no good to themselves or to anybody else. Father, if
> that remark was really made, forgive him, for he knows
> not what he's saying. I wish he could meet You.[143]

Robin gets the mumps and then encephalitis. She dies and is happy in heaven. The book ends with "And now, Father, please . . . could I just go out and try my wings?"[144]

Angel Unaware is the sad story of a child's death. Unlike books written by later parents, it does little to celebrate the worldly achievements of the child. But that is too much to expect of a child that young. Parents at the time certainly felt encouraged by the book. That was demonstrated by the help given to NARC by Dale Evans and Roy Rogers. Perhaps the image which most represents the time is a photograph of Dale Evans, singer, actress, and wife of movie cowboy star Roy Rogers, presenting a check for $5,000 to Gilbert Hanke, NARC president. The check represented the first royalties from the book.

Pearl Buck and Dale Evans had come out of the closet and pub-lished accounts of their experience as mothers. Until the Kennedy family story became known in the sixties, these women were the most prominent mothers of children with cognitive disabilities.

National Retarded Children's Week

The crippled boy advertisement of 1953 had demonstrated the

power of coordinated media campaigns. In effect, the ad served as the pilot for the National Retarded Children's Week, which was held for the first time in November 1954. Endorsed by President Dwight D. Eisenhower and co-chaired by Dale Evans and Roy Rogers, the event was the first national campaign to provide public information and education about persons with cognitive limitations and to help raise funds for them.

A year later in 1955 National Retarded Children's "Week" had expanded to ten days in November. The theme for the 1955 celebration was "Give Thanks...by giving to help retarded children." Jack Benny, star of television, radio, and the movies, served as national chairman and master of ceremonies for a national CBS telecast. Other well-known performers in the production were Irene Dunne, Bob and Cathy Crosby, Liberace, Dale Evans, Marge and Gower Champion, the Modernaires, and Art Linkletter.

For several years the National Retarded Children's Week became known as "The Big Week" among persons involved in the field. In Washington, as elsewhere, statewide and local events were planned accordingly. Outreach to service, business and other community groups peaked at this time, with many creative informational and fundraising activities taking place.

"Senator Bids NARC Challenge U.S. to Launch 5-Year Program."

So reads the headline in the December 1956 issue of *Children Limited*, now the NARC newspaper, which reported on a major speech by Senator Henry M. "Scoop" Jackson when he addressed the NARC convention in Seattle. Senator Jackson's proposal prefigured that of President John F. Kennedy six years later.[145] The speech is also interesting because it already accurately acknowledged the pioneering Congressional role of Representative John Fogarty (D, RI) who was the best ally that NARC had.[146]

Jackson urged the NARC not to delay, but to push ahead. They would find sympathetic ears in the current session of Congress.

Scoop suggested that the Executive branch should present a five-year plan to Congress that the Department of Health, Education and Welfare would develop by winter 1957. The program should identify problems that require emphasis in the field of mental retardation during the next five years, recommend priorities, and suggest legislation and revisions in the way the Administration dealt with the problem. Among the other projects that Jackson proposed was "Support pilot projects in care and training and contribute to promising lines of research." That sounds very much like what JFK proposed five years later. And very much what Washington state was already doing with a "pilot school," as discussed below.

Hired Help

Exploiting the potential of the media and hiring a staff went hand in hand. After Blumenfeld's six-month contract expired, Edythe Tucker was hired as WARC's first permanent employee. She worked part-time as WARC's executive secretary from a desk in vice-president Olaf Caskin's office at the Terminal Sales Building in Seattle in 1950. Local CBL leaders soon appreciated the value of an office to the organization and the first formal "state office" opened at that location a few months later.[147]

It soon became apparent that the skills of a writer and public relations specialist were needed to publish a newsletter and to conduct the other communications efforts. These requirements led to the selection of Leo Lippman as executive secretary in 1952. He was the public information director of the Community Chest and Council of Seattle and King County, the forerunner to today's United Way. Lippman had also been executive secretary of the coalition which successfully promoted a 1950 statewide bond issue that included $20,000,000 in construction dollars for Rainier and Lakeland Village. The fact that WARC sought and was able to hire someone with a solid resume shows that the organization was determined to be a real player among voluntary organizations. The fact that Leo Lippman applied for and accepted the position showed that he recognized that mental retardation was a field with real potential for professional growth.

In addition to his part-time position with WARC, Leo Lippman also had duties with the Seattle chapter. He remained with WARC for the next ten pivotal years and personally promoted and implemented many of its new initiatives.[148] As the association grew, Lippman's responsibilities evolved into that of an executive director for the association.

Tension between the paid executive and the volunteer leaders of an organization is to be expected; it occurred quickly. Harold Watkins was elected state president in August 1953. The following month, Lippman wrote to Watkins and proposed a WARC booth at the NARC convention. In a return letter, Watkins judged the suggestion unfeasible. Lippman continued to believe the booth was a good idea and found someone else who would arrange it, thus maneuvering around Watkins, his nominal superior. In October,

Lippman wrote to Watkins and asked that telephone credit cards be issued to the president and state officers; all except one of the officers were from outside Seattle. Lippman received no response from Watkins. Later in October, an ironic letter reveals his dissatisfaction with the pace of Watkins' leadership.

> Mr. Watkins
> Things look good here right now.
> A sensationally successful Carnival Bazaar—first approach made to Boeing Good Neighbor Fund—real enthusiasm for the national—cooperation from press, radio and TV—increasing public interest —new cooperation among our own chapters.
> What is next? Committee appointments and a board meeting?
> Leo

Volunteers need staff to remind them of their duties and to push for progress toward organizational goals. Yet voluntary organizations frequently offer only symbolic rewards for performance.[149] These rewards can occasionally elicit heroic levels of action, such as that exhibited by parent crusaders in the field of mental retardation. But stagnation will occur when motivation declines. Hiring an employee for the organization can provide a partial solution to this problem. Suddenly one individual receives "real" rewards, a salary. Being paid normally produces a consistent level of performance, efforts become more dependable, and the achievement of group goals is facilitated.

But there are counterbalancing negative consequences of having paid staff. Hiring staff adds a secondary, organizational maintenance goal. That is, the salary, benefits, office space, and other components required to support the staff position become a concern for the parent volunteers. At worst, the maintenance of the organization can become the primary goal to which the original objectives are subordinated. As long as the organization continues to add objectives and resources permit, more and more employees will be required. Adding staff will increase demands on the volunteers for their support. This outcome is inevitable, even without invoking Parkinson's Law that "an official wants to multiply subordinates."[150] Thus, as WARC continued to evolve and expand during the 1950s, so did the role of its employees. For example, when Leo Lippman distributed his annual report to the board of trustees in 1960, he noted a renewed level of activity in WARC, specifically the reorganization and reactivation of committees and the assumption of new responsibilities by WARC officers. This resurgence was due to the leadership of the first woman president, Mae Wise. Lippman complimented Mrs. Wise when he said it was "gratifying to be part of an observable forward movement." But he was openly critical when he added that the pressure on staff was reaching the point "where it brings inefficiency rather than greater productivity." There had been a lessening of some staff assignments because of the current officers' willingness to assume new responsibilities, but the clerical workload could no longer be accomplished by one part-time employee. Lippman told the board members that WARC's office secretary received pay for only sixty percent of her time and that the pressures of the job had caused the resignation of two successive secretaries in a one-month period.

Lippman offered several "suggestions." First, the "sorely insufficient" clerical staff had to be expanded. Second, the state association needed its own executive who was not also an employee of a local chapter. No conflict of loyalties was implied, he asserted; rather, the two jobs called for different skills. Third, having a separate state executive position meant that a redefinition of the job would be required. Fourth, and more radically, he proposed that the time had come to broaden the composition of the board of trustees. Expanding the board would supply the organizational machinery needed to "move the new mountains" which the decade of the sixties had brought into view. Lippman hinted that non-parent community leaders and professionals should be added to the membership of the board. Finally, the staff changes would require expanded office space. Lippman acknowledged that the lack of funds would make the reorganization of WARC difficult, but cajoled board members: "The challenge must be faced and met. It doesn't take money to begin thinking and planning. Then when you have the money, you also have a plan ready to put into effect."

The board accepted some of Lippman's recommendations. In 1962 WARC moved to a larger facility outside the downtown business district. Although still sharing quarters with the King County Chapter, WARC did gain more office space. A second change occurred in 1962—Lippman's position was upgraded to that of a full-time executive director. But after several of his requests were granted, Leo Lippman resigned the post with WARC to take a position in mental retardation created by the California legislature.

Lippman's successor was Van R. Hinkle, who had previously served as director of the Division of Child and Youth Services for the Department of Institutions. As executive director, Hinkle persuaded WARC to move its state office to Olympia. The new office opened in Olympia in 1964. The official rationale for the move was that, like many state associations, WARC was establishing its headquarters at the capital city "in order to achieve a close, working relationship with the key state agencies." While the move undoubtedly enhanced the relationship between WARC staff and state agency staff, it also increased the distance between the state ARC and the largest concentration of members and activists in Seattle.

In August 1965 Van Hinkle resigned the WARC position to become director of the Department of Consultative and Community Services of NARC in New York City. His replacement, Michael C. Kreider, had been executive director of the Michigan ARC for nine years. Elise Chadwick informed the WARC board that, while she was satisfied with Kreider's credentials, she was concerned whether WARC could afford the increase in the salary to $14,000. The board decided that it was necessary to pay the "going wage" in order to get the person they needed.

Kreider soon reported that, in his judgment, WARC was "not well organized to do many of the things that should have been done ten years ago." A list of the organizational problems he found in 1965 is illuminating, in part because of the regular recurrence of certain problems:

> The number of fathers involved was too low.
> A lack of enthusiasm was apparent in many chapters.
> Chapter attendance was too low, and the low attendance made a bad impression on guest speakers.
> Too many chapters were attempting to sponsor special projects and schools of their own, which was contrary to NARC's goal of promoting community responsibility for such programs.
> Too few "professional" people were active on local chapter boards; parents needed to make special efforts to obtain their contribution of volunteer time.
> Every chapter needed to reach out beyond itself, becoming knowledgeable of all community services and promoting development beyond their current "sample" size.

The comment about the chapters failing to attract "professional" people to lead the various chapters is the same criticism that Leo Lippman had raised five years earlier. The complaint reflects a continuing—and perhaps permanent—division within the organization over the nature of the group. Was WARC to be—is The Arc of the future to be—a parent or family focused group with major events involving parent-to-parent contact and having as a prime function developing self-advocacy by family members? If that was WARC or is The Arc, then there may no urgent need to ensure that there are professionals and influential people from community on the board of directors. Rather one needs plenty of space for family leadership to develop and not be overshadowed by professionalism.

Or should The Arc seek to be a comprehensive center of activities and services for persons with intellectual disabilities? Should it focus on developing programs that address gaps in the community support system and finding ways to fill the gaps with employment, recreation, education, and training? If that is The Arc, then broader community support is a necessity and persons with professional credentials and influence in the community will be critical to obtaining public and private grants and access to decision-makers like politicians and bureaucrats.

Although Kreider had ambitious plans, it is unclear whether the effectiveness of the association improved during his three years as director. Thus, when Dr. David S. Alkins assumed the duties of executive director in February 1969, he told the board that there was a need for "more communication" between local chapters and the state office, a typical complaint in organizations. In June, Alkins reported to the executive committee that he had mailed questionnaires to all WARC chapters and had requested information on their progress, problems, goals, and needs. Alkins hoped to establish "leadership workshops" in each region which would be conducted when he visited local chapters.

By the end of the sixties, the WARC executive's responsibilities had expanded far beyond the original focus on publicity to general association management. Problems of external effectiveness and internal inefficiencies were tackled by each new incumbent.

Leaders, Active Members, and Followers

In a famous boast the early Washington state labor radicals, the Wobblies, claimed "We're all leaders."[151] Unfortunately, WARC, like every other organization, was unable to realize such a proud claim. But when groups are small, most members do exert some influence in shaping organizational activities and policies. As groups grow, more differentiation between leaders and members occurs within the organization, and it becomes impossible for each individual to play a formative role.

Normally, the leaders of organizations such as WARC are the

elected officers. But during the early years of the CBL and WARC, women provided much more labor and commanded more influence than their absence from offices would indicate. In WARC, as in most other formally organized charities, the further down the hierarchy, the higher the proportion of females. Thus, women were in the majority among local members and held office in some chapters. For example, Ada Percival served as president of the Pierce county chapter for many years in the thirties and forties. But further up the hierarchy, it was not until 1959 that Mae Wise became the first female state president. However, since then there has been gender equality; indeed, most recent Arc of Washington presidents have been women.

The officers of the state organization were generally recruited from the ranks of the local officers. These men were often sought as candidates because of their relatively high social status. In addition, their flexible schedules allowed them time to devote to WARC. Finally, they had developed skills in their occupations which enabled them to be more effective leaders. The presidents elected in the 1930s and 1940s fit the profile of the small businessman: Monty Percival, automotive garage owner; Roy Fowler, automobile salesman; Harold Isenhath, bus driver and automobile salesman; Newland Reilly, newspaper reporter and editor; Alan Sampson, insurance agent; and M. P. Nolden, sawmill owner.

In the 1950s and 1960s, the presidents and their occupations were: H. N. Clifton, advertising and other businesses; Olaf Caskin, manager, lithograph company; Harold Watkins, owner, produce company; E. H. Riviere, banker; Mae Wise, office manager; Raymond Howell, public school music teacher; and Elise Chadwick, housewife.

In the 1970s and 80s, the presidents became more occupationally diverse: Frank Skerbeck, physician; Omer Carey, business professor; Harold Little, accountant and executive; Lou Healy, owner, office supplies store; David Foscue, attorney; Day, Lou, housewife; Hilty, Connie, special education pre-school director; Larry Jones, sociology professor; Melba Grau, special education pre-school director; and Jim Marick, industrial purchasing agent. And such diversity has continued.

Several trends are illustrated: proportionately fewer persons are small business owners and managers; women have achieved more equitable representation; and professionals in the field of mental retardation are emerging as a source for officers. The tasks which the group undertook probably influenced certain types of persons to become involved and served as a disincentive to others. The social criticism and litigation of recent years, for example, may not be the most popular activities of managers of small retail businesses. But such pursuits may appeal to a college professor or attorney. No matter what their profession, all Washington state Arc presidents were parents of persons with mental retardation until Linda Clark of Spokane, a community college instructor with special interest in adults with cognitive disabilities, became president in 1989.

Just as the context and type of leadership can vary, the meaning of membership can vary. An individual can be a "member" of the class of 1961 merely by finishing high school in a given year, while a credit union "member" may feel much like a customer. Some organizations, such as the Catholic Church, retain as members practically all persons who do not formally renounce allegiance. No monetary contribution or activity is required; one can forget that he or she is a Catholic for years. On the other hand, membership in a small and intense religious group can demand continuing hours of involvement per week and provide a primary source of personal identity.

What has it meant to be an ARC member? The minimal meaning is simply a name on the books which helps provide the appearance of strength as part of the "body-count." How many members has the ARC had? The organization claimed 3,000 to 5,000 members soon after its formation, and Superintendent Charles Parker of the State Custodial School reported 10,000 "registered" members in 1936. Registration apparently indicated consent to become a supporter of the organization and its efforts to assist the state school. A membership card was provided, but no dues were payable and contributions were entirely voluntary.

With by-law amendments in the latter forties, the meaning of membership began to change. In 1948, the membership committee for the first time distinguished between active, dues-paying members (1,115) and other supporters, termed associate members (1,915). The "active" membership claimed was thus reduced by two-thirds from the earlier figure of 3,000, and the concerned membership chair, Geraldine LeBlanc, protested that the dues were too high at one dollar. Unsuccessfully, she asked that they be lowered to fifty cents per year "like the PTA and women's organizations."

More committed members attended monthly meetings, listened to speakers, provided mutual emotional support, and socialized together. These chapter meetings across the state had an average of twenty persons in attendance, indicating that there were perhaps 200 to 300 core members state-wide. This figure approximates the number of people who attended the state conventions in the 1930s and 1940s. Since chapters were organized in support of the two schools which their children attended, there was a coherent focus for personal commitment. Commitment to your child, to the School, and to the parent organization fused inextricably together in their meaning. Membership had become an act of will, a way to express personal responsibility.

In the later forties and fifties, membership became easier. Families were more willing to join an association which was gaining widespread acceptance. Society had begun to acknowledge intellectual disability as a fact that families had to deal with and were dealing with successfully. Parents began to be relieved of blame. Society no longer viewed mental retardation as "their fault." This change in attitudes did not come easily. As Woodhull Hay had argued, a major motive in the early years was to demonstrate that, contrary to societal prejudices, parents could do something for their children. They could accomplish good for their child and perform a parental role of helping a son or daughter. Those physicians, educators, and others who said, "Nothing can be done for your child," would be proven wrong.

But, as Lippman pointed out, membership was not entirely a positive act of commitment; membership was only partially voluntary.[152] As one father put it, "my wife and I didn't join this organization; we were forced into it." No one chose to have a child with mental retardation. Furthermore, as long as the organization was focused on the state institutions, significant social pressures could be used to persuade parents to join. The other parents could find you easily, and, like kidnappers, they knew where your child went to school. Institutional staff were allied with the parents' organization, especially before the creation of civil service and before the unionization of employees. The staff's dependence on the parents' organization for support led to broad institutional collaboration with these families.

In absolute and in per capita terms, the Arc's membership has declined over the decades, due to several factors. One reason for the decline was the dispersion of persons with mental disabilities into hundreds of different programs. WARC had become a general purpose organization, not an institutional parents' club. In the process, the association lost members as families and professionals developed competing loyalties to the specialized new programs in the community. A second important dynamic in the decline was also tied to the proliferation of services. As more of their needs were addressed, there was less necessity for parents and their children to remain committed to advocacy groups. These first two factor scan be seen as a mark of the Arc's success. Through their hard work, Arc members have worked themselves out of a job – partial though that success has been. But the third factor is not due to the Arc's success. Along with other voluntary organizations, The Arc's membership has also been declining in important part to the entry of women into the labor force, which places a severe burden on finding the time to volunteer in any charity. Things will never be the same. Professional paid leadership and staff has seemingly thus become more critical to the success of the Arc.

Paying the Piper

At the first parents' meeting in 1935, James Oakley pointed out that no organization can get along on air. He struck a theme that echoes endlessly through the years. Because more or less everything is for sale in modern societies, a very large fraction of The Arc's work has been raising money. Early WARC members spent much time and effort to secure public funds to address the problems of persons with mental retardation. But the association also devoted a great deal of energy to raising money to assure the survival of the organization. In the 1930s and early 1940s, when most money was used to purchase supplies for the institutions and presents for inmates, contributing was more voluntary, less demanded. Little money was retained for "state work." But when the reformers in the late forties visualized larger goals, they felt they needed to raise more money as well. Membership became a matter of paying dues, assessments on local chapters began, and the need for funds loomed larger at meetings. Members and chapters were "expected" to pay their fair share. Budgets were prepared, and ways and means projects became a routine and necessary task. In the fifties support for the national organization and for staff salaries resulted in new budgetary demands. The state organization was expected to provide *its* fair share to the national Arc.

After World War II, most local chapters raised funds by soliciting contributions from service organizations and by holding bake sales, spaghetti dinners, and the like. In the late forties King County made a distinct improvement in fundraising when it decided to hold a bazaar which featured games, raffles, and merchant-donated items for sale. President Clifton engaged volunteers from the art departments of both major daily newspapers to decorate the reusable booths. Through his contacts with tolerant police officers, Harold Isenhath was able to set up quiet, but illegal, gambling by raffling off an automobile. The bazaar was a huge success. Rather than the few hundred dollars the chapter was accustomed to netting, $7,000 was raised the first year through the various bazaar events, and $14,500 was earned the next year. The King County chapter swiftly moved its meetings to higher quality rooms, and membership grew rapidly from 45 to 200. The bazaar was a large fund raiser for years, and the growth of Seattle's income was reflected in the increased state budget.

As noted previously, the development of National Retarded Children's Week concentrated the attentions of parents in Washington, as in the rest of the country. In the early and middle fifties, most local WARC chapters and their allies (dairies and milkmen one year) selected the NARC-organized Week as their largest fundraising event. Larger and larger amounts of money were generated as WARC membership increased, as more community needs for funds were identified, and as community acceptance increased.

But a problem plagued WARC: the state budget was often out of control. Even though support from local chapters increased, WARC encountered problems due to its dependency on them. WARC could not control contributions because of the lack of a true contractual relationship, and, likewise, the state office's budgeting practices were not effectively constrained by the local units. It was easy for the elected representatives of the chapters to vote for a state budget on the basis of what they hoped to gain, only to have shortfalls occur back at the county level. The budget irregularity from year to year, coupled with the lack of investment common in nonprofit organizations, resulted in perennial crises. For example, in a good year like 1961, 76 percent of the $10,180 budget had been received by the June board meeting. But in 1962, when the association had agreed to Lippman's plan to increase his position to full-time and thereby effectively doubled the budget to $22,600, only $4,000 had been received by June. The contributions due from the chapters ranged from $250 to $7,300 (King County). The budget crisis was over at the end of the summer when King County presented a check for its full share.

In 1965 the approved budget was $26,903, including $11,000 for the Executive Director. But when Michael Kreider insisted on $14,000 to accept the vacant executive position, a decision was made to tap a bequest of $28,224 to meet budgetary needs for the coming three years. Expenses, not surprisingly, soon ran ahead of even the adjusted budget, and a motion was passed authorizing the Executive Director to transfer an additional $3,000 in early 1966. WARC had hoped to use the bequest as an endowment, maintaining a principal balance of at least $20,000 at all times, according to board resolution. When pressing short-term goals arose, the association abandoned its investment goal and the bequest was quickly spent. A second sizable bequest was also expended on current operating expenses.

In 1967-68 WARC changed its method of assessing support payments from chapters. The previous system asked for approximately 20 percent of a chapter's income. Under the new system, local chapters were assessed one cent per capita. According to Treasurer Myron Marander, all of the units were meeting their assessments, except Stevens and Peninsula Counties, which were inactive. The new system seemed more equitable, because each chapter was assessed on a proportional population basis and chapters were not penalized for being effective money raisers. But a re-analysis of chapter incomes from 1964-66, compiled by Marander for the assessment system conversion, indicates other issues were at stake and reveals other regularities. As expected, there was a rough relationship between population size and income generated, with many chapters in small areas struggling to make any income at all. But a more negative effect of the assessment change was to shift more of the burden to the larger chapters. This was dangerous since the large units had not been contributing as much proportionately. Thus, the four most populous units, containing the cities of Seattle, Tacoma, Spokane and Everett, had not raised the state-wide average per capita level of income in 1964, 1965 or 1966. On the other hand, while some small units struggled, other small chapters were among the most effective of all units at per capita fundraising. Indeed, the mean population of the top seven producers (39,714) was only slightly more than the mean population of the seven struggling units (33,429).

These findings have both specific and general implications for such organizations. The specific short-run implication is that WARC was shifting its funding base to less solid ground by accepting a system which expected larger units to perform better than they had. Indeed the new funding system did not collect enough income. So in 1969, WARC had to begin charging a state membership fee of one dollar, in addition to that charged by NARC. Both fees were to come from whatever dues the local collected. In addition, each chapter's support payments were to be increased from one cent to two cents per capita, phased in over a five-year period starting in 1970.

There are broader implications of the lower per capita performance of urban chapters as well. These findings from the mid-1960s have been repeated more recently. Metropolitan ARC representatives in Washington and other states were often heard to complain that they could not raise funds as easily as in small towns. The "explanation" commonly given by the representatives of urban areas is that there is more competition for the charitable dollar in cities. While that is true, it neglects the fact that there is more money to go around, not to mention that per capita household income is higher in cities. Why do urban areas fare below average in per capita fundraising, while smaller units do better or worse? One important factor seems to be the impact of organizational size. A unit will be hard to start in a small community, and, if started, to sustain, because of a scarcity of volunteers. Yet volunteers, who work because of their dedication to the cause, periodically attain a burst of high achievement solely as the fruit of their dedication. But no little band of heroes can transform a large organization that has grown formal and rigid. A large association is far more likely to rely on the consistent, professional labor of its staff than on the uncertain performance of its volunteers. Such bureaucratic regularity will never match the performance of dedicated volunteers in the moment of their enthusiasm. On the other hand, although they do require larger overhead costs, larger units are likely to be there year after year to offer some support, while smaller units only give proportionately more as long as they last. Smaller units are prone to periods of death, hopefully to be followed by a rebirth, sometimes decades later.

Organizational Expansion and Differentiation

From the beginning the Children's Benevolent League activities differed somewhat between the state and local levels. But as the scope of operations expanded in the late 1940s, the League became more complex. The state organization not only continued to conduct the lobbying activities in Olympia, which it called on local members to support, it also began to produce public awareness materials for use by local chapters. Simultaneously, the national ARC emerged and added its own publicity and fundraising efforts, which states and localities implemented. The local chapter monthly meetings continued to raise funds and to provide the personal contacts which bound members together and gave membership the power to shape identities. Increasingly, local chapter meetings became a place where plans were developed, debated, and adopted to launch local programs. First, parents might work together to set up a school for their children. Then they would work toward gaining a recreation program, a sheltered workshop, and group homes. For many years,

WARC chapter meetings provided the central focus for planning and supporting local mental retardation services in most counties. The bigger the chapter, the more comprehensive the program.

The number of local units expanded along with the general organizational growth and increasing public acceptance of mental retardation at mid-century. This growth started from the low point in 1950-51, when conflict between East Side and West Side leaders had reduced the number of active chapters to seven: Seattle, Tacoma, Bellingham, Bremerton, Wenatchee, Vancouver, and Twin Harbors. By the end of 1952, Everett, Walla Walla, Long Beach, and Spokane had either re-formed or been founded. WARC recognized two new chapters in 1953—Thurston County, marking the first time for the capital city of Olympia, and Cowlitz Valley, serving Cowlitz and Skamania counties. A Skagit county group was considered a real possibility. While there were large rural areas of Eastern Washington which had no WARC chapters in 1953, King county had gained a second chapter in addition to Seattle, when the Society for Exceptional Children in the Shoreline suburb voted to join as the Woodhull Hay chapter.

By 1956 WARC had nineteen local chapters. Populous counties experimented with having multiple chapters. King county had three units—Renton, Seattle, and Woodhull Hay, and Pierce county had two—Tacoma and Puyallup Valley (Sumner). The remaining new chapters were Yakima Valley, Mason County, and Skagit County.

Adams and Kittitas County units were accepted in 1963. There were twenty-five active chapters of WARC in 1965: Adams County, Bellingham, Benton-Franklin, Chelan, Clark, Cowlitz Valley, Grant, King, Kitsap, Kittitas, Lewis, Mason, Okanogan, Olympic Peninsula, Peninsula, Skagit Valley, Snohomish and Island Counties, Spokane, Stevens, Tacoma-Pierce County, Thurston, Twin Harbors, Valley Section (King County), Walla Walla, and Yakima Valley. In 1966 Island County was admitted. Almost no significant population center in the state was without a WARC chapter by 1966.

Indeed, there were so many chapters that board meetings had become unwieldy. As Parkinson has suggested, it is difficult for a group of more than about twenty to conduct business effectively; as a result, the effective decision-making flows to an executive committee or staff. With the five state officers, WARC quarterly board meetings now averaged about thirty members, plus staff and guests. Consequently, the by-laws were amended in 1967 to divide the state into regions and to establish regional vice-presidents. President

Elise Chadwick argued that a new management structure was essential to in-depth communication "from the state to the local level."

The number of state committees also grew. In the 1950s, Education, Public Awareness, and special committees to coordinate National Retarded Children's Week activities were added. By 1960 the number of committees had grown to fifteen: Blood Program, Education, Game of the Year, Guilds, Institutions, Legislative, Medical Research, National Retarded Children's Week, Organization and Standards, Public Relations, State Convention, Budget, Fundraising, Nominations, and Personnel. Vocational Rehabilitation and Recreation were soon added. In the latter half of the 1960s, a Youth ARC division was developed. Members included young adults who were siblings or others who had become interested in working with persons with mental retardation, usually in recreational settings. The Youth ARC continued for the next decade, but never became strong in Washington.

Guilds of Community Women

By contrast, the guild movement became a very significant part of WARC. Begun in 1953, the guilds provided a vehicle for women interested in "serving the cause of mental retardation." These local groups were designed for women without a disabled family member, but included some of the latter as well. They were titled "guilds" in imitation of the high status Washington women's charity, the Children's Orthopedic Hospital Guilds. These "guilds for the retarded" were highly successful. Over two dozen were formed statewide in the following decade. Named after a particular son or daughter ("the Robbie Richards Guild") or more generically ("Hope Guild"), these groups raised thousands of dollars. In their most successful years the volunteers contributed tens of thousands of hours. The guilds raised money to found schools, to provide wheelchairs and recreational equipment, and to help establish the WARC mental retardation clinic at Children's Orthopedic Hospital.

No list of the statewide membership in the guilds has been found, but the scale of community involvement was large. By 1958, it was reported that Seattle had formed its twentieth guild for women working in the cause, Tacoma had formed its tenth and Spokane and Bellingham had each formed their second guilds *(HOPE*, April 1958).

Like the CBL in earlier decades, the guilds devoted their time and energy to fundraising and socializing. These women, often neighbors or acquaintances of a family with a child with a disability, were also newcomers, naive as to how progress might be made. Perhaps it was appropriate that the task of these good citizens was to welcome and support children with mental retardation. In the division of labor, parents were more natural candidates to challenge school boards over exclusionary policies and demand legislative actions. Guild members became the first large group of non-parents to join the movement in Washington state. They expressed the new acceptance of persons with mental retardation.

The 1950s and 1960s were the boom time for guilds. Afterward recruitment declined. Gradually, the membership aged and came to be predominantly older women. In the mid-seventies, the state ARC severed formal relationships with the guilds because the activities and interests of the two groups had diverged significantly. The Arc sought disability "rights" while the guilds provided charity.

Community Supporters and Donors

The guilds were the largest organized outpouring of community support for the work of WARC in the early 1950s. But another prominent example, one with national scope, was the 1953 adoption of mental retardation as the special work of the United (Airlines) Stewardess Alumnae, later called Clipped Wings.[153] The Seattle chapter of WARC not only had established a working relationship with the local branch of Clipped Wings, but had done such an effective job that the national service club adopted NARC as its project as well.

Lodge and service groups which also at times supported the association's work included the American Legion, Zonta, Eagles, Elks, Lions, Moose, Rebekahs, Rotary, Kiwanis, Washington Federation of Women's Clubs, the Junior Chamber of Commerce Auxiliary, fraternities and sororities, and innumerable others. Support from these groups, like that from the guilds, typically consisted of donations of money, needed items, and volunteer hours.

Problems can arise when the donor or supporter wishes to exert a significant degree of control over an organization. This was clear in the relationships between WARC local chapters and the various United Good Neighbor (later United Way) councils. Although at first reluctant to deal with intellectual disability, United campaigns soon became anxious to feature children and adults with Down syndrome as part of their program. The public appeal of helping handicapped children was much greater than for more controversial social welfare projects. United Way organizations viewed independent fundraising, especially during their campaign months, as a serious threat and exerted sufficient influence to reduce the effectiveness of some fundraisers. The high level of additional bookkeeping required to fit United Way forms had also been a consistent objection of ARC chapters. On the other hand, since United Way status had come to bestow legitimacy on the fundraising, and since it had evolved efficient collection techniques, the ARC chapters in most of the larger cities—Seattle, Spokane, Everett, and Vancouver—became a part of the United Way – at least for a period of time.

Support by United Way, in turn, tended to increase the local ARC's financial independence from the state and national ARCs. It also tended to favor developing and retaining direct service provision – such as housing or employment—as a major function, even though many ARC leaders called for such services to be "spun off" to other agencies once they were firmly established by the ARC. Advocacy is an amorphous and more threatening function for a United Way charity and thus harder to sell than bricks and mortar.[154]

The Game of the Year

Besides participating in the National Retarded Children's Week, the big public awareness effort by WARC in the mid-1950s was the Game of the Year. Ten years before Eunice Kennedy Shriver founded the Special Olympics, the citizens of Washington state were learning that persons with developmental disabilities had athletic ability. 1957 was the first year that the game between the men's basketball teams from Rainier State School and Lakeland Village went public. The Yakima Valley chapter of WARC hosted the game which was co-sponsored by the Junior Federated Women's Club and the Jaycee Wives, who also served as ushers. Lieutenant Governor John Cherberg was the Master of Ceremonies. Close to 2,000 people filled the Armory to standing-room only. The next morning the sports writer for the *Yakima Morning Herald* had a story on the front page that began "Yakimans saw last night how much retarded children can do. They can do quite a bit."

WARC immediately recognized that it was onto something with the 200 hundred speaking engagements that the women's groups had arranged in central Washington in the weeks preceding the game. The Game of the Year was covered by six radio stations and six television stations in Spokane and Seattle.

In 1958 the Game of the Year was held in Tacoma and attended by 3,500 spectators. About 100 residents of Rainier and Lakeland

Village participated as players, cheerleaders, or in ancillary activities like tap dancers, madrigal singers, Western dancers, and musicians. The Emcee of the event was Congressman Thor Tollefson, whose remarks at the game included thanks to the officers and their wives at the local McChord Air Force base for hosting the visitors from Lakeland Village with rooms, meals, and a dance with "bop music."[155] Tollefson's remarks and a supporting article "Air Force Helps Retarded Children," were inserted into the *Congressional Record* and mailed to every Air Force base in the United States, as well as every unit of the National Association for Retarded Children.[156]

(Of course, this provided good exposure for the Congressman, as WARC knew it would. Never one to miss an opportunity, WARC, presumably working with NARC, persuaded Tollefson to introduce two bills in 1959. H. R. 4100 proposed an additional income tax exemption for a child who is permanently disabled and H. R. 4541 would have established a Federal Agency for the Handicapped.[157])

The following year the game was played in Spokane with 2,500 attending in the Coliseum.[158]

Each year the publicity surrounding the Game of the Year was huge, with widespread newspaper and live radio and television coverage of the game. The climax came in 1960. The Master of Ceremonies was Jim Owens, the most popular celebrity in the state as coach of the Rose Bowl winning, national champion Washington Huskies football team. Governor Rosellini rode down the main street of Everett in a parade of cars and floats showing the players and other school performers. According to the WARC newsletter[159]

> It is believed that this is the first parade in which retarded persons appeared and were featured for their abilities rather than their limitations.

WARC produced a 15 minute *Game of the Year* feature film that was widely circulated. The first showing at the Olympic Hotel in Seattle was attended by 70 people, but it was immediately circulated to organizations as far away as Honolulu, Hawaii and Southbury, Connecticut. Professionals nationwide read of Washington's successful public awareness of athletic competitions in an article by WARC Executive Director Leo Lippman in the AAMD *Project News* of May 1960.

The film showed not only the game but the women cheerleaders from the two Schools. Its narrative praised the potential of the men and women, given the proper training. After four major years of the Game, WARC, and the institutional superintendents in particular, felt that the point had been made and no longer wanted to put out the tremendous effort to continue it as a public relations event.[160]

Allies and Alliances

An inevitable relationship which has its own ambiguities is the coalition or coordinating group. The first ambiguity is a question of identity: when a group decides which other "similar" groups to join with, it decides what kind of group it is. From the beginning of the Children's Benevolent League of Washington, the question of its primary identity had been troubling: was it a PTA-like educational group, or was it essentially an association with health concerns, such as the 1935 proposed name of Purple Cross had suggested? Neither answer was formally adopted and no alliances were formed in the 1930s. After World War II, the CBL pondered whether it should affiliate with the American Association on Mental Deficiency, but it soon found a home of its own in a national parents' organization.

In 1954 the Coordinating Council for Handicapped Children became Washington state's first disability coalition.[161] County-level coalitions were formed first. In King county, sixteen local handicapped groups appeared at the first meeting in May (*Seattle Times*, June 13). Coordinating Councils were formed in Tacoma, Bellingham, Everett, Seattle, Grays Harbor County, Spokane, Cowlitz County, Wenatchee, and Thurston County.

Kirkland was the host city for a statewide organizing conference in November 1954. Orlando Thomas, president of the Woodhull Hay/Shoreline chapter of WARC served as the temporary chairman, and Mae Wise of the Grays Harbor WARC chapter was selected to head a committee to define the objectives. Even though the bulk of the state's population was covered by its units, the Coordinating Councils were almost all dead and gone by the end of the decade. Why did this happen?

Coordination, like motherhood and apple pie, may seem unobjectionable. Such is not the case, however. As one official from the National Association for Mental Health put it, "everyone wants to coordinate but nobody wants to be coordinated." [162] Issues of power and principle are at stake in making the decision to join with other groups or to continue alone; this decision-making is the second ambiguity of such alliances. In 1956 President E. H. Riviere, speaking for WARC, officially rejected the Coordinating Council on the

114

grounds that its by-laws did not permit "true co-ordination" (HOPE, July), and the coalition began its swift decline.

What were the other disability groups? In newspaper accounts a Coordinating Council statewide membership of over seventy groups was claimed. In addition to the State League for Blind Children, the PTA for the Deaf, and the WARC chapters, there was one other developmental disability group, United Cerebral Palsy (UCP), which was of special interest to WARC.

United Cerebral Palsy. The first known parent advocacy in cerebral palsy in Washington state began in 1940 when Blythe and Charles Lawliss persuaded the Olympia school district to open a special classroom so their son could attend school ("Seattle's Honored Mother," 1956). The Lawliss family moved to Seattle in 1942. Together with other parents and an interested physician, H.J. Wyckoff, they established a school and in the following year the school district was persuaded to adopt the program. In 1945 the Washington Spastic Children's Society was formed. It succeeded in attaining state funding for special classes in 1947. By 1949 the Society had moved beyond being just a parents' organization when Atley Nelson, who had cerebral palsy, was elected the Seattle president.

WARC had a number of membership meeting exchanges with UCP, but not with any other disability group.[163] Separate State Schools for the Blind and for the Deaf (both in Vancouver), and for the Feeble-minded (at Medical Lake), illustrate the long separation of these groups. For one thing, those with sensory disabilities did what they could to avoid any connotation of mental retardation. The Washington State Association for the Deaf, although it once had chapters across the state, focused on supporting the State School for the Deaf. Their involvement with local school districts, which other groups were launching into during the post-war decade, remained restricted. United Blind of Washington State was founded in 1935, although a Spokane group of blind adults existed as early as 1920.[164] No record of cooperative efforts with the CBL or WARC is apparent. (Organizations addressing other neurological problems were founded later in Washington state: epilepsy in the fifties, learning disabilities in the late sixties, and autism in the seventies.)

Professional groups. There were also professional organizations concerned with disabilities at mid-century. The National Rehabilitation Association's local affiliate promoted the Employ the Physically Handicapped Week. The Washington State Society for Crippled Children and Adults, which had been set up to qualify for funding under 1935 federal legislation, was an advisory body to the State of Washington made up of health professionals and representatives of women's and men's service groups.[165] After the war, it expanded its scope of operations by opening a deaf pre-school (*Seattle Times*, October 27, 1949). But probably the most important professional organization to join the Coordinating Council was the Council for Exceptional Children (CEC). Organized nationally in 1922 for special education teachers and administrators,[166] CEC published the influential journal *Exceptional Children* and popularized the terminology of "exceptionality." Although scattered efforts had occurred before, the first Washington affiliate was Seattle (1936), followed by Tacoma, and, in the fifties, by Rainier. Finally, in 1959, a state federation was formed.[167] The three WARC chapters most involved in promoting local school district programs in the early fifties—Kirkland, Shoreline, and Spokane—all had adopted the phrase "exceptional children" in their original names. Special education teachers were becoming an important source of ideas and values for these groups.

Dr. Ross Hamilton, state director of special education, was one of these opinion leaders, and he played a critical role in promoting the Council. Besides serving on its state executive committee, Hamilton also assisted the organizing meetings of the Tacoma, Seattle, and state councils. He was a good friend to the special education advocates in Shoreline and Kirkland, not only speaking to their groups, but visiting in the leaders' homes and playing with their children. Like Superintendent Parker in the 1930's, Ross Hamilton provided critical assistance to a new parental initiative.

In contrast, others did not promote the Council. Orlando Thomas was president of the Shoreline chapter and of the Washington State Coordinating Council. Thomas reported that WARC leaders Leo Lippman, E H Riviere, and Olaf Caskin were angry about the large turnout.[168] Thomas saw the Council as a tremendous opportunity for all persons concerned about handicapped children to speak with one voice, but the Council was a rival consumer-based statewide organization, and WARC saw it as a threat. Some WARC parent leaders certainly saw increasing community programs as direct competitors to the institutions where their children lived.[169]

After WARC's rejection of the Coordinating Council, the dream of unity crumbled. True, Council backer Hamilton served on the NARC board of directors and Orlando Thomas was on the NARC Education Committee. But the contention with WARC led rapidly to the decision of the Shoreline group to withdraw from WARC and to Kirkland's decision to drop affiliation. Of the three local units that had begun in the search for special education, only Spokane stayed with WARC. Ross Hamilton left the position of state director of special education in the same year. With the withdrawal of his support and the opposition from WARC, the Washington State Coordinating Council collapsed. It was more than a decade before another special education coalition was formed.

Maturity

By the beginning of the seventies, WARC had reached a level of maturity as an organization. The signs were obvious. An assistant director was hired. An administrative manual for the board was produced. With smart three-ring binders lettered with the WARC name, the contents were organized according to a detailed numerical code. In 1971 the assistant director was promoted to director. He was authorized to lease an automobile for his exclusive use, reimbursing the ARC for his personal mileage.

Besides these and other indications of organizational formalization, maturity was reflected in another manner. The ARC, as a respectable group, was asked to respond to another social issue – race and its frequent companion, poverty. So WARC invited Dr. Robert Aldrich, Vice President of the President's Committee on Mental Retardation (PCMR), to address its Spring Conference.[170] Aldrich told the audience that about 75 percent of cases of mental retardation were not due to disease, genetic disorder, or injury. Aldrich said this fact meant ARCs should pay new attention to the arena of culture, social affairs, and general environment. He felt that the time had come for the Association for Retarded Children to do an in-depth analysis and re-evaluation of the organization so that a new image might be adopted which "befit the times" (HOPE, February 1970).

But it was unrealistic to expect such a comprehensive transformation. WARC had no constituency demanding that it fight racial injustice or join the war on poverty. To begin with, Washington's population was about 90 percent white, with the minority population very divided among blacks, Asians, Hispanics, and Native Americans. The minority membership of WARC was miniscule, but, following the lead of the PCMR and the NARC, a black man, Mel Jackson, was appointed to the board of directors to represent minority interests.

Although WARC did discuss lead paint poisoning and malnourishment as causes of mental retardation in children, most members were middle class and did not have an immediate concern about such poverty-related causes of mental disability. And it was also true that WARC families correctly believed that most children with environmentally caused retardation had only mild disabilities. They believed their own children had greater troubles.[171]

WARC began the seventies with the same kind of financial problems it had faced in the sixties. Support from local units was not dependable. In 1970, for example, contributions from local chapters were the same as the previous year, but the state association was operating on a greatly increased budget ($61,180 for 1970 compared to $39,080 for 1969). Once again, there was a mismatch between the budget the board approved and the money which chapters contributed. It was necessary to draw from the savings account. Following a pattern established a decade earlier, the Executive Committee discussed what fundraising assistance to offer and what sanctions to apply to units in arrears. According to Treasurer Yancy Reser, WARC was forced to deplete its entire savings account balance in 1971 to offset the assessments owed by some chapters.

Insufficient money was a recurring problem throughout the seventies, and WARC often turned to fundraisers as a solution. In July 1971 executive director Perry Liljestrand announced that A. Ludlow Kramer, Washington's Secretary of State, had agreed to become chairman for WARC's fundraising. Kramer promised to become actively involved in the recruitment of volunteers in fifteen targeted counties. His participation was welcomed by WARC and he received an appointment to the board of directors. With a successful fall campaign, WARC ended 1971 in the black—a 30 percent excess of income over expenses.

WARC had enjoyed great success with its fund raiser, the Walk-a-thon, in 1970 and 1971. In March 1972 Lud Kramer revealed his plan for an even larger WARC Walk-a-thon. Kramer proposed that $20,000 be allocated for projects such as Special Olympics out of a goal of $150,000. The Walk-a-thon would be the state association's project, with local units invited to participate. If the chapters did join the project, the funds would be divided as follows. First, fifteen percent of the gross would be set aside for campaign costs. Once these debts were settled, the local unit's ordinary assessments from WARC and NARC would be paid. Some of remaining money would be used for special projects, such as the Special Olympics. The balance would be split evenly between the state and local units. The Board adopted Kramer's proposal.

President Harold Little, perhaps elected in part for his training as an accountant, announced at the December 1972 board meeting that WARC had finished a second year in the black. Forty thousand dollars was in the savings account, almost a half year's budgeted expenses. Lud Kramer reported that the fall Walk-a-thons had raised approximately $160,000 in pledges. However, he concluded that the Walk-a-thons would not be the best way to raise funds on an ongoing basis and proposed that a permanent fund raiser be hired on a percentage basis. Kramer projected that within three years WARC could be raising a million dollars a year. The largest project would be a "Spring Fling" of chain parties. He had met with the guilds and Junior Federated Women who would do much of the necessary work on the event. He proposed that the vast majority of funds raised would go into matching monies for local programs rather than to state office operations—a feature that would appeal both to the women's groups and to local ARC members.

At the June 1973 meeting, President Harold Little reviewed the history of WARC for the assembled board members. According to Little, the association had been on the verge of bankruptcy in 1969, there was little or no support for it, and the public image of WARC was almost non-existent. WARC then embarked on a five-year plan. By 1973 the credibility and stature of WARC was "ten-fold greater" than it had been. Projecting into the future, Little foresaw annual fundraising receipts of $1,500,000.

Also at the June 1973 meeting, Lud Kramer reported that WARC's Walk-a-thon would probably be merged into NARC's Hike/Bike in 1974. However, by September Kramer reported that progress toward the three-year goal to raise $1,000,000 was falling short. Even so, the personnel committee recommended a number of salary and staff increases which the board approved. The executive director's salary was raised; a field representative and resource services consultant were hired at $17,000 each per year.

In 1974 the Hike/Bike campaign was no longer headed by Kramer, but was still highly organized. The Washington Education Association provided much help by contacting the media across the state. Television spots and full-page ads on the Hike/Bike appeared in Seattle newspapers. Public service announcements were mailed to radio stations throughout the state.

The Later Seventies

In the later seventies, the financial and organizational resources of WARC began to decline. Perry Liljestrand resigned as Executive Director of WARC late in 1974; the following March funds were so low that WARC accepted a $5,000 loan from the Grays Harbor chapter. But interim Treasurer Harold Little reported that WARC was still in serious financial trouble in June. The association needed $17,000 just to keep its head above water. The total monies received by June for the 1975 (and final) Hike/Bike totaled only $43,108, of which $27,661 was distributed to the chapters. Thus, just two months after Patricia Wilkins was hired as executive director in April, the board strongly considered laying off some staff members. Wilkins recommended against the action and expressed hope that the crisis would be over by the end of the summer. The board agreed to give her the extra months.

Lud Kramer resigned from the board, but the directors finally gave Wilkins the authority to hire a professional fund raiser as Kramer had suggested three years earlier. This time the advice had come from WARC's newly-formed Financial Advisory Committee (FAC). The FAC was a group of fifteen prestigious Washingtonians, including some of the most wealthy, prominent and powerful individuals in the state (including George Weyerhaeuser and Dorothy Bullitt, a leading Seattle television owner). In August 1975 Bill Borah became WARC's Finance Director. Borah and members of the FAC met with Greg Barlow of the Medina Foundation, a major Washington charitable foundation. Barlow promised that if the FAC raised $70,000 by December, Medina would add another $5,000 and would look favorably on larger requests for the subsequent year.

Although contributions from FAC efforts were included in the budget the following year, WARC failed to take advantage of the golden opportunity the FAC seemed to represent, and Borah was laid off in the spring of 1976. It is unclear why this fundraising effort failed, but several factors seem to have been at play. For one, there was some lifestyle mismatch between the middle class WARC board, on the one hand, and Borah and the FAC, on the other. Some board members felt uneasy around these persons of greater means and prestige. Secondly, the board and the ARC members probably were not as fully committed to fundraising as they might have been. This lack of commitment stems from two perennial differences between the ARC and other health groups to which it has been compared, such as the cancer, polio, heart, and muscular dystrophy associations. Most of the other health groups do not have extensive activities other than fundraising in which local lay volunteering makes sense. By contrast, many parents, teachers, and others (and especially the leaders among them) are involved in the ARC because of the opportunity for direct service activities which it provides.[172] Additionally the ARC has a federated, rather than corporate, organizational structure, at least in fact, if not officially.[173] The diversity of character and activities among state and local ARCs makes it hard to plan a unified national program. This feature is magnified within the states—each local unit has a strong tendency to go its own way and become committed to its own projects. Thus, an effective, unified response to the opportunity presented by the Financial Advisory Committee may have been impossible.

As usual, WARC's response to the budget crisis in 1975 involved trying to compel more financial support from local units that were behind in their assessments. A formal policy of provisional, suspended, and expelled statuses, modeled on the NARC's standards for state units, was adopted. But most chapters also felt hard-pressed. In August, Treasurer Little announced that local units had increased their payments to the state, but it had still been necessary to borrow $18,500 from Seattle-First National Bank. Little claimed that the financial crisis had done more to bring the association together than the last proposed bill in the legislature to make parents pay for the supportive services for their children had done. By the end of July, 45 percent of the "Fair Share" support by local units had been received; five units were 100 percent paid and some were more than 50 percent paid. But the year-to-date income projections were behind. The crisis remained in December, and WARC entered the new year with only $10,000 in cash. The association needed $16,000 a month to operate current programs. Despite objections from King and Clark county ARCs, which had their own traditional Christmas appeal letters, the board approved a December letter to all members requesting special contributions.

Organizational health continued downhill in 1976. In January the staff included Patricia Wilkins, Executive Director; Bill Borah, Finance Director; Lucille May, field consultant for organizational development; Gary Neill, field consultant for governmental affairs; Mike Wilson, field consultant in employment (running the On-the-Job placement project); Ann Lenzie, office manager; Anne Seaburg, secretary; and William "Mac" McKinney, bookkeeper. By the end of the year, Wilkins and Neill had resigned and Borah's contract was terminated. Other members of the staff were soon to go. Even the president resigned, the first to do so in the history of the association.

Two outstanding debts, left over from the fiscal difficulties of the previous year, were a problem for the board. Seattle-First National Bank demanded repayments of $1,000 a month on its loan, while WARC was hard pressed to pay $500. In addition, $9,500 was owed to Central Washington State University for facilities and fare for the 1975 Special Olympics spring games. It was many months before the debts were totally retired.

However, two major new WARC funding sources began in

121

1976—government grants and bingo. For several years, WARC had had a federal On-the-Job training contract to place adults with mental retardation and other disabilities in competitive employment. In June a second large grant was received when WARC received a contract with the State of Washington to produce informational brochures (the "Where-to-Turn" Project), material for a media campaign, and a resource directory of handicapped services in the various regions of the state. Such public grants provided resources that often allowed it to accomplish auxiliary aims like organizing supporters and disseminating political information. WARC was able to obtain additional public grants in the latter part of the decade, including multi-year contracts for pre-school public awareness and a number of smaller one-year grants.

In March 1976 the ARC decided to open a bingo game and take advantage of a new state law which legalized them for non-profit organizations. WARC patterned its game after the Pierce county Arc's very successful bingo game, which netted over $100,000 a year and made that ARC financially strong for the first time in memory. However, the state's game did not do as well. Relying on a start-up loan from the Pierce county chapter, the state association barely stayed in the black.

Since finances had not improved, a task force on the budget met over the summer in 1976 to resolve budget problems. At the state convention, Harry Carthum reported that long-term liabilities had been reduced by 31 percent and short-term debts were being handled on a 30-to-60-day basis. WARC's executive committee accepted King County's proposal to loan the state $25,000 without interest, to be credited to King county's past due assessments at a rate of forty two cents on the dollar. Projections were nevertheless made that by the end of the year the state organization might have to fold because of its debts.

WARC accepted the task force's recommendation that the association should try to raise $140,000 from the local units under a further revised fair share assessment plan. An additional $35,000 would have to be found elsewhere to continue current programs. A reduced operating budget of $80,594 was adopted for 1977.

Withdrawal from NARC

Some leaders contended that budgetary constraints called for withdrawal from the national association. This decision was reached at the end of 1976 after a heated debate among WARC members. Withdrawing from NARC pleased no one, especially those who remembered the crucial role that Washington had played in founding the NARC. The decision based on the hope that unpaid NARC assessments on the state would stop piling up. The board resolved to work toward rebuilding the state organization so that WARC could rejoin NARC as soon as possible.

Under the executive direction of Stan Baxter, hired in March 1977, multiple fundraisers were employed to gather the funds which the board felt were needed. Having abandoned the Hike/Bike, WARC: made direct-mail appeals to the membership, sought unsuccessfully to open three thrift stores in partnership with a for-profit management operation in 1977, held a dance marathon jointly with King county in 1977 (losing $5,000), netted nearly $10,000 from raffling off a Hawaiian vacation (and much less when repeated in 1978), collected pledges from a series of backpacking Mountain Treks, sold advertisements in the WARC newsletter, and was assisted by special events organized by local chapters in 1978 (a ball and a horserace in Yakima, a Casino Night in Spokane).

In July 1979 reaffiliation with NARC was achieved, accompanied by a renewed sense of optimism. The board of directors set a goal the following December to strive for the state ARC's financial independence from the county chapters through a series of monthly fundraising activities. Both the board and the staff were optimistic enough about the ARC and its mission to tackle the perennial problem of undependable local support. But it was not a problem those leaders solved.

CHAPTER FOUR:
AN INSTITUTION HAS A LIFE OF ITS OWN

> I have been in this school just about four years, and in the years I have been a good boy. I have worked hard and made a lot of friends. Our school is really a fine place to live when you come right down to it and the sooner all of us realize it the better off we are all going to be. Now you take our beautiful trees, grass, and all our shows to go to. So you see we're not so bad off as some of us may think. So all in all I think if we keep smiling we will all come to find out that life can be beautiful.
>
> — Jon F.
> "The Children's Column" *Rainier School News*
> February 24, 1950

The F. family had made a choice about where Jon would attend school. It was an unusual choice in Washington, since the state had very few residential schools. Not many pious parents sent their sons away to religious schools, nor did socially elite families have many boarding schools to choose from. But the F. family's situation was different. Jon was mentally retarded. Sympathetic professionals encouraged Jon's parents to send him away to a "state school" so he could receive the training he needed. His parents decided it was right thing to do.

Jon didn't really enjoy being separated from his family or being excluded from the world he had come to know. He tried to make sense of his personal problem, and he wanted to believe that life at the school was not as bad as it seemed. Beautiful landscaping and lots of movies helped compensate for the losses he and his friends had suffered. Jon's family hoped that he would learn to become happy there, and Jon was trying to do so.

Professional people had likely advised Jon's parents to send him to a residential school. But it was not just professionals who were responsible for the choice which the F. family made. The Children's Benevolent League members had created Rainier School when they lobbied through the bill for a West Side institution in 1937. These parents had sent their children away to school. They believed an important part of their job was to encourage other parents to make the same choice, and to help them feel better about it once the decision was made.

At mid-century some parents who were plunging into advocacy in other areas of the United States chose a different approach. They kept their sons and daughters at home and tried to get the public schools to provide an appropriate education. If they could not get the proper education, they set up their own special day schools in their hometowns. After decades of this hard work, the passage of the 1975 comprehensive federal special education act, P.L. 94-142, provided the symbolic achievement of full educational opportunity, discussed in the next chapter.

In Washington the situation was atypical. Because the League had a fifteen-year tradition of providing parental support for institutions, it continued to be a major force behind their expansion, not only in the 1950s, but even through most of the 1960s. Washington parents probably pushed for institutions longer than leading parent advocates in other states who wanted their children in the public schools. On the other hand, the pre-existing strength of the CBL enabled the League to gain the necessary authorization and funding from the state to assist those families who wanted local education. As a result, by the 1970s Washington was a leader in providing expanded local educational opportunities for children with disabilities.[174]

As noted, some Washington parents worked hard in the 1950s to achieve a public school education for their children. Their story will be told later. But in the decades following the formation of the CBL, many parents sought institutional expansion and upgrading. They also attempted to maintain parental control over the small financial obligations required by the state and over the admissions and release process. These parental rights anticipated the due process guarantees for families which were eventually incorporated into state and federal special education law.

Always a Minority Choice

The peak of institutionalization in Washington was reached about the same year as the national peak. But even in those years, it was truly a minority choice. In 1968 Washington state schools numbered their all-time high, 4,197 residents. In the closest prior census in 1960 the total state population was 2,853,000.Thus the rate of institutionalization was about 1 person in a thousand at its peak. Using a straight IQ test will result in IQs below 70 for about 3% of the population. In 1948 the CBL put out a pamphlet called "One out of Fifty," which equates to 2%. It is often said that only about 1% of the population is identified as some special education or adult support services. But even 1% of the state's population in 1960 would have been over 28,000 people institutionalized! Even if these figures are slightly off, the results are striking. Only a small minority of people were institutionalized. Most parents never sent their children away.[175]

Life at Rainier State School

If some parents wanted expansion of what they had, what did they think they were choosing? What were Rainier State School and other institutions like in 1950? To many parents, the answer was simplicity. They wanted a simpler, less stressful, more protective environment, with a modified program of education which would meet the special needs of the residents. But the places where this simplicity was provided were complex, formal organizations that were part of a public bureaucracy.

At mid-century, institutional life was in full flower[176] and the imagery of a prison was hard to avoid.[177] These "children," who were required to be less than 50 years old at admission, were committed because they were judged to be misfits or problems in their homes, schools, or communities. Children were admitted, usually at parental request, by juvenile court judges. Parents gave up their legal rights once their son or daughter was committed to the state's custody.

A 1950 informational brochure from Rainier School took pains to assert that "this commitment is <u>not</u> a sentence." But the brochure also directed parents to write to school officials before visiting, so that their children might be "ready." The school was a controlled space, severely restructing access to its residents and facilities. Visiting hours were limited: 9:45 AM to 11:00 AM and 1:30 PM to 4:30 P.M. Parents were allowed to visit their son or daughter in the residence halls on only four holidays. During the remainder of the year the child was "brought to Center" to meet family members or guests.[178]

> This is absolutely essential. It is upsetting to the children on the halls to have parents of other children visiting in the day rooms. Also, it distracts the attention of the attendants and it requires their full time and attention to supervise the children in their care. There is also the danger of spreading contagious diseases in the institution.

Even though parental visitations were limited, supposedly to curb the spread of illness, an epidemic did break out at Rainier State School in March 1950. At least 177 residents contracted hepatitis by the end of the summer. Parental visits were entirely suspended. There is no record of parental objections to many aspects of institutional regimentation, but shutting off visitations was a serious blow to those caring families who wished to see their children. During the quarantine, which lasted several months, the Children's Benevolent League kept the pressure on Rainier State School for the earliest possible change in visitation policy. All residents recovered from the illness.

It was not only face-to-face contact that was restricted. The mail was censored.

> This is to prevent a child from receiving mail of which a parent might not approve, or mail from persons with whom the parents might not wish the child to correspond. No child should receive news which might prove upsetting to him, or which would interfere with his progress.

Because the mail was censored, each resident was limited to two outgoing letters a month. Families were told that this was all that the budget allowed with the time-consuming job of censorship which was necessary to prevent their children's correspondence with undesirable persons.

Unavailing Institutional Criticism

The parents continued to lobby for expansion during the fifties and sixties, but they were not entirely happy with the idea of residential schools. In fact, institutions for persons with mental retardation have always been criticized and they have rarely been popular establishments. In the 1920s some parents had to be coerced by the school districts to choose institutionalization. James Oakley felt pain over the situation of the inmates in 1935. In the 1940s Newland Reilly called unnecessary institutionalization "a great crime." But parents were not the only ones who felt the pain. The fact that the *Rainier School News* editor chose to use Jon F.'s letter in 1950 indicates that sensitive members of the school staff knew that being at Rainier was essentially tragic. Jon F.'s brief composition did not strike the editor as incomprehensible. On the contrary, the letter described a real problem and showed how one person was dealing with it. Those who worked in the institution knew its reality; it was the place where services were delivered to those strange and imperfect persons society wished to avoid.

The superintendents of state residential schools also periodically showed their unease, while they continued to support expansion to address lengthy waiting lists. For example, Superintendent Barber expressed the hope that Rainier could imitate Southbury in Connecticut and "return some of these children to the community." Concurrent comments by L.F. Mason, Lakeland superintendent, betrayed awareness that institutions were bad options for both residents and staff (HOPE, October, 1953).

> Our staff is motivated by the slogan: "Let's make
> Lakeland Village more of a home—less of an institu-
> tion—for the children." Our personnel standards are
> rising; no longer is a job at our school considered "the last
> hope."

Ironically, as Superintendent Mason says, even though this was a decade when hope was the watchword for WARC, employment at an institution still threatened to tell the old story: it was the last hope for a job, when nothing else could be found, working with that kind of people.

Of course, Mason's comments show that he knew that ideally everyone should live in a home. And he also recognized how devalued his residents at least had been during his tenure – human beings so disliked that to be forced to take a job working with them was "the last hope" a person had. Clearly, the pool of persons from

128

whom staff would be drawn could hardly make these institutions progressive educational centers.

The CBL itself brought in known critics of institutions. *Woman's Home Companion* staff writer Edith Stern gave the most anti-institutional speech in the CBL records when she addressed its 1950 convention in Seattle.[179] As a parent herself, Stern had credibility. Yet many of her listeners must have been distressed, or at least surprised, by her words. Although she began by complimenting Rainier State School as the second best facility in the country (after Southbury School in Connecticut[180]), she proceeded to criticize the school and other institutions. Stern asserted that the nation was at "a fork in the road." Adding more buildings was not the answer. Programming and adequate staff support were needed more than fancy equipment.

Stern had heard that few, if any, residents were ever released from Rainier State School. She declared that this situation should be changed and gave suggestions on how the League could move toward reducing the school's population. The CBL could sponsor prevention programs. Methods of admission should be revised to insure that only the results of scientific screening would result in placement. (Washington was the only state Stern had ever seen where admissions were gained by "pull"—a measure of the strength of the parent organization, with much of the pull exercised by the League.[181]) Stern argued that an interdisciplinary team of specialists was needed at the schools to provide treatment and training. She said, "All should join together to give the children the Total Push to release them from the institution."

Stern believed communities could be made to work. Communities, public schools, home teachers, diagnostic and guidance clinics, and special intervention with fathers to help them adjust. In addition, Stern acknowledged that household help "often makes the difference between being able to keep the children at home and having to send them away." For those who could not care for their own child, foster care could be provided as an alternative to institutions.

Also, some families found that their children could return to their homes after a period of institutional training was completed. However, many "high morons" were being retained and not released simply in order to reduce the labor costs of the school; Stern strongly condemned the practice as slave labor. Finally, after release, these people would need expanded social service departments in the community.

In conclusion, Edith Stern argued that buildings were the most expensive way possible to deal with the problem of mental retardation. Rather, investing in education would prove a far more beneficial approach.

> The assets of the state will be increased if these people
> can be taught to be productive even in the most minor
> way. We can count it as an asset if these lives are even
> partially fulfilled—all have this right.

Stern's use of the concept of rights may have been new, but in several ways her vision of the future was similar to Newland Reilly's from a decade earlier. It was comprehensive; it looked toward a future of more family and community services; and it emphasized the benefits of investing in training programs. However, neither asserting the rights of persons with mental retardation nor building a new service system were as yet on the agenda of the CBL in 1950. They were merely the words of a banquet speaker.

One leader who did attempt to take these words seriously was future CBL president, Harold Watkins. With the assistance of Stern, Mr. and Mrs. Watkins visited New York three months later and inspected a program of foster care placements for institutional residents. Harold Watkins was impressed. With care, it could work in Washington state. Admittedly, there were problems with community acceptance ("even over church attendance of the patients"). Yet over time, neighbors had grown tolerant. Watkins expressed his support of foster homes in a letter to the CBL.

> We feel that every solution to this problem must be
> considered. It is our belief that the State—even if that
> were the solution—can never build room enough at Rain-
> ier to care for all the mental deficients. We must
> investigate ways of getting the higher types out of institu-
> tions and economically at least partially productive.

In 1951 Harold Watkins continued to work on the topic, writing to state legislators and to Rainier School about his interest in developing placements in foster homes. R. Sid Justice, a Rainier social worker, replied to Watkins that his letter

> does point out many things for which we are striving.
> With proper ground work in the community, we are sure
> this plan of colonization can be made very successful.

At the April 1951 Board meeting, the question of whether the CBL should attempt to set up standards for foster homes for mentally retarded children was extensively discussed. Presumably this discussion was initiated by Watkins. However, the idea was effectively tabled by a decision that President Clifton would consider the matter at further length. With the exception of foster care, residential alternatives to institutions were almost inconceivable in the early 1950s. Even the election of Harold Watkins as president in 1953 did not bring about rapid changes. Institutions have inertia, which keeps them expanding, even after a persuasive rationale for their existence has collapsed. In Washington it took years before the parents' organization shifted its attention away from institutional growth.

Bigger and Better, with Waiting Lists

The move away from institutions was not the road taken. Instead the CBL got waiting lists, expansion of existing institutions, and construction of new ones. This meant two kinds of funding were regularly sought: capital construction and operating expenses. In 1949 the CBL had faced a fiscally tight legislature, and the League quickly abandoned hopes for additional construction of residence halls. Concerned parents had worked hard on the operating budgets hoping to avoid the worst, but both Rainier and Lakeland Village suffered reductions. CBL members were consoled somewhat when their legislative committee chairman, Alan Sampson, pointed out that other facilities received more severe budget cuts. Sampson noted that the state training schools for delinquent boys and girls had no advocates at all.

Bond issues placed on the general election ballot were a frequently used device for public construction projects. In 1950 the League worked with a coalition that succeeded in passing four state bond issues. Referendum 8 included $20,000,000 for institutional construction, including work at Rainier and Lakeland Village.

A branch of Rainier School was opened in Yakima in 1951 to accommodate demand and to provide a facility located in central Washington. CBL leaders and local members attended the opening. In 1954 Van R. Hinkle, supervisor of the Division of Children and Youth, announced that reduced legislative allocations would force its closure. The newsletter of the Washington Association for Retarded Children (WARC), as the League had been renamed in 1952, reported that approximately 120 residents at the school would be transferred back to Rainier School at Buckley.

Concern over steadily increasing waiting lists at the residential schools intensified when the residents were returned to Rainier School Governor Albert D. Rosellini addressed the issue at the 1957 state convention in Wenatchee. His speech, "The Future for Washington State Institutions," was broadcast live by television station KPQ. Rosellini's words elicited a warm response from his audience. He asserted that "the mentally retarded have a top priority in my book" and acknowledged the hardship that waiting created for families. He pledged early action to house retarded children at two former tuberculosis treatment facilities, using contingency funds. Although he was generally optimistic, the governor cited difficulties which still lay ahead:

> It is not anticipated that even these actions will provide an ultimate answer to the needs of our retarded children. Our waiting lists cannot be abolished without action on every front to meet these needs. What I think we should interest ourselves in is a clear-cut program for the future by which we can avoid such situations as now confront us. To me, the basis of that program must be the policy that is now being accented in all our institutions: that of rehabilitation, of restoring patient and prisoner to society as quickly, and as successfully as possible.

Indeed, the state policy during Rosellini's tenure (1957-65) was highly favorable to institutions. He was nominated the best governor ever by a long-time institutional advocate and WARC legislative chair, Erik Froberg.[182] But even such a governor knew that isolation is a sin, as he confessed in a speech to the regional meeting of the AAMD, the professionals' association.

> I am afraid that. .for many years past our institutions for children were deemed custodial schools with little of interest to the public and they thus remained separate and apart from the community. This besetting sin of isolation, I sincerely trust, is permanently behind us. Today all our residential schools are endeavoring to take their place in the community as facilities offering special training and education to a large group of children who cannot be taught or adequately supervised in the regular day school program.[183]

With the support of Governor Rosellini, the branch of Rainier State School re-opened at Selah near Yakima in January 1958 for 220 "grossly handicapped children." At the dedication of the Yakima Valley School on March 23, 1958, Governor Rosellini and 800 guests toured the new facility. The governor was optimistic that the opening of Yakima Valley School was a start to reduce waiting lists and was "a significant step forward in solving a problem that has

has been with us much too long." The residents of the new school were drawn from Rainier School and Lakeland Village and from the waiting lists of the two schools. The opening of the school helped somewhat, but the waiting list remained high at 800 people. Even with Yakima Valley and Fircrest School, which was opened in 1959, the waiting list was expected to grow.

No one was surprised when the WARC newsletter reported early in 1961 that "the space situation is desperate for Washington's mentally retarded residents, particularly for the younger age groups" (HOPE, January 1961). But the Department of Institutions statistics did not show the predicted growth yet since it cited a shortage of 740 beds at the four state residential schools. The average waiting time for an admission was two years and two months.

By July 1961, the number on waiting lists had reached 1,007. Dr. Garrett Heyns, Director of the Department of Institutions, said the figure was an "all-time high" and added that there was no indication that there would be a decline or leveling off of applications in the foreseeable future. Even though Fircrest School had been expanded in 1960, there was still an increase of 51 on the waiting list a year later.

The situation remained similar in 1962, when attention to community placements increased. For example, in 1955 there were 87 people placed outside the institutions. That number had risen to more than 250 in 1962, with an additional 200 people ready for placement for whom no community services were available. Although many of the residents were placed so they could gain employment in the community, the Department of Institutions was beginning to place older residents out of Fircrest and into nursing homes in order to relieve overcrowding (HOPE, April 1962). Moving residents into nursing homes was controversial, and Frank Junkin, Fircrest superintendent, was cross-examined by WARC officers about the use of nursing home placements.

The community placements by the Department of Institutions were consistent with a 1960 Legislative Budget Committee report to the Legislature, "State Aids to the Mentally Retarded," which explored the future of facilities which served persons with mental retardation. The budget committee, composed of five senators and five representatives, suggested several components of an alternative system of care. In some ways, these legislators re-invented the wheel previously wrought by Reilly and Stern, i.e., the committee recommended that prevention and expanded services to families needed to be considered. Two new elements discussed in the committee report were "halfway houses" (community living centers) and "sheltered workshops" for persons with milder disabilities.

Although steps had been taken to alleviate the problem, lengthy waiting lists had not gone away by mid-decade. Governor Daniel J. Evans addressed the issue at the WARC convention in the late summer of 1966. The *Port Angeles Evening News* quoted from governor's speech.

> A section of Eastern State Hospital at Medical Lake will be transferred from the Department of Institutions' division of mental patients to its division for handicapped children. The former mental hospital buildings, containing full facilities to care for 400 retarded children, will form a separate institution distinct from Eastern State Hospital and Lakeland Village School for the Retarded. I realize this might arouse controversy, but I am convinced those who need help the most must be helped now. This will not detract from the ultimate goal, but will be a means of attaining it.

But the WARC board of directors' resolution on August 22, 1966 showed much hesitance about institutions. WARC accepted the expansion and expressed appreciation for the "genuine interest of the Governor in the pressing needs of those on the waiting list." But the state's proposal "does not reflect full consideration of the recommendations of the President's Panel on Mental Retardation, with regard to institutional placement *and the use of community facilities.*" Furthermore, WARC's resolution insisted that the state should develop a plan for the most effective use of existing space in the institutions "*as well as the most effective use of community facilities.*"

Evergreen Snake Pits

Evans' concern with waiting lists was soon overtaken by a need to react to Washington's first modern national public scandal about institutions. In 1966 Burton Blatt and Fred Kaplan had published their national institutional photographic expose *Christmas in Purgatory*, with its Auschwitz-like images. Their book inspired inquiries in state after state. In the fall of 1966 feature articles on Washington's institutions dominated the news across the state for weeks: "Shame of Fircrest" (editorial, *Seattle Post-Intelligencer*, September 18, 1966), "Mess at Buckley Shocks Probers; Solons Ask Emergency Measures" (*Seattle Post-Intelligencer,* October 1,

1966), and "Candidates Inspect Lakeland Village" (*The Spokane Spokesman-Review*, October 20, 1966**). WARC members were among those who read the stories—some with more shock than others, some perhaps with guilt. The scandal immediately gained so much media attention that one third of the state legislature, 58 members, toured Rainier State School – certainly the first (and last) time that has happened.

Having long been the chief supporter of institutions, WARC would naturally be expected to have a strong, leading role in addressing the scandal. But such was not the case. According to minutes, the WARC board of directors did not even discuss the topic either at its August meeting before the scandal or at the December meeting afterwards. A special meeting of ten leaders was held at the WARC office on Sunday, October 23, 1966. A partial, informal set of minutes survives, which reveal which topics were discussed and which ideas were floated, though no formal votes were taken. Here are a few excerpts:

> Beatings of residents, ask department – what are the disciplinary methods used? Request procedure of program. ...
>
> Ward supervisors, concern of parents as to treatment, try and get detailed report. If physical marks on child find out when it was first recorded. Find out daily hearings, certain girl was told to mop floors, was this a privilege or a punishment? ...
>
> Example: (difficult hall) some detail workers run safety pin across child's back. Recommend, investigate situation. ...
>
> Another ex[ample] – resident restrained in straight jacket for over 8 hours. Causes; for this type of treatment; lack of personal [personnel]. ... [184]
>
> Complaint; too heavy sedation, again, lack of in-service training. ...
>
> Every parent have appreciation of difficulty caring for this type of child and give a helping hand. ...
>
> Parents must give idea to public and legislators (and be able to describe actual conditions.) Get a new set of standards. (Qualify according to AAMD standards. Policy has been way below AAMD standards concerning institutions. ...
>
> Rules for institutions seem well designed <u>but are not carried out</u>. ...
>
> <u>There are to be no threats to parents in</u> trying to have

135

better care for their children. ...

Why shouldn't parents have the right to go into the halls where their child resides and see where child's clothes are and where he or she sleeps ...

Grievence committee keep alert. Too many delinquents admitted to schools for retarded. ...

According to Joe Thomas, who in 1963 was a beginning psychiatric social worker at Rainier State School, conditions for residents were bad. Often the attendants were elderly and afraid of the stronger and more violent residents. Thus, those residents often wound up running the ward as they wished from a favored spot outside the attendant's cubicle – a practice that continued at least through the late 1970s. Persons with more severe disabilities who were incontinent lay in their urine and feces for long periods, before the days of absorbent diapers. Residents who could stand were hosed off in groups in the showers which had no individual stalls.[185] After a parent brought dozens of socks to replace the missing socks of a son or daughter, had been lost, the socks would be divided up as needed among all those without them. There was then no provision for private property and most families never brought replacements.

Thomas estimated that only one third of the residents ever had family visits. Of the third who did, many visits occurred only once a year at Christmas. They might be home that one day, but they always came back the next, "even though they [had] the ability to live at home."

A smaller fraction had more regular visits. The Friends of Rainier, an institutional parents' group formed in the late 1940s when some parents disagreed with the decision of the CBL leadership to go public and engage the community, would come by bus once a month. They would "have their meetings there and after their meetings they go and see their children and if they want to they'll take them out, you know, ice cream cones or something special for them, and then return them" to the institution.[186]

Forty years later, Kathryn Epton felt that the worst decision she ever made was to cave in to her mother-in-law's pressure (she lived with them) and place Johnny in Lakeland Village for 20 months. He lost 40 pounds. She believed that because Johnny had cerebral palsy and could not eat quickly, the residents who had been assigned the duty of feeding him ate much of his food themselves.

Most of the news stories focused on the lack of staff needed to perform routine attendant duties. The staff shortage functioned as the official "explanation" for the problems. It was true that inadequate professional personnel had plagued the residential schools for years. For example, in 1960 WARC had pressured the State Personnel Board to correct the salary inequities for the schools' social workers to bring their wages in line with comparable positions at the state mental hospitals. (The ineffectiveness of parent advocacy to effect basic changes in institutions is evident when one recalls that in 1936, a quarter century earlier, the very first CBL political handout attacked the inequities in the budgets of the various institutions with the Custodial School at the bottom. The same complaint was heard here thirty years later.) Staff salaries were a high fraction of the varying costs of institutions then and later.[187]

Low pay was one reason the schools could not retain quality staff. The situation regarding non-professional employees was even worse. The Legislative Council Subcommittee on State Institutions and Youth questioned why 102 of 380 attendant counselors had resigned in the last year. Rainier superintendent C.H. Martin, replied, "We're in an economic boom. People won't apply for these low-paying jobs."[188]

The newspaper horror stories could not be ignored. 58 members of the state legislature – one third of the total—toured Rainier School. Governor Evans tried to allay fears when he spoke to a crowd of nearly 500 people, mostly parents, at a meeting in Seattle in the fall of 1966.[189] The meeting was sponsored by the Division of Handicapped Children of the Department of Institutions. In his speech entitled, "The State's Participation in Programs for the Retarded," the governor proposed a three-part program for "mentally retarded and handicapped children": increased salaries for institutional employees, upgraded and expanded facilities, and better coordinated management by state agencies. Evans called the waiting lists at the state residential schools a distressing state of affairs. But the governor also asserted that many of the 1,200 people awaiting admission could be cared for in their homes if the "right kinds of community resources" were made available.

Nearly 600 people represented emergency cases "in which the parents needed immediate relief and in which the child himself cannot be best served except in an institutional setting," Evans said. Referendum 15, which the legislature had already placed on the November ballot, would provide three new wings at Yakima Valley School to accommodate 270 more "blind, deaf and non-ambulatory retarded children," a new laundry at Rainier School, and a recreation building at Fircrest School. The WARC board had unanimously endorsed the referendum at its March 1966 meeting. That was inevitable; the board had been instrumental in persuading the legislature to place the issue before the voters.

Governor Evans pledged his support for the referendum and urged his audience to "campaign actively for this important bond issue during the next two weeks." The problems of mental retardation would be placed on the state's priority list, Evans said. Like each bond issue which WARC supported over the years, Referendum 15 passed, and the institutions were enlarged and improved.

But neither WARC nor the Friends of Rainier had controlled the coverage of the story. The most important public media event in the state's recent history of developmental disabilities was apparently initiated by journalists who were reading stories in the national media.

Parent Rights

The voluntary admissions act of 1957 was the most valuable piece of legislation ever, in the judgment of Erik Froberg, a lawyer and, for many years the most prominent parent lobbyist. Although not originally proposed by parents, the law increased their control over institutional placements. It provided a voluntary entrance procedure which was compatible with the image of a school. After all, who ever heard of being involuntarily committed to the University of Washington?

Earlier some parents *had* sought an involuntary commitment bill. In 1949 the Children's Benevolent League had lobbied in favor of a combined mental illness and mental retardation institutional commitment bill. The bill passed, and a comprehensive mental illness reform act was enacted, but only after the phrase "mental deficiency" had been totally eliminated. The words were reportedly stricken because of fiscal concerns that, if the phrase were included, the state would have been forced to accept every mentally deficient person into a state school. Thus, the parents' inability to keep mental deficiency in the bill prevented them from achieving a true involuntary commitment act for all persons with mental retardation.

In 1955 the Department of Institutions submitted a bill to alter the current commitment procedure. Instead of requiring all placements to be made as commitments ordered by a juvenile court judge, parents would be able to apply for the admission of their children through a petition to the superintendent. The Department had not consulted WARC in drafting the bill. Froberg, chairman of the WARC's legislative committee, testified that "intelligent recodification of the existing laws" was needed, but this bill contained too many weak and negative aspects. Without parental support, H.B.

293 failed to pass.

Between legislative sessions, WARC members worked on another admissions bill that was offered to the state legislature in 1957. Erik Froberg, Van R. Hinkle, and Dr. Edgar A. Doll drafted Senate Bill 122. Froberg, the lawyer, presumably put the bill into legalese. Hinkle provided critical ideas and backing as supervisor of the state Division of Children and Youth Services.[190] Doll, who had retired to Bellingham, was a nationally prominent mental retardation authority, formerly at the Vineland School in New Jersey.[191] Doll created what is now the Vineland Adaptive Behavior test which measures functional abilities and deficits not captured by an IQ test. The new admissions bill passed both Houses of the Legislature without a dissenting vote and was signed into law by Governor Albert D. Rosellini on March 13, 1957. In a special address, Rosellini called S.B. 122 "an expression of the state's social conscience on behalf of children with an especially challenging handicap."

Supplementary legislation enacted in 1959 established the legal category of "parental successor." According to HOPE (April, 1959), Senate Bill 335 was the major legislative concern of WARC in this session. Parents of institutional residents could now designate an individual, bank trust officer, or church official to exercise parental rights to protect the child's interest and welfare" upon the death of the parents. This legal category was separate from guardians of the estate or of the person and was distinguished by the lack of ordinary court review. No guardian ad litem needed to be appointed to represent the potentially separate interests of the institutional resident. Parent rights trumped resident rights.

In later years when the ARC sued for deinstitutionalization, Froberg responded by successfully leading institutional parents to lobby for additional appeal procedures. These included court hearings, that would be required before a resident could be placed in the community—even if the son or daughter wished the placement (RCW 72.33.161, commonly known as the Froberg law). Parental control over institutional admission and release was as complete as they could make it.

Institutional Parent Pay

What is known as "parent pay" legislation aroused just as much parent emotion as waiting lists and outlasted the latter issue by many years—lasting from 1947 till the present. Over the forty-year period there have been two-dozen legislative sessions and three-dozen bills seeking "financial responsibility" of parents to pay for services for their sons and daughters with developmental disabilities. Only a few sessions have seen no parent pay bill. Yet because of parent opposition, no significant legislation in that respect has yet been enacted.

The first bill successfully opposed was introduced in 1947. In his speech to the national AAMD convention Alan Sampson proudly cited the bill as an illustration of parent power. In 1951 Erik Froberg judged that Senate Bill 165 "concerned members of the CBL probably more directly than any other." To help defeat this bill, a sixteen-point series of objections and a two-page cover letter had been sent to all CBL chapter presidents and other interested parties.

In 1953 Froberg again led the opposition and again a list of arguments against parent pay was circulated, and opposition from other groups was obtained. Generally, the opponents felt little relief would come to the state budget from such a fee, and it would do an injustice to a small group of persons. Over one thousand letters objecting to parent pay were sent to Olympia, and more than one hundred parents attended a hearing to express their displeasure (HOPE, May 1953). The bills died in committee.

The topic of parent pay emerged once again in 1956. WARC President E.H. Riviere met with Erik Froberg, Alan H. Sampson, executive director Leopold Lippman, and others at Froberg's Seattle home on June 22, 1956 to discuss the renewed effort by the legislature to enact a parent pay bill.[192] The WARC leaders recognized that the legislative proposal was a very real possibility and agreed that steps should be taken to meet the challenge with a "counter campaign." WARC's list of objections to parent pay, revised in 1953, was discussed, and the group felt the list should be updated and reissued.

By July 1956 Erik Froberg had gathered information from other states on parent pay. Froberg solicited a contact person in each chapter to work against any such bill in the 1957 legislature. Froberg's strategy was to take a "low profile" approach. He wanted to avoid mobilizing potential supporters of parent pay. WARC's tactics were outlined in a memorandum from Leo Lippman to WARC President E.H. Riviere:

> Meanwhile, there is no big campaign and we seek no
> publicity. We are not recommending letters to the editor,
> or public meetings, or open protests. We are only after a
> clarification of thinking—first for the chapter leaders,
> second the membership, and third (in some cases) the

Legislators.

The approach Erik suggests on contacting Legislators is that it be done most informally, and on a personal basis. He doesn't think our members should seek appointments, but should rather use the casual contacts they already have. For instance, one member may be a fraternity brother, or fellow Reserve officer, or co-Rotarian with a local member of the Legislature. Or they may sit together on the PTA board, or in some other service organization. If the opportunity comes up—and we are not urging that members go out of their way to create the issue—the idea is simply to say: "You know, John, this proposal is kicking around again, and really it's most unfair. Did you realize—and here's another angle—and so forth."

This form of "soft lobbying" is exactly what Felicetti found effectively used by the NARC at the national level. [193]Felicetti also found NARC to be very influential in its sphere. Similarly, according to Representative Kay Epton, WARC was one of the most powerful lobbies in the legislature in the 1950s.[194]

In 1959 parents opposed each other on the issue of parent pay for the first time. Representative Kathryn Epton was the parent of a child with disabilities and an active advocate for expanded community services. She introduced the session's most viable bill to assess parents for the costs of institutional care. Epton's friends and constituents in Spokane struggled to raise funds to begin a new school for children with learning disabilities in the community. Other parents sent their children to nearby Lakeland Village and paid nothing for their care. Epton felt it was grossly unfair for some families to be working very hard to gain services for their children while other parents turned their children over to the state and got services for free. The bill was defeated again, although sentiments of a similar nature have continued to be voiced by parents whose children live in the community.

The 1965-66 Study Divides WARC Again

Although another parent pay bill was defeated in 1965, the topic was given a new lease on life when the Legislative Council authorized an interim study of the issue. WARC offered its full cooperation with the study. Additionally, WARC was on record in favor of increased taxes so that needed services could be funded. This theme, too, was repeated in later sessions as a means to deflect the argument that the parents wanted something for nothing.

"Probably no phrase generates more heat and at times raises more smoke among members than the parent pay bill," WARC Executive Director Michael Kreider wrote to chapter presidents and the WARC Executive Committee in 1965. And some WARC officers also had begun to hint that a parent pay bill might be the responsible course of action. It was argued that WARC could best continue to play a strong leadership role by showing "responsibility." This would help to gain support from the general public and the legislature. WARC's past opposition to a parent pay bill had "distorted the WARC image, for many did support the use of funds from Social Security, pensions, etc."[195] Some WARC officers argued that, "It is time that we take a positive approach, stating our position on this matter." They believed that WARC must impress upon the legislature the need for better programs, more community services, and support in the home. It was felt that the appropriate time to discuss these issues with the Legislative Council was when the parent pay issue was presented. A trade-off might be mutually acceptable.

John Weiks, chairman of the Governmental Affairs Committee, agreed that WARC should move in a "more positive" direction. By now, separate parent groups had emerged at the four state institutions, outside of WARC. They were less politically powerful, but they might well be opposed to parent pay. WARC agreed that the Legislative Council should be made aware of the fact that not all parents were speaking for WARC when they expressed their concerns.

But the more favorable comments toward parent pay by some parent leaders came to a swift end. At the Executive Committee meeting on March 12, 1966, WARC President Elise Chadwick reported on the results of a questionnaire which had been sent out to local chapters regarding parent pay. The results indicated that parents overwhelmingly opposed any new statute. They claimed they were already accepting financial responsibility. Chadwick noted that Washington state had passed a parent pay bill long ago; since the turn of the century, the law had required parents to supply clothing for their institutionalized child. Chadwick said, in addition, that most parents paid for their child's major doctor and dental bills even though these responsibilities could not be found in the law.

In May, Chadwick presented WARC's opposition to a parent pay bill to a joint meeting of the Legislative Budget Committee and the Legislative Council at Shelton, Washington. The topic was discussed again on November 12, 1966 when Chadwick and Executive Director Mike Kreider met with the Subcommittee on State Institutions and Youth Development of the Legislative Council in Seattle. Five of the seven members of the Subcommittee were present at the Seattle hearing. They unanimously passed a resolution opposing a parent pay bill and sent such notice to the Legislative Council. The Subcommittee's resolution effectively ended the political threat posed by the legislative study of parent pay.

As a consequence, 1967 was one of the few sessions in which a parent pay bill was not introduced. On the other hand, Senate Bill 40 was enacted; it required payments by *residents* of institutions to pay for their care if they had personal assets of more than $1,000. This bill was approved by WARC at its February 1967 Executive Committee meeting. The action was consistent with the interests of WARC: the association was primarily a *parents'* organization for Washington state. These parents could support pay by residents, just as they also supported parent pay by those families who lived out-of-state but had children in Washington state institutions.

According to Chadwick's annual report in the fall of 1967, WARC had proven its case; parents generally were doing their fair share for their institutionalized children.

> Parents now support their children in terms of clothing, medicine, and incidentals to the amount of $525,000 yearly and spend an additional $215,000 in transportation to visit their children. The amount of $525,000 is entirely exclusive of volunteer hours, gifts from parents and chapters, and solicited gifts chapters from other organizations in support of the institutions. I sincerely hope we established the fact that there is a parental responsibility law in the State of Washington and that parents are more than meeting their requirements to their children.

However, the state agency leadership continued to propose the idea and the WARC leadership continued to examine parent pay as a live option. It was reported at the March 1973 board meeting that President Harold Little and Executive Director Perry Liljestrand had met with representatives from the Department of Social and Health Services concerning a parent pay bill. According to the board meeting minutes, it was "felt by the Washington ARC leadership that one year's preparation and one year's 'selling' is needed on this item before we could support such a bill." At the June board meeting President Little again declared that WARC would be willing to form a joint committee with State of Washington people "to explore justification and economics of a parent pay bill."

In December 1974 David Foscue of WARC and Steve Hosch, Assistant Attorney General for the Department of Social and Health Services, discussed the parent pay issue at the WARC board meeting in Olympia. A new parent pay bill was being prepared by Hosch. He went over the bill carefully and asked for questions from board members, staff, and guests. WARC referred the issue to the Executive Committee for study and urged those attending the meeting to notify the state WARC office as soon as possible with their comments in favor or against the bill. Once again the outcome from the grass-roots was overwhelmingly negative, and WARC wound up opposing the legislation. The association continued its successful record in opposing at least four more such bills during the rest of the 1970s.

In the fall of 1981, House Bill 759 was stopped by the ARC and its allies during the special session of the legislature. The topic was a familiar one, parent pay, but the scope of affected services now included all community programs. The cover story on the *ARC News* intentionally stirred up anger and fear by headlining the question: "Would you like to pay $300 a month for group home care? Up to 100% of cost for respite care and other services?" Readers were alerted to what would have happened if the bill had passed and urged to continue working to defeat another parent pay bill which would be considered at the 1982 legislature in January. Readers were warned that the Republican leadership in the House had given the parent pay bill a high priority for passage and that legislative and state agency staff would be working diligently on the bill over the holiday break.

But Governor John Spellman's administration and Republican legislative leaders waged a losing battle. The parent pay sections of SB 4418, termed the Financial Responsibility Act, failed to pass during the 1982 legislative session, although fees and collection procedures for mental health, juvenile delinquency, and other programs were changed.

Given the importance of the issue to the parent movement over the decades, it might be argued that the frequency with which WARC chose to battle parent pay expended vital resources and thus significantly diminished the other concessions it could wrest from the legislature. But it seems more to the point that this issue of narrow self-interest mobilized many parent members to action who were otherwise apathetic. Indeed, the leaders of WARC can occasionally be seen moving toward an accommodation with the state on the issue, only to be undermined by the grass roots, who felt otherwise.[196]

Institutions in the Community?

Parental attitudes had begun to shift and more ambiguous support for institutions became the rule. WARC had approved the conversion of a former tuberculosis sanitarium which became the Fircrest School in 1959. But unlike other state residential schools, Fircrest was not isolated in the country. It was in a middle-class residential area just north of Seattle city limits.[197]

Again in 1963 WARC chose to pursue new residential options in urban areas. At the urging of the local Kitsap county chapter, the WARC board approved a state purchase and conversion of Harrison Memorial Hospital in Bremerton to a mental retardation facility— but then the motion was reconsidered and defeated. Later in the year the board again reversed its position and approved a motion presented by Kitsap County calling on the State of Washington to fund the hospital as a new model "community-oriented facility for the retarded." On the surface, the battle was over the notion that it was so important to provide services to families who were demanding them, that substandard facilities were acceptable. In truth, the controversy reflected growing unease with old-style institutions.

With strong WARC lobbying House Bill 288 passed in 1965. The bill designated Harrison Memorial Hospital as a combined mental retardation and mental health center. When Governor Daniel J. Evans signed the bill into law, he expressed hope that the facility would become a prototype for Washington state and the nation. "Olympic Center" opened as a multi-service center, with in-patient mental health housing, information and referral for a broad range of public services, and some day programs for persons with mental retardation.

In 1967 WARC weighed legislation to create a "new school" in Kitsap county and another near Spokane, which later opened as Interlake School. Both facilities were the subjects of serious debate among WARC members, in part because each involved use of old buildings. The Kitsap county delegate urged the WARC Board to adopt a position that the center should become a resource facility, including a full residential school for 100 to 300 persons, for the families in that region of the state.

After a long deliberation, neither an approving nor a disapproving motion could attain a majority, and the board recessed. When the board members met the following day, a motion by vice president

Frank Skerbeck was passed. The proposal called on Governor Evans to create a model regional center to serve Kitsap, Clallam, Jefferson, and northern Mason counties, provided that as an interim measure only, the buildings at Olympic Center be used. No mention was made of Interlake School.

According to the resolution, WARC supported the concept of "regional centers" providing comprehensive services for persons with mental retardation. Such centers would have the full array of services as described by the President's Panel on Mental Retardation. These were: diagnostic services, day care programs for more severely retarded individuals, family counseling, information and referral, special education and rehabilitation, supervised living accommodations for persons who were moderately and mildly retarded, residential care as determined by the needs of the area, recreational programs, and staff training.

In WARC's message to the Governor, the association urged that the proposed Olympic Center be developed, in part because of the Bremerton area's commendable community efforts to design a model comprehensive regional center and thus achieve the first really significant development in reversing the long standing pattern of constantly rising waiting lists.

This proposal did not succeed, but the energy in the Kitsap chapter for such a solution, coupled with the legislative support the chapter received from Senator Frances Haddon Morgan,[198] eventually resulted in the opening of Frances Haddon Morgan Children's Center for Autistic Children at the Olympic Center campus in 1972.

Waiting lists were the political pressure point. They represented the demands which legislators and other governmental officials heard from constituents. Similarly, waiting lists were the main reason many parents joined the Washington Association for Retarded Children. They expected the organization to lobby for expanded institutional facilities. This reality is reflected in the insightful conclusions of President Chadwick in her 1967 annual report. The board had set policy; it

> resolved its position on Olympic Center from the
> standpoint of its being an institution in keeping with
> WARC's state policy regarding new beds for the mentally
> retarded—that such facilities be located in or very near
> communities, the buildings be designed for the specific
> resident to be housed, and that they house much smaller
> numbers than institutions have in the past.

However, she added,

during the heat of the controversy, there were movements of mental health patients into Interlake School...and it was not clear at the time that these persons would not become part of the population at Interlake and hence would fail to reduce the waiting list to the extent originally intended. Therefore, WARC did look at Olympic Center far more in the light of a regional institutional facility which would help relieve the waiting list, than that of a multiple use community facility.

This era was, in fact, the high point of institutionalization in Washington state. In 1936, when the parents' movement began, there was only one institution with 1,530 residents. By 1968, the number of residents at the state's five schools had reached 4,197. Per capita institutionalization in public facilities for persons with intellectual disabilities peaked at 13.4 residents per 10,000 Washingtonians in the mid-sixties—an increase of roughly fifty percent since the CBL had begun its work. Institutional populations then began to decline as more parents chose community options for their children. Waiting lists for institutional placement faded from WARC's attention. In concert with national shifts of opinion between 1963 and 1967, WARC's leaders became convinced that new state institutions for persons with mental retardation should be more closely tied to the community.

Yet the institutions have continued to live on with a life of their own, with more declines in resident population due to deaths than to placements in the community. A gradually aging resident population becomes progressively more expensive with the fixed cost overhead associated with the institutional facilities. When will the last "school" close?

CHAPTER FIVE:
A SPECIAL EDUCATION FOR ALL

In mid-20th century America, including in Washington state, parents of children with developmental disabilities began to demand entry to the local public school systems. These parents thought they were pioneers, coming out of the closet for the first time. To some extent, they were, but special education had its antecedents that had largely been forgotten.

It is true that the earliest special education was institutional. In Washington a year after a Presbyterian minister in Tacoma started the first school for deaf children, he led a group which petitioned the territorial legislature for funding. The 1886 legislature agreed to the petition and established the Washington State School for Defective Youth at Vancouver, to which the deaf pupils moved. From the beginning, children with other disabilities attended as well.

Education for All in 1890: Parents as the Problem

The state of Washington not only appropriated funds for institutional schooling, it also created legal authority for special education. In the state constitution (1889) education was declared the "paramount duty" of the state, a provision now interpreted to include special education. In 1890, consistent with this notion (and because the School for Defective Youth had not attracted sufficient pupils),

148

a *compulsory attendance* law was passed. It became the duty of clerks of local school districts to report to county school superintendents all "feeble-minded children" between the ages of 6 and 21, under penalty of fine; the report was then relayed to the state school. The term feeble-minded was not defined in statute, leaving interpretation to local school districts.

In addition, by this law, parents were *required* to send their children to the school—violation of which was made subject to a fine of up to $200, almost $5,000 in 2010 terms! An exception was provided: if the county commissioners judged that the child was receiving an adequate education locally, the child need not go to the state institution. However, in such cases, monitoring the child's continued progress was required.

Thus, from its first full year as a state, Washington had a mandatory education act for all defective youth, as well as a mandatory registration and referral system. Mandatory education and registration both fell into disuse long before the statutory basis was repealed in 1957. But after 47 years, the state renewed the mandatory education provision in 1937, when the statute authorizing Rainier School was enacted. Limiting institutional capital and operating budgets also constricted formal educational opportunities, since the superintendent was not expected to admit all applicants. But comprehensive registration continued to be practiced through the 1930s.

In 1891, two years after statehood, the legislature appropriated $20,000 for a special building on the campus of the School for Defective Youth,

> which will be a home and school for such feeble-minded children as possess germs of intelligence, capable of being developed into active mentality, who are free from vicious habits and are not afflicted with loathsome and incurable disease.

There were twenty-six feeble-minded children at the institution during 1892-93. In the following year there were forty-three, almost half of the total enrollment.[199]

In 1907 a separate State Institution for the Feeble-Minded was organized at Medical Lake near Spokane. The institution served eighty-seven "idiotic" children through a "custodial or asylum department for the care of such as can not be benefited by educational training." The statute implies that some children could not be educated, a belief that had its precedents. In 1892 the superintendent of the combined School for Defectives had praised the decision "to discriminate against the admission of the epileptic, paralytic,

149

and profound idiot," whose entrance would likely "defeat the ends for which the school was established."[200] The superintendent had contended that accepting the custodial cases tended to undermine the scholastic nature of the institution, and thus make parents of the feeble-minded more resistant to having their children at the facility. No one wished to accept responsibility for "the uneducable," neither the local schools nor the institution.

However, succeeding superintendents expressed other opinions. E.G. Bixler felt the 1917 name change to the State *Custodial* School had not gone far enough and suggested the name be altered to "State Custodial *Home*," since eighty percent of the residents would stay for life unless the families took them back. Bixler asserted:

> Parents reading the present style of the Institution
> name are inclined to believe that their hopelessly defec-
> tive child, upon being sent here, will be educated and
> reclaimed by us through several methods in education and
> training.[201]

In this sentiment, Superintendent Bixler was in tune with national thought. The superintendent of New York's large and prominent Rome State Custodial *Asylum* wrote that

> I firmly believe that no feeble-minded person should
> be taught to read and write…I have seen any number of
> feeble-minded children, who, if they had not been taught
> to read and write, would have been happy in an institu-
> tion. They are making their parents unhappy when they
> come to visit them…We are sorry that we ever taught
> any of them to read and write, because they find what
> they are losing in the world and are constantly hankering
> after it, and it makes them miserable…[202]

Parental hopes and desires created other problems for the school as well. Wanting their son or daughter to come home, parents showed up at the school and demanded a release. Samuel C. Woodruff, superintendent from 1907-20, complied with these requests, claiming that the mandatory admission law did not authorize retention over parental objections. Such a practice caused him to be "sometimes censured by county superintendents and commissioners" who argued that these children were unfit to associate with normal children or that they had inadequate home environments. Still, he could see no objection to parents taking their children home during the summer, when the school department was on vacation.[203]

The development of special classes in local school districts was not viewed with competitive alarm by Superintendent Woodruff, in part because he believed that they would become a feeder system for the state institution. If students failed special classes, their "parents...would feel that everything had been done and would feel more resigned to sending them away from home to the institution."[204] Woodruff was right. Because of their universality and credibility, the public schools probably functioned as the most effective referral system for institutions until after World War II. Thus, institutionalization rates rose at the same time that enrollment in special education classes did.

Early Special Education in the School Districts

From the beginning of public education, sensitive teachers and administrators have responded to children with special needs. For example, in about 1902, Hoquiam public schools enrolled a three-year-old girl to insure her proper language development, since both parents were deaf-mutes.[205] Attending with a friend, the child took a long nap at school in the afternoon. But such "individualized education" was soon accompanied by the development of formal programs.

Several of the larger "first class" school districts began to offer handicapped programs before World War I. Hoquiam Public Schools opened the first special education class for mentally deficient children in 1909. The superintendent was enthusiastic about its success.[206] Nellie Goodhue taught the first class for Seattle students with mental disability in April 1910, two years after a private school for deaf students was absorbed into the public schools.[207] In the fall of 1910 Margaret Horton taught a class for "mental defectives" at Tacoma's McKinley School. By 1914, there were twenty-five pupils. Spokane schools joined the movement in February 1911, while Everett's programs began in the mid-1920s. After two years of experimentation, Olympia opened a class in 1929.[208]

Part of the impetus for the rapid development of classes was a favorable state funding formula. In 1909 the legislature declared that districts with schools for "defectives" would receive *five times* the per capita apportionment as that due for regular students – a formula never matched in later years. The records from Tacoma Public Schools show that the state paid forty cents for each student in the handicapped class, but only eight cents per day for regular students. The state's contribution was more than half of the total cost of education. A financial commitment to special education was evident on the other side of the state as well. Spokane proudly offered a $100 bonus per year for special education teachers to insure the highest quality instruction.[209]

The Washington Educational Association recognized the new field of special education by creating a Section for the Study of Defective Children in 1913. In 1914 Nellie Goodhue became its first president.[210] In 1927, Spokane special education teachers formed their own local group with the motto "Every child deserves an education suited to his needs and his capacities."[211]

How disabled were the children? The classes were designed for the large majority of students, whose disability was mild or "borderline." This is hardly surprising, because, then as now, the number of children with mild disabilities exceeds the total of those more severely affected. Curriculum guides suggest that the classes were similar to remedial coursework today. Poverty among many families of children with mild disabilities is suggested by the fact that those children who needed it were fed and bathed at school.[212] But by the mid-1920s, school districts across the country began to use the new intelligence tests to formulate cut-off points, below which children would be excluded. Typically, the line was an IQ score of 50.

In Seattle, that was indeed the situation. Nellie Goodhue asked Superintendent Frank B. Cooper, a notable Progressive in general educational matters, what policy she should adopt toward "imbeciles"—that is, children who were not educable, but who might be trained to do some things in an acceptable manner. Both Goodhue and Cooper were concerned about the impact of excluding the children. In "a number of cases" the parents "had finally been induced" by Goodhue to institutionalize their children. The parents who accepted institutional life for their children were a distinct minority. There had been 128 students "debarred" from schools, but most parents had refused to send their children away. Cooper worried that there were "now at large in Seattle, 170 low grade imbeciles and idiots. This constitutes a considerable social menace."[213]

Seven Seattle children were about to be discharged as uneducable. Nearly all of their parents were resisting, and several had threatened legal proceedings. It was clear that a policy was needed. Thus, on January 16, 1917, the Seattle School Board formally approved an exclusionary policy; a child would be barred or expelled if Ira Brown, the school physician, and Nellie Goodhue concurred that a child was uneducable. Dr. Brown was adamant on excluding all imbeciles and idiots, even from the Observation class.

He believed they belonged in institutions.[214] Since Brown and Goodhue battled over which discipline, medicine or education, had primary authority in regard to disabling conditions, it was natural that they disagreed on numerous specific exclusion decisions. Eventually, Seattle decided to exclude those with IQs below 50.

However, children with substantial intellectual deficits were being educated in other Washington school systems. The reports of "defective youth" to the Superintendent of Public Instruction reveal a number of districts in which "morons" (or children with roughly 50-70 IQ scores) were in school. A follow-up study of students enrolled in Tacoma "special rooms" between1922 and 1930 revealed that seventy-nine people had been individually administered the Binet-Simon tests. Nine had IQ scores between 40-55, thirty had IQs of 55-70, and forty received scores above 70. The investigators judged that they could not interview 13 individuals because of their "low mentality."[215]

The number of all children with disabilities who were enrolled in the public schools grew irregularly, a situation complicated by the lack of standardized definitions. Before the outbreak of World War I in 1914, only about 500 such students were enumerated statewide. During the relatively prosperous decade of the 1920s the number of defective youth in school tripled—partly, and perhaps mostly, due to the increase in labeling.

County superintendents of schools were required to report defective children to the state annually. In 1930-31 Pierce County (Tacoma) reported 40 defective children. The descriptions of the children used at the time were: paralytic, feeble-minded, blind, deaf, deaf and dumb, moron, "mind of a child," "born defected," "nervous trouble," spine, sick, "intellect of a six year old," "deaf in one ear, blind in one eye, brain not developed," dwarf, "vicious," epileptic, mentally deficient, and "defective vision." Only nine children were supposedly in school in one setting or another.

But the Depression reduced tax revenue and funding for special education was curtailed. The 1933 legislative session reduced the state apportionment ratio of handicapped students from five times to twice that for students in regular education—although the excess cost apportionment was extended to medium-sized ("second class") districts. Perhaps as a result of the funding shifts, the number of "subnormal" students enrolled in large school districts leveled off, based on a comparison of six cities in 1930 and 1936. In 1935 the state Superintendent of Public Instruction reported an enrollment of 3,052 special education students; 2,354 were classified as subnormal, 422 crippled, 159 deaf or faulty speech, and 117 blind.

However, growth resumed in the latter half of the decade, with 5,490 students served in 1937-38.

In 1938, Seattle had 1.4 percent (or 783) of 56,000 students enrolled in 54 special education classes. Spokane had .6 percent of its total (117) in 14 classes, for an average class size of 12-13. Olympia's special education enrollment was relatively large at 3 percent, or 60 students out of 2,000.[216]

The 1937 legislature authorized rural and small ("third class") district co-operative special education programs. The state would pay 80 percent of transportation costs required by the co-ops, as well as "the usual double amount allowed for attendance in schools for defective children." At a meeting of county superintendents of schools, those in attendance felt that they were pioneers in implementing a truly statewide special education system. They quickly seized their opportunity, with 49 small districts establishing a total of 53 classes with an enrollment of 2,200 students in the 1937-38 school year.

World War II was accompanied by a re-direction of fiscal priorities away from children with disabilities. In a report to the AAMD[217] Tacoma teacher Mae Williams stated that the war brought "a shortage of teachers and a need for curtailment of classes." Special education classes were abolished, and the students were gradually absorbed into regular classes. Williams crisply rendered judgment on this involuntary mainstreaming. "To their detriment? Convincingly yes! To their state of happiness? Emphatically no!" It was hard, Williams wrote, to mix those with third grade reading skills with those in the ninth grade Remedial English class. But she had to admit the special students *liked* knowing their classmates and *liked* learning the ninth grade vocabulary as they had not done before. She reported that the students' slogan was: "Be your age! No one can be better than we in courtesy and good nature."

The State Division of Handicapped Children

In 1943 a Division for Handicapped Children was created within the office of the state Superintendent of Public Instruction. A supervisor was hired to coordinate and supervise handicapped programs in the various school districts. Handicapped children were defined as those of common school age "who are temporarily or permanently retarded in normal educational processes by reason of defective hearing, defective sight, defective speech, or by reason of other physical handicap." Why this act excluded children with

154

mental disabilities is unknown, but this separation of such children from other children with handicaps, may help explain why post-war parents felt they were starting from scratch legislatively. In fact, however, "mentally retarded and slow-learning" children continued to be educated in the state's classrooms, comprising 54 percent of the identified 5,824 children in special education in 1942-43.[218]

In response to new parent activity, the 1947 legislature explicitly authorized boarding schools, special classes in day schools, and other similar programs for children with cerebral palsy and who were unable to take advantage of regular education.[219] The act appropriated $200,000 for the medical and educational needs of these people "to enable them to become normal individuals."

In 1949 pre-school programs were authorized for most handicapped children. Senate Bill 296 extended the regular school district apportionments, and such special allocations as provided, to handicapped children of "pre-school age," defined as those three years and older.[220] Unfortunately, the law built upon the 1943 and 1947 act and excluded children with mental retardation. That is, pre-school was funded for those children whose learning was temporarily or permanently limited due to "defects of hearing, speech or sight, cerebral palsy, or other physical handicaps."

Education is Blowing Your Nose

The first public school legislation which the League supported was House Bill 310 in 1951. The impetus behind the bill was the rebuff, and then the encouragement, that Anna Magnuson received from the Kirkland School District Superintendent when she tried to enroll her daughter in school in 1949. Assuming her child needed a special class, the superintendent told Mrs. Magnuson that he could not possibly start a class for just one child—but he did suggest that a classroom might be possible for ten children.

Anna Magnuson took the superintendent's response as an expression of support. In her Model A Ford, she began to track down parents of other children who were excluded from school. She knocked on doors when neighbors relayed rumors, and approached them in parking lots when she spotted them with their children. She often dealt with rejection. In fact, as she recalled it,

> the parents were the hardest to deal with, because the
> kids weren't out of the closets yet. I would knock on a
> door and say "I understand you have a child who is not

in school." "Who told you?" they would reply. I answered "I have four of them in the car right now."[221]

In all she found 28 children.[222] Magnuson eventually formed a Society for Exceptional Children, a group of parents in the Kirkland and neighboring Bellevue and Bothell districts. They met and drew up a petition with signatures from 43 families and presented it to their school superintendents.

Again they were rejected, this time with the explanation that state law did not explicitly mention educating this particular type of child. The school districts urged them to seek changes in the law. Four determined parents drove to Olympia and met with Ross Hamilton, director of handicapped education. He and his staff drafted a bill immediately to revise the laws of 1943 and 1949 to include students with mental handicaps. Hamilton, who emerged as an effective advocate for such children, found Anna Magnuson's surname to be a lucky coincidence with that of Washington's senior U.S. senator Warren Magnuson.[223] The identical surnames proved helpful in gaining access to state legislators, who were taken aback at the idea that such children might attend local schools.

After House Bill 310 was introduced, Magnuson began lobbying. She reported that she was the only parent; "the others thought I was nuts, crazy." The Superintendent of Public Instruction strongly supported the bill, as did sympathetic others. Among the supporters was the Children's Benevolent League, although Magnuson reports there was substantial internal opposition within the CBL.[224] Some parents feared that the bill would detract from efforts to support Rainier School. The CBL legislative committee noted the bill's special importance to parents whose children were not in the institutions.

According to the League's legislative report for the session, House Bill 310 passed the House without much trouble, but it ran into strong opposition in the Senate Committee on Education. The report noted that CBL President Clifton spent "a day in Olympia working primarily in this regard and is entitled to credit for the Bill passing as it did and becoming law." However, it was acknowledged that "Mrs. Magnusen [sic] from Kirkland and her group and the school authorities in that area worked many hours" and "...are entitled to the greatest credit for the passage of this law."

The argument Anna Magnuson made to the state senate committee for educating her child in the public schools illustrates the governing assumptions of the day. Yes, her daughter would eventually go to Rainier School when the family could no longer care for her through parent death or other circumstances. But if her daughter had gained self-help skills, the total lifetime cost to the state would be reduced. Magnuson's major problem was convincing senators that it was education she was asking for; "education is not just reading and writing, it's blowing your nose," she argued repeatedly. The support received from the state Superintendent of Public Instruction was critical in legitimizing self-help skills as a component of education.

As passed, Chapter 92 of the Laws of 1951 provided that special education could be offered by school districts to children down to the age of three who were educationally delayed due to "physical or mental handicap, or by reason of social or emotional maladjustment, or by reason of any other handicap." A proviso was added, perhaps by the CBL, which stipulated that no child could be removed from the jurisdiction of the juvenile court for training or education without permission of the superior court of the county. This stipulation meant that there would be no wholesale deinstitutionalization from Rainier and Lakeland Village.

The legislature made a biennial appropriation of $875,000 for the education of children covered under the 1943 and 1949 acts, and an additional $125,000 to implement the provisions of House Bill 310. Thus, special education in Washington state first reached an appropriation of $1,000,000 in 1951. This compares to a total regular school operating fund appropriation of $124,000,000. (Rainier State School and Lakeland Village each had operating budgets of $2,500,000 in 1952.)

Just passing the bill and obtaining the funds did not bring a school into being in Kirkland. The Society for Exceptional Children had to struggle to obtain a building and a qualified teacher. Anna Magnuson sought out the help of a professor in the Education Department at the University of Washington to locate qualified teachers. According to Magnuson, the professor yelled at her, "What the hell do you think you're doing? Do you think teachers go to school for eight years to waste their time on imbeciles?"[225] Magnuson was rejected again, but again she did not give up.

By the following year Anna Magnuson could report progress. Stewart Heights School in Kirkland served forty-one children, ranging from four to twenty-one years, "and in mental age from two years to twelve." Over 40 percent of the students had IQs below 50. Disabilities included Down syndrome, epilepsy, cerebral palsy, visual and hearing defects, and brain tumors. According to Magnuson (HOPE, May 1953):

For many of the children this is their first attendance

157

in any form of group activity. For others the absence of too keen competition makes learning possible for the first time.

Good progress in special education programs was reported elsewhere in Washington by 1952. President Olaf Caskin particularly praised the work of the Spokane and Kirkland chapters on behalf of school programs. Spokane CBL president Joe Kolb reported their satisfaction with their school in which one privately paid teacher supplemented parent workers. Programs were also under way or planned at Bremerton, Shoreline, Bellevue, Wenatchee, Walla Walla, and in Okanogan county.

At Western Washington State College in Bellingham, where Edgar Doll was associated, special training was conducted for special education teachers. CBL members were urged to contact their local school boards and request that such in-service training be included in next year's school budget.

In 1952 Pearl Wanamaker, State Superintendent of Public Instruction, addressed the CBL convention for the first time. Wanamaker had taken the lead in organizing a meeting between the CBL and representatives of cerebral palsied, blind, and deaf groups, about the need for special education for children at the Firlands Tuberculosis Sanatorium in Seattle. The next year, a state conference was held by the handicapped division of the state Office of Public Instruction and the superintendents of the state schools. Conference participants discussed how educational opportunities could be extended to children in the institutions.

In 1953, for the first time, WARC's legislative program included adequate appropriations for the handicapped division of the Public Instruction office. Seven school districts had opened programs for children with mental retardation, and almost all districts were interested in doing so, according to Ross Hamilton's speech to the convention. "There are now some 600 severely retarded children under these school programs, and we expect 2,000 by Christmas" (HOPE, October 1953). Hamilton did not report that Seattle, the state's largest district, opposed this expansion of special education.[226]

Thus, in Washington, the early burst of progress in special education brought mixed results for children and their parents. Some superintendents and school boards were sympathetic and opened classes for most children. Others continued to practice broad exclusion, or, if not exclusion, lack of effort. Washington's law provided partial state funding for children with mental disabilities if the district wanted to provide classes, but the law did not require it to.

Parents Start Their Own Schools

In the 1950s Orlando Thomas became president of the Woodhull Hay WARC chapter in Shoreline. His daughter Bonnie had a disability and she had difficulties.[227] The Thomases told how the neighborhood children came to the house and teased her, taunting her as a clown.

Bonnie told her mother Jean, "I like animals, but not people. Animals don't tease me."

Although they lived in Shoreline, just north of Seattle, when the Thomases heard of a play group in White Center, south of Seattle, they drove their daughter Bonnie there. They also tried enrolling Bonnie at Broadview School in Seattle until one day her mother found her crying under a bush on the playground.

Bonnie said, "Mommy, they're all my enemies and I thought they were my friends."

After that they tried Oak Lake School in north Seattle, but when Jean came to school to pick her up, she found Bonnie in the back of the class with her coat still on. Bonnie said that the teacher had ignored her all day. A boy had hit her on the shins with a 2x4. So her parents pulled her out.

Later a better opportunity developed at Rose Hill School in Kirkland. It was a decrepit 1922 building, but at least it was something. Jean had to drive 50 miles a day, from Shoreline to Kirkland, back when that was far more difficult and indirect than it now is, sometimes staying overnight in Kirkland.

Rosemary Hunt, a psychologist and principal of the Kirkland school, helped convince the Shoreline district to send their pupils there. Finally Shoreline permitted them to use a plain old house in their own district as a school. The parents were thankful to get it. According to the Thomases, Mrs. Saunders, the first teacher, was bad, and the superintendent was even worse. Superintendent Howard had the school sign burned and destroyed other things that the parents had erected.

Jean started a parents group at the Woodhull Hay school (which they named for the recently deceased NARC president). Forming the group was tough but rewarding.

> I approached [another mother] Mrs. Gilly and she
> slammed the door in my face. I said that I was a parent
> and she just wilted. Finally she relented. It was a won-
> derful moment to have witnessed. Some wonderful
> leaders have picked up the torch.

When Jean had 10 to 15 families, they went to the state capital and lobbied Pearl Wanamaker, state superintendent of schools. Upon their return, the Shoreline district heard the parents describe their wishes. While they offered coffee, and talked sweet, "they made fun of trying to educate such children." The superintendent of Shoreline Schools, Dr. Ray Howard, refused any funding for special education. According to Orlando Thomas, Howard said, "We're not pouring money down a rat hole."

Next Howard persuaded some of the parents to form a PTA in attempt to split the parents and control them. The Thomases resisted the PTA move, encouraged by Ross Hamilton, the state director of education for handicapped children, who agreed that it would be a disaster.

Educating these children required significant additional labor beyond that which other children required—mothers became teachers and fathers became builders of special equipment. But in large measure, the parents' efforts seemed less a burden than a privilege and an opportunity. The same was true, at least at first, in those communities where parents encountered total rejection from school officials, but managed to open their own alternative schools.

Throughout the 1950s and 1960s, the situation remained similar in Washington and across the nation. A typical story from the October 1957 WARC newspaper described two new programs. The account reflects both the restrictions of the time and the pride in what had been achieved.

> A new school for trainable retarded children has been started in Yakima. The public school system is furnishing the teacher, and the Yakima Valley Chapter of WARC underwrites the rental cost of the building. The program started this fall, with registration limited to 20 children on half-day schedules.
>
> A play therapy school, for seriously involved children unable to attend special classes in the public schools, has been launched by the Twin Harbors Chapter. While the chapter is paying most of the cost, parents of the children in the group also are charged small fees.

Education for All in 1971: Parents as Partners

A quarter of a century after the national parents' association was formed in 1950 all children with mental retardation could finally go to school. But families in Washington and other states had envi-

160

sioned that goal long before it was realized. In 1952 the CBL adopted an education for all policy at the state convention:

It shall be the duty of each organized unit and each individual member of the League to assist the counseling and educating of all handicapped children, wherever they may be.

But this resolution called for action at the local level, not at the state level. After all, before considering mandatory state legislation, parents first needed to learn that they could not persuade each local district to offer education on a permissive basis. They also had to learn how much work it was providing the schooling themselves.

By 1959 parents had gained more experience, and "inclusive education" – though not the terminology of the time—was emerging as an issue. Representative Kathryn Epton introduced a bill in the legislature to provide some funds for children excluded from public school who were attending the parent-run private schools which were developing around the state. The bill failed. WARC's legislative and executive committees met to debate a bill mandating that all local school districts offer education to children with mental retardation (HOPE, January 1959). The legislative committee reserved judgment, preferring to concentrate, once again, on institutional policies and appropriations. Presumably Erik Froberg, still the committee chair, correctly sensed that a statewide system of local educational alternatives would eventually spell the doom of residential schools.

Years later Representative Epton who had not been a WARC member, recalled that it was due to WARC's strong efforts and political skills that they achieved 17 times as much funding for special education as when she had first become involved ten years earlier.[228]

A keynote speaker at the state convention in August 1959, Alton Lund, past president of the National Association for Retarded Children, called mandatory education one of the major pieces of unfinished business facing WARC and proclaimed that, "The day of education of all children—whether retarded or not—is at hand." A panel moderated by Joe Kolb, WARC vice-president, debated the issue of pressing for such legislation. Convention participants later formed small discussion groups to talk about the education for all issue. Their ideas would be presented at the "Little White House" Conference on Children and Youth for Washington to be held in Seattle in October. Summaries of the three discussion sessions were printed in HOPE (October 1959). One group stated:

There seems to be no question of a law of this type, since our present law clearly states that education shall be provided for every child. The question therefore is enforcement and how far shall we go. The consensus in this group is that education should be provided for the trainable as well as for the educable child, that it will be invaluable to the child's well-being and happiness in being a part of a group.

Another group concluded that a total overall program like that envisioned by Governor Rosellini was necessary. "Public acceptance of a total program should automatically solve this problem" in the school system. This approach suggested that attitudes should be changed first, rather than relying on the coercion of legislation.

An unenthusiastic report by the third group listed problems which could be created by over-hasty mandating of services and the benefits to be derived from a slower and more gradual approach. There would be better facilities with time and "better programs for children if time is given for training of personnel and understanding on part of the community." According to this group, programs were "progressing so well in the state we do not want them to be slowed by mandatory rules."

The failure of WARC to accept the need for a mandatory bill must have frustrated the minority of WARC members, such as Kathryn Epton, Anna Magnuson, and Joe Kolb, who were laboring so hard for schools in the community.[229]

Support from National was also nuanced. In an August 7, 1961 letter, NARC executive director Gunnar Dybwad wrote that Washington people needed to educate first themselves, then the other interested parties, that education of "trainables" (those children with more severe disabilities) was "no longer a vague and daring experiment but a well established and amply documented procedure." But, on the other hand, WARC should proceed with "orderly growth and development" and not rush into legislating mandatory education because such legislation did not suffice in Kentucky and Massachusetts, states which already had mandatory laws on their books

In June 1961 exclusion was formally extended. In accordance with a newly passed law, the State Board of Education for the first time established "Criteria of Eligibility" to determine which residents of the state residential schools might benefit from funds appropriated to the Office of the Superintendent of Public Instruction (HOPE, July 1961). The bill was a result of the legislature's "hold the line" budget and limited education to those children in

162

institutions who were educable; that is, a child who

> possesses the potential to respond to and benefit from
> educational experiences in terms of such factors as social
> competence, emotional stability, self-care, a degree of
> vocational competency or intellectual growth.

Yet universal education was an idea that would not die. In 1962 WARC's annual meeting was held jointly with the Council for Exceptional Children, the special education teachers' organization. President Raymond Howell moderated a panel on "progress toward education for all handicapped children." At their annual meeting the WARC board authorized drafting a bill to mandate education for all handicapped children for introduction in the 1963 Legislature. But the state's budget fell apart. Far from making advances, WARC licked its wounds after the session.

In 1967 WARC sponsored and funded a large conference on special education at Central Washington State University in Ellensburg.[230] The educational issues presented included day-care centers, pre-school, and separate versus regular school facilities, but the main aim, according to the July HOPE, was

> to point the way for a Special Education public policy
> for the mentally retarded in the state of Washington
> which can be understood and supported by parents,
> teachers, teacher training institutions, school administra-
> tors, and policy making and appropriating bodies.

Two hundred persons attended the conference, hearing addresses by Louis Bruno, Superintendent of Public Instruction, as well as by two nationally known educators. At the August board meeting, President Elise Chadwick reported two major themes had emerged from the exciting dialogue between parents and professionals:

> 1. a parent from WARC should be a member of
>   the state Curriculum or Guidelines committee
>   of the Department of Public Instruction, and
>   the same thing should be true on the local
>   school district level; and
> 2. special education should be available to all
>   MR persons at the same age levels as for the
>   normal child.

Two clear principles emerged at the Ellensburg conference: universal education and a legitimate parental role in special education curricular planning.

WARC's governmental affairs committee recommended at the state convention in September 1969 that the association push for mandatory education. At the next annual meeting, Elise Chadwick, head of the Education Committee, reported on a proposed mandatory education bill that the Executive Committee adopted. It stated

> that the policy of the State of Washington with regard to the provision of education and training shall be mandatory for all children, except that in the case of handicapped children, it shall be mandatory from the age of 3 to 21, and to this end directs that WARC in conjunction with other appropriate groups shall propose a bill to the Legislature of the State of Washington,...said bill to provide mandatory education in each district, or combined districts, for all handicapped children.

The "other appropriate groups" mentioned above especially included the Education for All Committee in Seattle, consisting of Evelyn Chapman, Katie Dolan, Cecile Lindquist, and Janet Taggart.[231] The committee had evolved out of the Northwest Center Mother's Guild, a group whose children had been excluded from Seattle schools.[232] Seattle, like many other districts, excluded children who were not toilet-trained, who lacked other self-help skills, and who had behavior problems. The parents grew tired of their children being excluded from school, and they grew weary of trying to operate their own program with assistance from the Seattle Parks Department.

The leaders of the Education for All Committee met every Sunday throughout 1970, organizing and overseeing the drafting of legislation by two law students, George Breck and Bill Dussault. When the session began in January 1971, they not only had sponsors for two parallel bills lined up, but also had won the endorsement of Governor Evans, the Superintendent of Public Instruction, and the interim joint education committee of the legislature. At their May meeting, the WARC board discussed the successful passage of H.B. 90. President Omer Carey claimed that the mandatory education bill had passed because of WARC's heavy involvement. It is true that WARC had worked hard to obtain mandatory education. But there is no question that Chapman, Dolan, Lindquist, and Taggart provided the leadership both before the session and in the day-to-day shepherding of the bill past obstacles.[233] According to Evelyn Chapman,[234] WARC's statewide organization allowed the Education for All Committee to mobilize supporters to pressure recalcitrant representatives and senators. This

persuasion was especially critical with several Spokane legislators –
a compliment to the strength and educational focus of the Spokane
chapter.

In their search for the legal mechanisms to guarantee educational opportunity, Breck and Dussault had surveyed the laws of all
other states. They found that every one of the laws contained large
loopholes. For the first truly universal education act, they decided
upon several provisions. First, universality and appropriateness of
education were mandated.

> The superintendent of public instruction shall require
> each school district in the state to insure an appropriate
> educational opportunity for all handicapped children of
> common school age....For purposes of this chapter, an
> appropriate education is defined as an education directed
> to the unique needs, abilities, and limitations of the han-
> dicapped children.

Next, the Superintendent of Public Instruction was given the
power to withhold any portion of state funds if a school district
failed to comply.

School districts were allowed to retain their right to exclude
children who were "physically or mentally unable to attend," but
were required to show that no other neighboring district or other
specialized program in the state could accommodate the child. If the
district made such a decision, the parent could appeal to the state of
Washington, and the state had the duty and authority to assist the
parent. Due process had been defined to ensure inclusion.

There was one omission from the ideal of education for all
children of common school age that reflected the territorial prerogatives of competing public agencies. Every school district had to
offer education for all, but the state institutions did not. The state
Superintendent of Public Instruction was allowed, but not required,
to offer special education to institutionalized children. As it turned
out, educational advocates were able to convince the state superintendent to expand programs to these children as well.

Although the act had an implementation date of 1973, Washington was already far along. For the 1971-72 school year it was
estimated by the national Council for Exceptional Children that 81
percent of Washington children with handicaps were in school, the
highest figure in the nation. The other inclusive states were Florida
(75%), Illinois (71%), and Minnesota (70%); nationally, only 39
percent of such children were receiving an education.[235] The successful passage of the bill may have been due in large part to the

fact that Washington was already providing programs for all but 5,000 children—either through the schools, through other day activity programs, or through institutional care.[236] Fewer dollars were needed to complete the inclusion of all.

However, the 1973 budget for special education which was sent to the Governor proposed a substantial increase in the school district operated programs. A total of $62.3 million was requested for existing programs, with an additional $47.6 million to implement House Bill 90. Of the latter figure, $5.6 million was requested for pre-school programs, which were permitted although not mandated. Thus the total cost of the special education budget was $109.9 million. Had the budget been adopted as proposed, the figure would have represented a hundredfold increase over a twenty-year period. But full funding was not achieved. In 1974 a $100 million budget was still the goal proposed by Ellen Foscue of WARC's Education Committee.

In 1974-75, however, much of WARC's attention focused on the accelerating pace of action on the national level. In October 1971, just a few months after Washington had passed its legislation, a landmark decision in a federal district court granted children with all disabilities in Pennsylvania broad rights, including a free public education; procedural rights including notice, hearings, and periodic re-evaluation; and avoidance of unnecessary labeling. *PARC v. Pennsylvania* 343 F.Supp. 279 (1972). This decision inspired many imitative lawsuits and provided a further stimulus to state and federal legislation. Partly because the decision was in a state in the mid-Atlantic seaboard, it gained more media attention, and it is usually credited with the origin of education of all.[237] The assessment of Washington's contribution to the enactment of national law, whatever it should be, should include the fact that, within months of the passage of Washington's House Bill 90, Breck & Dussault were summoned to Washington, D.C. to explain the legislation. They wandered the corridors explaining the legislation to crucial members and staff under the sponsorship of Washington's two powerful senators, Warren Magnuson and Henry "Scoop" Jackson.[238]

The culmination of the process was reached in the passage of the federal "Education for All Handicapped Children Act of 1975," Public Law 94-142. New sources of funding and new program components were mandated. In Washington, as in most states, the latter were more important. Of most importance to parent advocates, the procedural rights from the Pennsylvania decision were revised and incorporated, and an "Individualized Educational Program" (IEP) curricular planning model was adopted. Advocates intended that the IEP be a contract which brought together a parent and child, an administrator who was authorized to make financial commitments, and a teacher who would have the responsibility to decide how to implement the agreement. More parental power was thus gained than in any earlier act. Parents would work with the other team members to establish the following:

- a statement of the present levels of educational performance of such child;
- a statement of annual goals, including short-term instructional objectives;
- a statement of the specific educational services to be provided to such child, and the extent to which such child will be able to participate in regular educational programs;
- the projected date for initiation and anticipated duration of such services; and
- appropriate objective criteria and evaluation procedures and schedules for determining, on at least an annual basis, whether instructional objectives are being achieved.

P.L. 94-142 controlled much of the action of the parents in the following years. A major parent education campaign was undertaken by the WARC Education Committee, which drafted a lengthy manual on rights and responsibilities. Local chapters across the state engaged in a prolonged course of self-education and training of other parents in their new rights.

With the passage of H.B. 90 and P.L. 94-142, the achievement of educational programs for all children seemed almost complete. Succeeding years saw the ARC fight to maintain programs in the face of budget cuts and other regressive legislation. The ARC continued to struggle on three topics. First, WARC unsuccessfully urged the legislature in the late 1970s to provide compensatory education for handicapped adults who had been excluded from the public schools when they were children. With the passage of time, the issue faded from view.

Second, parents sought guaranteed pre-school opportunities in every school district across the state. After pre-school bills failed again in the 1979 session, the ARC worked with members of the Developmental Disabilities Planning Council's Pre-school Task Force in organizing the Pre-school Planning Board. The new board was an organization of parents, advocates and professionals who were striving to improve educational and related services for children with mental disabilities from birth to age five. The coalition of advocates, led by Laila Hammond, failed again in 1981 and 1983. Most legislators favored these special education programs and even believed that early intervention was a good investment. They simply claimed an inability to fund a cost-effective program—even though 80 percent of the eligible children lived in districts where pre-school was already offered. In 1984 the advocacy coalition finally secured mandated pre-school services for three- and four-year-old children. Below that age, education remained permissive.

Finally, ARC members followed with great interest the efforts of general education advocates to find a constitutional basis for adequate state funding of the public schools. At least since the postwar baby boom, Washington State had relied extensively on local school districts obtaining a significant part of their funding through local property tax levies in special elections. However, this had resulted in substantial funding differences between richer and poorer school systems. Seattle School District complained that it was unable to get enough funds through the levy system, because it had more poor families than did the wealthy suburbs. In 1977 Judge Robert Doran of the Thurston County Superior Court found the system of financing public schools unconstitutional because it failed to fulfill the provision in the Washington state constitution that public education is the "paramount duty" of the state (not the localities). In response, the legislature enacted the Basic Education Act of 1977, a move that was designed to retain legislative prerogatives over education and not allow the courts to decide funding issues. The following year the state Supreme Court upheld the Doran decision. The legislature complied by enacting a funding formula that was primarily state dollars (some calculations are 84%).

After the testimony of Arc parents and others, in 1983 a second decision by Judge Doran expanded the definition of "basic education" to include special education, bilingual education, remediation assistance, and transportation. However, the ARC, as part of the Special Education Coalition of parent and professional groups, was not happy with the special education funding formula that the legislature had adopted. It filed another lawsuit in 1985 seeking a decision from Judge Doran on the special education funding formula.[239] ARC leaders provided testimony in support. After an earlier oral ruling, in 1988 Judge Doran issued a decision that the current state special education funding formula was unconstitutional because it relied on statewide averages to set an upper limit on funding. Instead, the state had to devise a funding formula based on the individualized educational program (IEP) needed by each stu-

168

dent.

That decision was very welcome. It meant that, regardless of the budgetary constraints on a particular legislature, there was a new level of protection behind basic special education funding. A degree of immunity from the vagaries of citizen lobbying from session to session had been obtained. The parents and teacher of students with mental disabilities could afford to relax a little.

Conclusion

In the 1950s the nation and Washington state witnessed a surge of parent advocacy in public education which eventually provided a true alternative to state residential schools for children with mental retardation. Initially, Anna Magnuson did not find much help from the institutionally oriented Children's Benevolent League when she sought to educate her daughter. The re-formed Spokane unit's leaders at first felt closer to parents in other states who sought local schooling than to the CBL in their own state. State Representative Kathryn Epton, a leader in the Spokane unit, even introduced a parent pay bill in direct opposition to WARC, thereby expressing her irritation at those parents who escaped financial and other responsibilities through institutionalizing their sons and daughters.

But the parents did not pose the issues in a vacuum: whether they realized it or not, they were part of a larger debate that involved the self-interests of competing state service systems as well. Thus, in 1956 the Department of Institutions proposed to open a third state residential school, a goal high on WARC's agenda. But Ross Hamilton, head of the handicapped children's division of the state Office of the Superintendent of Public Instruction, declared an institution would not be needed for another decade, "if the Legislature would appropriate enough funds to care for as many handicapped persons as possible through local school districts."[240] Hamilton argued:

> if sufficient educational and medical services were
> provided on the local level, the need for long term residen-
> tial schools could be reduced to one-tenth of one percent
> of the population.

This statement implied that the current institutions were already too big by a third. Hamilton's general theme was neatly captured in the familiar phrase "education for all children," the topic on which he spoke to the Woodhull Hay unit of WARC in March 1956.

An irritated Van R. Hinkle, director of the Institutions' Division of Children and Youth Services, countered that a delay would be irresponsible "in light of the tremendous need for facilities to care for many severely retarded children now kept in their homes with great hardship to their families." He had a point since there were no community or family support services, outside of local schools, for children with severe disabilities, and most schools would not admit them either. But to simply continue to build more institutions begged the question of what the children and their families really wanted.

In fact, in her original declaration of candidacy for state representative Kay Epton struck the theme forcefully. She had met another mother whose daughter was about to go to Lakeland Village. Although she was not severely disabled, the daughter was going "because she will learn quickly and not be much trouble." Epton drew a conclusion:

> It is the institution that needs the child and not the child who needs the institution. But this is not an isolated case. If people knew about these things, I know of an absolute certainty there would be a complete re-appraisal of the function of a custodial institution....
>
> But it is not only the humanitarian side of the problem that concerns me. It is also the economic. Up until a few years ago, the handicapped and disabled were a waste product so to speak of humanity. But, as in many a well established billion dollar a year industry, if we take a second look and try to do something with this "waste product" we will find they, too, are a rich and valuable resource.[241]

Over the succeeding fifteen years, Kay Epton and the other mothers became teachers and aides, gradually broke down the doors to the local schoolhouse, and got their children admitted. In the process, they built an alternative life for themselves as advocates. Women moved clearly into the forefront of the Washington parents' movement for the first time in the 1950s. Epton played a special role in creating community day programs where, hopefully, the "waste product" could be recycled into proud, productive, human beings.

CHAPTER SIX:
BUILDING A SYSTEM OF
COMMUNITY SUPPORTS

> Mental retardation today has a new face. No longer is
> a mentally handicapped person's behavior—impaired
> speech, unsteady gait, faulty reaction—viewed merely as
> a tragic but isolated symptom. His condition is recog-
> nized as part of a larger problem. When he suffers, his
> family, his community, the whole of society suffer. Simi-
> larly, the response of agencies to the problem of mental
> retardation cannot be isolated. It must constitute an inte-
> grated web of services. Programs must accept
> contributions from widely different disciplines in order to
> serve the best interests of the mentally retarded, their
> families, the community, and the state.
> —Washington State Interagency Subcommittee on
> Mental Retardation,
> *Everybody's Child,* 1961

In the 1960s WARC members began to concentrate on developing a
"comprehensive" system of supportive services for persons with
mental retardation. It had to be comprehensive to counter the cri-
tiques of institutional advocates who claimed that they had found

the only truly complete system in specially designed institutions.

Of course, there had been earlier dreamers, pioneers of a broadening vision. For example, in 1941 Newland Reilly advocated a comprehensive approach to mental retardation services. And in the 1950s innovative parents spent much of their time trying to gain public schooling for all children with handicaps. Once the idea of education for all children was securely grasped, parents quickly identified additional needs, including training and employment for adults, residential options other than parental homes and institutions, medical research, prevention, and recreation.

At first, the various services sought were not unified into any theoretical framework. But soon the Arc and other advocates came to envision a system of supports for persons disabled by intellectual deficits with many of the components organized along a "continuum of services" from "least restrictive" to "most restrictive." The idea of a continuum had emerged out of the mental health field where professionals battled the ACLU and like-minded libertarians over the constitutional right to liberty of persons with mental illness versus the state's public safety interests. The result was that the courts and legislatures made decisions about involuntary commitment which reserved it to only the most dangerous cases.

When introduced by professionals in the field of mental retardation, this idea conformed to the common idea that individuals with more severe disabilities should live in institutions, while the others could live in the community. In fact, the notion that only individuals with severe disabilities lived in institutions was a misconception, as evidenced by the many able individuals who joined the schools' basketball teams, bands, and dance groups. Nevertheless, for a while this belief allowed parents with children in institutions and those whose offspring lived at home to work together, at least while lobbying at the state legislature. The state facilities did increasingly serve more severely disabled individuals as more people moved from institutions to the community through the deinstitutionalization process. But there were always far more people with severe disabilities living in the community in the family home than there were in institutions.

The Role of the Federal Government

Without support from state and federal treasuries, a consistent, quality array of programs was not conceivable. Parent associations were attracted to the federal government's extensive resources and its vocational rehabilitation and New Deal welfare programs. Apparently, the first parent group to appeal for federal support was the New York Association for Help to Retarded Children. In 1949 these New York families wrote to President Truman and asked him to include handicapped programs in his health proposal.[242] In a second instance, the newly formed National Association for Retarded Children requested federal aid for special education in 1951. The National Society for Crippled Children and Adults had secured sponsors for a bill to fund education for the physically handicapped, and NARC sought to expand the bill to include children with mental retardation.[243]

Not long after these two unsuccessful efforts, Rhode Island parents and the NARC[244] gained the support of Congressman John Fogarty (D, RI), who used his position to earmark $600,000 for mental retardation research in fiscal year 1956. Further success was achieved when the secretary of the U.S. Department of Health, Education, and Welfare responded to Fogarty's inquiries by creating a committee to review what the government was doing in the field of mental retardation.[245]

More and more appropriations were obtained in the next few years, and the Kennedy administration provided an even higher level of support. In 1961 John F. Kennedy created the President's Panel on Mental Retardation to plan federal policy and programs and to begin "a comprehensive and coordinated attack on the problem of mental retardation." Three years later President Lyndon B. Johnson reported on the progress being made in the field of mental retardation. Johnson gave credit to Kennedy for creating the panel, and with his characteristic ebullience, Johnson added: "I believe we will accomplish more toward overcoming retardation in the next five years than the world accomplished in the last five hundred years" (HOPE, December 1964). In retrospect, his prediction was wrong factually, but of value as a statement of public commitment, an easy standard to meet.

State Government

As the national government began to take steps in mental retardation, progress was evident at other levels of government as well. The states were moving beyond support for schools and institutions, and looking toward the development of a system of social services. In Washington, Governor Albert D. Rosellini, speaking at WARC's 1959 convention, reaffirmed that long-term planning was necessary for developing adequate services. To accomplish this planning, the governor assigned his two-year-old Inter-Agency Subcommittee on

173

Mental Retardation the task of producing a comprehensive report. Five WARC leaders served on advisory panels which worked on the subcommittee. *Everybody's Child,* published in 1961, was a milestone that clearly showed the government's commitment to addressing the problem of mental retardation. The five priority issues recommended by the subcommittee were: research, prevention, diagnosis and prognosis, services, and professional training. The medical and scientific orientation of *Everybody's Child* was striking and no doubt reflects the burgeoning interest of the medical profession and the University of Washington in mental retardation.

Interest in planning and coordination continued to increase on both federal and state levels for at least the next fifteen years. In 1970, the states were required to establish "developmental disabilities planning councils" to oversee the distribution of federal dollars. These councils have brought together, on a continuing basis, agency staff, parents, and other interested parties, eventually including persons with disabilities themselves. In the meantime, the 1965 Washington legislature had created an Advisory Council on Mental Health and Mental Retardation Planning, composed of the directors of four state agencies (Health, Institutions, Public Assistance, and the Superintendent of Public Instruction) and seven citizens appointed by the Governor. The Council advised the governor on the creation of community service programs. The last important planning and coordination function within state government was provided by the Governor's Committee on the Employment of the Handicapped. In the early 1950s, this committee had been composed solely of businessmen who were supportive of hiring persons with physical and sensory disabilities. But by the mid-1970s, the committee had been taken over almost entirely by persons with disabilities themselves, a few parents, and providers of community services, none of whom limited themselves to employment concerns.

Local Government: Washington's Mixed System

How did the third level of government, counties and cities, address the issue of mental retardation? There is considerable variation among the states. Some developmental disabilities services and employees are part of county government, while others are state agencies. In 1967, Washington adopted a mixed system of state and county mental retardation services in the process of creating the community mental health service system. The state was the primary source of funding for residential services, while county millage dollars derived from property taxes would provide the primary funding for employment services. With federal leadership provided in the 1963 Mental Retardation Facilities and Community Mental Health Centers Construction Act,[246] the nation was quickly becoming sold on the idea of expanding these two localized service systems.

According to an editorial in the March 3, 1967, *Seattle Post-Intelligencer,* Washington ranked *last* in the nation in per capita public expenditures for community mental health services, although it was eighth in institutional expenditures. It was time to correct the shameful lack of community services according to the newspaper. Two companion bills, Substitute House Bills 303 and 304, were enacted. They enabled counties to establish, respectively, mental health and mental retardation programs financed by a one-tenth of a mill property tax assessment per year. The "Community Mental Retardation Services Act" also established county boards to coordinate, plan, and recommend to the county commissioners or executive the expenditure of funds available from county, state, and federal sources. WARC, which had not originated the idea for these bills, endorsed them as creating coordinating mechanisms in the communities. In the late 1960s, parents were increasingly told that planning and coordination were critical functions. WARC recommended that its members apply for membership on the county mental retardation boards to assure that county millage funds would be properly spent. Thus, the counties began to provide some limited programs in mental retardation, often using their funds to supplement state funds or to fill in service gaps. With their guaranteed income flow, they actually were independent of the parents' groups and thus were not as beholden to the Arc as the latter leaders wished at times.

In retrospect, the beginning of some county responsibility for mental retardation services seems to have been a positive step in the development of community services. However, confusion over the inevitably intersecting responsibilities of county and state agencies was long a problem in Washington.

By turning some functions over to the counties, state government delayed its own evolution toward community services and helped it stay tied to institutions. Governor Daniel J. Evans (1965-1977), under whom community services expanded more rapidly than before, was a Republican and more sympathetic to private sector initiatives. Community services, as they developed, tended to be provided by private (usually non-profit) groups. On the other hand, the institutions were allied with the Democrats through the state

175

employees' unions because a large fraction of their membership worked in institutions.

Government does not simply respond to the demands of its constituents; it also provides jobs. Employees who quickly and effectively develop new programs earn the respect of their colleagues and are advanced in their careers. This career advancement is one of the few rewards available to a bureaucrat who, unlike an owner or stockholder, cannot keep the "profit" made by his or her agency.[247] Thus, in this favorable climate, public sector employees began to make a significant contribution to the development of programs for persons with disabilities. Parents had gained new allies. This is shown not only by the fact that mental retardation professionals began to serve on local and state WARC boards of directors, but also by the frequency with which employees began to move both ways. ARC executive directors Leo Lippman, Patricia Wilkins, and Judith Devine left the association for state employment, and state disability agency heads like Van R. Hinkle, Ross Hamilton, and Sue Elliott took positions with the ARC.

But it wasn't just public employees who helped parents construct the community service system. The general public had heard about the need for support and pitched in. With the proliferation of helpful groups and individuals, the system was truly in the community.

Jobs for Adults

As did other states during the Progressive Era, Washington passed programs for adults disabled by industrial accidents. Washington's 1911 act provided funds to the disabled worker or to the spouse and children in case of death. In 1920 the National Civilian Vocational Rehabilitation Act was signed by President Wilson (who by this time was disabled himself). The law provided a 50 percent federal reimbursement for state expenditures for training, guidance, placement, and prosthetic devices. Although the act was terminated after four years,[248] it was revived in the 1930s and eventually incorporated into the Social Security Act of 1935. Thus, vocational rehabilitation was made a permanent piece of federal policy and appropriations increased. However, none of this legislation applied to workers who with mental retardation until the act was further amended in 1943. Even after the war, only a few hundred such persons (many of them in Michigan) received such training until the mid-1950s.[249]

Several events contributed to the expansion of rehabilitation for adults with mental disabilities in the fifties. Salvatore DiMichael published the seminal *Vocational Rehabilitation of the Mentally Retarded* (1950) and soon thereafter became the first executive director of the NARC in 1954, assuring that rehabilitation would gain a strong hearing among parents nationwide. Mary Switzer, director of the federal Office of Vocational Rehabilitation, successfully urged amendments in 1954 to broaden support for persons with mental retardation. She publicized the idea that federal rehabilitation funds would repay the investment at a 10-to-1 ratio in terms of increased employment of persons with mental retardation (HOPE, April, 1959).

Sheltered Workshops

The first idea about the right way to employ adults with intellectual disabilities was the idea of "sheltered workshops." In Washington state, the first formal sheltered work training programs for such individuals were apparently provided by Goodwill Industries. Although Goodwill had been founded in Boston in 1902, the organization had not originally focused on persons with disabilities, and it was not until 1953 that the Spokane and Seattle locations began serving a few adults with specifically cognitive disabilities.

In the 1950s WARC members were beginning to talk about sheltered workshops around the state, but progress was slow at first. For example, parents in the mill town of Shelton were interested in finding work for their sons in the forest products industry. They sought and received encouragement and advice from Van Hinkle of the Department of Institutions. Local leaders Bob Kimbel and Warren Richard invited WARC President E. H. Riviere to talk with them about sheltered workshops in 1956. Convinced they were on the right track, they organized Exceptional Foresters, Inc. in 1957. Later it claimed to be "America's first community-sponsored habilitation program for the mentally handicapped."[250] The group struggled in its early fundraising efforts. It was not until 1963 that the first five young men received regular work and training in planting and harvesting Christmas trees.[251] The claim to be "community-sponsored" was in contrast to operations which are dependent on government funds (funds which were almost non-existent when it started anyway). Not that the Exceptional Forester operations were entirely free of government support. For example, as a non-profit organization, it paid fewer taxes. It leased public lands from the county, and tried to lease more from the state, on favorable terms. But until the mid-1960s, the Shelton group operated without substantial direct government funds.

177

When a state funding program was approved in 1959, it was authored by parent-legislator, Representative Kathryn Epton, serving her second term from Spokane. House Bill 612 authorized the Division of Vocational Rehabilitation and the State Board for Vocational Education to provide grants to agencies for sheltered workshops, supervised work opportunities, or similar facilities for the rehabilitation of severely handicapped persons. The authorization for such "independent living rehabilitation" grants was originally limited to projects lasting not more than thirty-six months.[252]

Developments followed rapidly. NARC rehabilitation consultant William A. Fraenkel visited Washington state in March 1959. HOPE, the WARC newsletter, ran numerous stories on rehabilitation at the time. The newspaper highlighted Fraenkel's visit (and his return in 1960) and Governor Rosellini's tour of the Tacoma Goodwill in August 1959 to meet workers with mental disabilities. In 1960 WARC chose rehabilitation as the theme for its convention. A convention speaker, Ross Hamilton, proclaimed that Washington was leading the way in vocational rehabilitation. Hamilton, now Chief of Special Services for the State Board for Vocational Education, Division of Vocational Rehabilitation, was the former Washington state director of special education. He contended that the successful legislation in Washington State had produced action at the Congressional level. Modeled after the state act, Washington's U.S. Senator Warren Magnuson had (unsuccessfully) introduced S. 1265 in 1959, which would have extended federal assistance to workshops.

Three sheltered workshops received the first funds under the new state law in 1960. At Kitsap Sheltered Workshop in Bremerton, workers constructed gardening materials such as flower boxes and trellises. In a "supervised work opportunity," they performed lawn work and were employed in the Christmas tree industry. In the workshop's first three years of operation, significant achievements in worker productivity were claimed; 16 of 88 severely disabled persons (about half of whom had mental retardation) had graduated to competitive employment. Monthly earnings per worker grew from $9 in 1960 to $73 in 1963 (HOPE, July 1963).[253] The second grant was awarded to United Cerebral Palsy of Pierce County in Tacoma where subcontracting was done with manufacturing industries. A typical job was assembling boards for displaying hardware. A third grant to Occupational Rehabilitation, Inc., in King County, enabled workers to be employed by a laundry, cleaning towels and similar items for local schools. Another project of the workshop involved a

178

subcontract with the Boeing Company for the salvage of airplane parts.

Adult Developmental Centers

The second primary component of specialized adult education for persons with mental retardation in Washington was again proposed by Representative Epton. These programs for more severely disabled persons, who were not then thought eligible for vocational rehabilitation funds, were called "Adult Developmental Centers." Many of them began under the funding provided by this act. Some of the centers honored the legislator by calling themselves "The X County Epton Center for the Handicapped," names that were often retained for many years. This act provided $100 per month, funded by the Department of Institutions, for "day training centers" for mentally or physically deficient persons "accepted for admission to a state residential school." Ironically, these programs which served adults were begun primarily to serve children who had been excluded from public schools. For example, in the early sixties the three Seattle centers developed from the parent cooperative preschools of the previous decade and served children from three to twenty-one years old.

In the legislature's one-year authorization for the 1962-63 fiscal year, $30,000 was divided between Central School in Seattle, New Hope Training Center in Spokane, and the Spokane Parents' Cooperative Society for the Handicapped. The three facilities served eighty persons and all had waiting lists (HOPE, October 1962). However, in 1963 the state budget was once again in crisis. Not surprisingly, the legislature rejected WARC's request for $200,000 for Epton Center programs—a sevenfold increase. However, the Epton Center program was made permanent and the budget was slightly increased to $70,000 for the biennium. In 1965, the budget was doubled to $140,000, the per capita reimbursement rate increased to $125 per month, and the eligibility criterion revised from "persons accepted for institutional admission" to those "acceptable for" admission. Thus, the charade of institutional application was no longer necessary for parents who wanted this community service for their children.

In 1966, fourteen centers served nearly 300 young people, but there were substantial waiting lists. WARC recommended that $300,000 in Epton Center funds be appropriated to develop and strengthen additional "community programs to provide training for severely retarded children living at home as well as to alleviate the waiting list." WARC's lobbying proved fruitful. In the 1967 legislative session the appropriation for "Day Care Centers," doubled again from $140,000 to $300,000. However, by October 1967 WARC President Elise Chadwick reported that three months of demand had already more than exhausted the allocation for the full twenty-four months. Clearly, the demand for community services was rapidly expanding.

The passage of the Education for All Act in 1971 ended the expansion of the separate Epton Center system of education for children severely disabled by mental retardation, which had grown to 63 "day care" centers serving 2,000 persons, mostly children.

The citizens of Washington state became strong and regular supporters of adult work and training programs in the 1970's. This public support was invaluable, since few facilities could then operate without continuous direct giving and United Way contributions. The combination of products and services offered by the Adult Developmental Centers and the financial support provided by the government did not suffice to balance the budget. Thus, it was natural that, in 1971 WARC President Omer Carey, a business professor at Washington State University, tried to create a separate, non-profit Small Business Investment Corps. Carey proposed that the Corps function without its own staff, relying on local business people to start sheltered workshops and group homes. Two banks were involved in negotiations, but the project failed to materialize.

With strong support from the public for programs for persons with "handicaps," the time was right for introducing the first state bond issue for community facilities. However, in 1972 the "Boeing recession" was affecting Washington state so severely that a billboard reading "Will the last person to leave Seattle please turn out the lights?" received national notoriety. In the face of the downturn, Governor Evans proposed the "Washington Futures" bond issues, which went on the ballot in the fall of 1972. Referendum 29 passed, providing funding for the construction of community health and social service facilities, including many sheltered workshops.

Vocational proposals. The creation of sheltered workshops and developmental centers met only part of the state's vocational rehabilitation needs. WARC identified other needs in a special 1966 legislative issue of HOPE. The association recommended that the Division of Vocational Rehabilitation hire additional skilled personnel to help local communities develop training centers. In addition, WARC asked that a study be undertaken to determine the state's vocational rehabilitation needs, with established goals and timetables.

One of the specific goals WARC hoped to achieve was increased cooperation between the public schools and the vocational rehabilitation system. In Tacoma and Auburn, the public schools and Division of Vocational Rehabilitation had begun to offer cooperative work-study programs. WARC believed that these cooperative programs, operating at the high school level, represented "the greatest resource" available to train most persons with mental retardation. WARC proposed that these programs be expanded across Washington. [254]

In 1966 WARC also suggested that a job classification, called "Service Worker," be established under Washington Civil Service to provide positions for persons with mental retardation.[255] The new category could include such jobs as manual labor and routine clerical tasks. WARC felt that a review of state government job classifications was needed to determine which jobs could be performed by persons with intellectual disabilities without requiring a state civil service exam.

Community Colleges. Washington has a strong system of inexpensive community colleges serving all adults, regardless of previous educational achievements. The 1966 WARC legislative platform proposed that community college programs could prepare students with intellectual disabilities for state civil service jobs as "Service Workers." In the ensuing years, the association remained convinced that generic adult education programs should serve persons with mental retardation. WARC's Vocational Rehabilitation Committee conducted a survey in 1974 to determine if fifteen percent of the vocational education money allotted to community colleges was being spent for students with disabilities, as required by federal law, and also to find out how the money was being spent. The committee had completed its survey by early spring and was generally satisfied. At the June Board meeting in Seattle, the committee reported that the colleges had spent $266,000 to instruct students in skills such as how to get about in the community and how to use public transportation.

NARC On-the-Job Contracts. But training, regardless of what kind, was not enough, and state government alone could never provide enough employment. Other incentives were needed to help obtain private sector employment for workers with disabilities. These incentives arrived in the form of federal on-the-job training legislation. In 1970 Van R. Hinkle, who had returned from duties with the National Association for Retarded Children in New York City, became the Washington state coordinator for the NARC On-the-Job Training Project. Funded by the Department of Labor, the program's initial goal was to secure employment for adults in the selected states of Washington, Texas, Maryland and New Jersey. The On-the-Job Training Project was later expanded to include all states. Employers were reimbursed for 50 percent of the salary paid during the first four weeks of training and work and for 25 percent during the next four weeks. It was hoped that the trainees would be retained as regular workers after their training period. Through separate grants, WARC was able to hire its own staff to supervise additional on-the-job training projects during the latter half of the 1970's. This training was one of the few direct services ever provided by the state association to persons with mental disabilities.

Community Residences

Before there was advocacy by families, there were people with mental retardation living outside institutions and away from family homes. Some adults lived in non-specialized facilities, such as county poor farms and private, charitable arrangements. Children, too, shared these facilities. For example, in 1930 fourteen "feeble-minded" children, aged six to thirteen, lived at the Parkland Lutheran Children's Home in Everett.[256] It is difficult to determine how widespread such arrangements were, and this system of care never became a model for future service systems in Washington. Foster care was another older model, but WARC had maintained since the early 1950s that foster care could only be considered a temporary arrangement.

In the 1960s, new, specialized community residences opened. The Epton Center Act of 1961 granted funds for "group training homes," defined as providing "full time care, training and maintenance of mentally or physically deficient persons." But group homes did not expand rapidly under the 1961 act because the limited funds were primarily allocated to day training programs. Also, in the beginning, group training homes were only temporary residences since residents were required to be on a waiting list for institutional admission.[257]

The pressure for change continued to build. In December 1966 WARC recommended that the state fire marshal and the state departments of Public Assistance, Public Health, Institutions, and Vocational Rehabilitation jointly establish "supervised boarding homes" with staff standards and licensing procedures. The following May, President Chadwick announced she was setting up a Group Home Committee, because the Residential Care Committee continued to be preoccupied with institutions. The new committee set to work, meeting with the Legislative and Executive Committees, and with group home committees from chapters like King county. After a year, much discussion had taken place, but agreement had not been reached among the parents. Institutional parents usually did not support deinstitutionalization. Parents with sons and daughters living at home wanted them in the group homes. They did not want group homes reserved just for persons coming out of state facilities. Neither group was pleased.

House Bill 465, expanding the group home section of the Epton Act, was introduced by executive request in the 1969 legislature. The bill was consistent with the position of the Evans administration that Washington should move away from state institutions as the answer to every person's needs. At the March 8, 1969, Executive Committee meeting in Pasco, the Governmental Affairs Committee presented the case for the bill and handed the Executive Committee a dilemma. Too many amendments might hamper passage of the bill this session, but the concerns of some institutional parents were unaddressed. Some members of the Executive Committee argued that WARC should let the bill fail and wait till the next legislative session for a new bill. Given the disagreement over the bills, WARC President Dr. Frank Skerbeck appointed an ad hoc committee to study the matter. This device worked as intended. The ad hoc committee's report affirmed the support for the bill originally proposed by the Governmental Affairs Committee and its chair, Elise Chadwick. The opposition of some Executive Committee members was overcome.

WARC adopted the position that it "heartily supports the concept of group homes ...as a necessary component of the continuum of services," but that there should be a continuing state responsibility for "retardates" placed in the community. The recently created county mental retardation boards should play a role in "planning, programming, and supervision" of deinstitutionalized persons, but WARC distrusted their ability to provide the full security of operations which state government had furnished. So instructed, the Governmental Affairs Committee returned to its lobbying duties and, before the bill passed in April, had secured two amendments. The first assigned responsibility for program quality to the Department of Institutions. The rules and regulations to be formulated

> shall include standards for care, maintenance and training to be met by group homes. In addition, the department of institutions shall be responsible for coordinating state activities and resources relating to group home placements to the end that state and local re-

sources will be efficiently expended and an effective community-based group home program may be created.

The second amendment required the Department of Institutions to evaluate the resident's adjustment to the placement "at reasonable intervals." A decision could then be made on whether the individual should remain, return to the institution, or be given some other placement. Harmless enough, this face-saving device could buy needed support for reluctant supporters of institutions.

The passage of the legislation in this amended form (along with an initial biennial appropriation of $405,000) did not cause all concerns to evaporate, since the implementing administrative policy and regulations had yet to be developed. On June 19 and 20, 1969, a WARC Conference on Group Homes and Related Services for the Retarded was held at Western Washington State College in Bellingham to "clarify the problems inherent in community-oriented supervised living for the mentally retarded" and to develop an ARC policy on the regulations to be drafted. Five representatives of various state agencies and forty-five resource people participated in the conference, which was keynoted by Gunnar Dybwad, Brandeis University professor and former NARC executive director.

The Group Homes Committee continued its work after the conference. After surveying the chapters for recommendations, the committee prepared a position which was adopted by the Executive Committee on September 6, 1969. WARC's position was presented at the hearing on the Department of Institutions' proposed administrative rules. WARC agreed with the four basic criteria of the Department's final proposal, namely, that group home placement

> is recommended if parents have given approval, and residents indicate they would like such a placement and do require sheltered living (close supervision),
>
> requires that a person demonstrates minimum behavioral problems,
>
> is recommended for those who can enter regular public school, special education, or a sheltered work experience, and
>
> should be open to those who have received successful core training from the institution, but may still demonstrate some inadequate emotional and/or social behavior in new or stressful situations.

Since the Department of Institutions had been politic enough to include a parental veto in the group home placement criteria, much of the most hostile institutional opposition had been silenced. Indeed, it was really those parents who were favorably inclined to community residences who had the most to be concerned about, because they were venturing into unknown waters. WARC and Washington State were now exploring a new continuum of services model which matched persons with particular settings, depending on the nature and extent of their disability. [258]

WARC's official compromise position was that the entire program was experimental and should be reviewed at the end of two years. In addition, consistent with its amendments, WARC demanded that the state supervise and inspect the group homes to insure quality of care equal to that in institutions. Each time a resident was placed in a county, the relevant county mental health and mental retardation board should be notified. But this was not enough, because the boards had no authority or capacity to exercise case work or case management. Therefore, WARC proposed

> that the Department of Institutions establish or cause to be established a central point of referral in each community where the retarded are placed and where voluntary contact by the retardate may be made. That the retardate be trained to use the referral center while a resident of a group home, and that the county boards be notified when the retardate is released from a group home. Further, that the Department of Institutions shall be responsible for educating other concerned staff and community agencies (i.e. police, etc.) in understanding the nature of and meeting the needs of retarded individuals.

Group home expansion continued, while the concerns of many remained. These persistent anxieties were evident at the next annual meeting in Spokane in 1970. Dr. Frank Skerbeck, now chairing the Group Homes Committee, moved that

> WARC, in cooperation with the [regional] American Association on Mental Deficiency and the County Mental Retardation Board Association, form a body to accredit group homes and approach the Governor for authority to issue accreditation and conduct annual reviews.

The successful motion would have created an analogue to the national standards developed by such groups as the Joint Commission on the Accreditation of Hospitals (JCAH), the Council of Accredited Rehabilitation Facilities (CARF)), and the Accreditation Council for Mentally Retarded and Other Developmentally Disabled Persons (AC/MRDD) for various types of programs. But neither an accreditation board nor an official WARC monitoring role was achieved in the state of Washington.

The state did make one large change to meet the concerns of parents: a case management system was created for clients who were living in the community. The initial move toward a state community service role was the WARC amendment to the 1969 group home law requiring that the Department of Institutions coordinate the group home program and periodically re-evaluate residents living in the community. New state employees were added to the staff at Rainier School to aid in the group home placement process. The agency included a regionalized system of case management for clients living in the community.

In 1970, Governor Evans merged the Departments of Institutions, Health, Public Assistance, and Vocational Rehabilitation into one "super-agency," the Department of Social and Health Services (DSHS). Initially this change concerned WARC parents, especially those tied to institutions, because the merger threatened the clear state commitment to their children's distinctive programs. However, the creation of first an "Office," then a "Bureau," and finally a "Division" of Developmental Disabilities indicated the continuity of state concerns, but without the word "institutions" in the name.[259]

The state had failed to satisfy all parental concerns and had not established an independent quality assurance device. But this failure did not deter WARC members, especially those whose teenaged and adult sons and daughters lived at home, from plunging into the new and unknown area of creating and operating group homes. Parents had been forced for some years to make pro forma application for institutional admission to gain entrance to a group home. Gradually, the local WARC chapters stepped into the group home process. A survey at the June 1973 Board of Directors meeting in Tacoma revealed the fragile and uneasy development of community services. WARC Region I Director Dorothy Skerbeck reported that the Bremerton chapter had recently developed a group home. She noted that the Port Angeles chapter had problems with the continuing success of a local workshop and was behind schedule in starting group homes. Boyd Winter, Region II, reported that his area wished to start a group home but was unsure of the proper steps to open one. Region III Director George Drake blasted nursing homes for not meeting the needs of persons with mental retardation. He argued that group homes should replace nursing homes.[260] According to Kink Barnett, a group home had been planned for King county. Construction had nearly begun, but had to be halted because the bank withdrew the loan. Barnett believed that some type of government-guaranteed mortgage backing for group homes was needed. Grace Gould of Region VI reported that a private group home was opening in Longview and that the Clark County chapter was considering opening two group homes, one for children and one for adults. Region IX Director, Agnes Schiffner, reported that plans had been developed in Spokane to start a group home.

From this slow beginning, WARC parents moved forward and picked up speed. By the end of the 1970s, most chapters could point with pride to the group homes which they had started. Sometimes the chapter owned and operated the home. Just as often, consistent with the long-standing NARC policy on "spinning off" services, a separate non-profit board of directors was created. Some of these boards were truly independent, while in others, ultimate control was still vested in the ARC through control of the nomination or amendment procedures.

Since a new funding source had been created, WARC soon noticed that others were starting group homes. Only a few operations were explicitly profit-making ventures. Others qualified as non-profit, but provided their founder-operators with a comfortable, if modest, living. Still others were started by small groups of parents who had no affiliation with the ARC. Group home populations continued to grow, in accord with the state's deinstitutionalization policy. From 417 persons living in 29 group homes in November 1972, the state projected growth to 850 persons in 60 homes (for an average of 14 individuals per facility) at the end of the 1973-75 biennium.[261]

New Federal Funding Supports Institutions

In 1958 the federal Hill-Burton Act had been amended to add many mental retardation facilities to those "medical facilities" that could qualify for federal cost-sharing in construction buildings. This legislation, partly an outgrowth of the parent-led advocacy efforts on Capitol Hill, supported further construction of institutions. But construction costs were only a part of the necessary funding for programs. The largest part of the budget in institutions was staff salaries. These costs were dramatically impacted by the 1971 amendments to Title XIX of the Social Security Act (the Medicaid program), which authorized funding for a new category of "Intermediate Care Facilities for the Mentally Retarded" (ICF/MR). This program provided a federal match (50 percent for Washington state) for facilities which provided developmental care to persons with some medical needs. The act, in effect, meant that the federal government would *match* the state's costs for the institutions. Heavy capital and staff expenses had to be incurred, because the intent of the Medicaid program was to require compliance with a highly medicalized version of health and safety standards (nursing etc.) Consequently, only a few of the private, non-profit group homes in Washington would qualify. Thus, the effect of the successful lobbying of NARC and other groups to gain Medicaid funding provided substantial new incentives for the state to turn its attention and its funds back toward the large public institutions.

If cheaper alternatives to institutions than ICF/MRs were being established, why did most states want to spend the money, even if the federal government would pay half? The states chose to support ICF/MRs to "capture" a proportional share of the federal appropriations which, naturally enough, were based on the taxes paid by individuals and companies in each state. Non-participating states found that their taxpayers were subsidizing programs in the other states. Such a fiscal incentive was enough to gain the compliance of most states.

The ICF/MR regulations were finally published by the Department of Health, Education, and Welfare in 1974. At their March 1974 meeting, WARC board members discussed the new rules and regulations and voted to ask the governor that the state of Washington participate in the ICF/MR program.

Regional Mini-Institutions Rejected

The turn toward community residences and new federal funding provided both the opportunity and the resources for state administrators to devise new programs.

In 1975, the legislature authorized the Bureau of Developmental Disabilities to formulate a plan to reduce the populations in the current institutions by moving individuals into community facilities which would meet the requirements of the new Medicaid ICF/MR funding. The plan initially called for 80 group homes and 26 training centers to be operated by the state. At its December 1975 meeting the ARC directors concluded that the plan was not acceptable, as it had not been determined where the centers would be and who would be in them.

In response the state of Washington formed an ad hoc advisory task force on "State Residential Training Centers" (SRTCs) of which WARC executive director Patricia Wilkins was a member. Wilkins felt the plan, as presented, had no continuum of services and no genuine alternatives.

188

At its December meeting, following Wilkins' recommendation, WARC decided to insist on a reformulation of state policy to allow for the development of a "full continuum of care" in which placement would depend upon the severity of a person's disability. At the same time, the board also passed a motion that

> The Washington Association for Retarded Citizens strongly opposes further placements of any developmentally disabled persons to any community residential facility unless that placement is: 1) made to an appropriate facility of highest quality standards for the needs of the placed individual; and 2) is accompanied by funds adequate to provide an appropriate community-based program for the individual.

What was happening in WARC? What was happening to the SRTCs? The proposal was getting clobbered by advocates from both institutional and community sides. The former said SRTCs and the state's general policy of deinstitutionalization was going too far, too fast. The other side felt it was not going far enough. A motion by one WARC board member, Frank Wastradowski, in December 1975 had put WARC on record as opposing residential placements until quality standards and adequate funds were available. The following June he complained that no action had been taken to implement the board's position. An unsympathetic President David Foscue explained that the Long-range Planning Committee had recommended that, prior to taking action, the ramifications should be studied by the Residential Services Committee. Wastradowski then moved that the Residential Services Committee implement his December motion. However, board member Linda Rolfe, supported by Harry Carthum, successfully amended the motion to instruct the Residential Services Committee to gather information on ramifications and submit a report on implementation to the August Board meeting. Rolfe, Carthum and others were concerned that SRTCs would be "mini-institutions" and would impede the development of truly appropriate housing in the community.

Rolfe, a regional administrator for the Bureau of Developmental Disabilities,[262] and Carthum, director of a special education cooperative for public schools in the Aberdeen area, were representative of the non-parent members who had been elected to the WARC board in the mid-1970s. They helped bring a new ideologically coherent voice for normalization to WARC. Many family members on the board of directors struggled to keep up or flatly rejected the new ideas, while other laypersons were excited by their ideas and strove to put them in place. It was a decade when the best professionals led the way.

Governor Dixy Lee Ray took office in 1977 and included the State Residential Training Centers in her legislative package. Again the board debated the issue at its March meeting. The proposal had been revised to specify that there would be sixteen SRTCs statewide, each containing a central training facility and three contiguous, fourteen-bed residences. The WARC board voted to support the SRTCs, if an amendment could be agreed upon which would provide for community input and control. No such amendment was forthcoming, and a decision was made by the state not to resubmit the proposal to the next legislature. SRTCs, new institutions in the community, were dead.

That did not mean that the ARC had given up on getting federal ICF/MR funding however. In fact, the ARC continued to believe that it was a good move.[263] In 1978 Washington State agreed and approved the contract with the federal government. Almost as soon as ICF/MR was in place, however, the ARC was complaining about it. In testimony to the Senate Social and Health Services Committee on August 28, 1960 the ARC told the legislature that the ICF/MR promise of "active treatment" for persons in ICF/MR funded nursing homes and state-operated institutions would be lost if the state continued with planned budgetary cutbacks. Eliminating day training programs would leave the ICF/MR facilities with a solely custodial function.

Funding Medical Research

Education, employment and housing have loomed so large as topics of family concern that other early and persistent actions of parents have sometimes been overlooked, notably their promotion of medical research and the improved diagnosis of mental retardation. But it is not unusual even today for a parent's autobiographical account to begin with a complaint against a physician. Not surprisingly, the events surrounding the diagnosis of intellectual disability is still loaded with powerful emotions. How did parents cope in prior decades when many felt that the diagnosis was the social equivalent to a death sentence for their child? Confronted with such an assault on the potential worth of their children, parents have often shopped around for another diagnosis. The professional literature has too often treated this parental searching as a personal, irrational response to the diagnosis of mental retardation. But these families

190

were also demonstrating a well-founded skepticism about professional opinion physicians knew little.

In Spokane, Kathryn Epton, whose son Johnny had cerebral palsy, was one of those parents who rebelled when told "there is nothing that can be done for your child." She searched till she found a physician operating a school in the East who offered some hope. She asked him whether he or someone he knew would be able to open a school in Northwest. He said, "Why don't you?"[264] So she in 1946 she and other Spokane area parents formed a parents group and the following year opened a parent cooperative school.

Years later Epton still recalled the searching experience of another Spokane family. Having taken their son Bobby to an East coast psychologist, they were told by him: "Put this child in an institution, as far away from where you live as you can put him, and forget you ever had it."

The K family went back to the motel where they were staying, but when bedtime came, they couldn't find Bobby. Finally they went in the bedroom and heard a funny noise in the closet. Mr. K opened the door, and there was Bobby huddled in the corner, crying,

> Please, Daddy, don't throw me away. Please don't
> throw me away.

Forty years later Epton said, "I cry every time I think about that."[265]

In their anguish, ARC parents did shop around. But, working together through the organization, they also funded medical research into causes and treatment of mental disability. Out of their optimism about what could be accomplished, the Children's Benevolent League formed the world's first trust fund dedicated to research on intellectual disability. (The Joseph P. Kennedy Foundation, formed in 1945, did not fund research until 1958, although some have later claimed otherwise.[266])

As early as the 1947 amendments to its by-laws, the Children's Benevolent League listed research among its goals. CBL literature repeatedly dealt with the topic of research. For example, its 1948 brochure *One Out of Fifty* stated that each state institution should become "a laboratory devoted to investigations into the causes, treatment and prevention" of mental retardation. By the early fifties, the parents called for the establishment of "diagnostic clinics," that could become a community center for research and insure that parents could learn the facts in a professional, up-to-date fashion. Although the CBL members could not yet know the times were propitious, they determined to move ahead. President "Cliff" Clifton recalled (1986) approaching the University of Washington Medical School in about 1949 with the idea that the children of the CBL members could be treated and studied there. The university administration first rejected the idea, because the children might fall on the stairs from "a fit" or for another reason and file a lawsuit. But the CBL was not deterred. King county CBL leader Bob Leavitt knew some physicians including Norman Clein, a prominent pediatrician. Leavitt garnered support for the project from these sympathetic professionals, and the times began to change.

Thus, on August 4, 1950, the CBL created its Research Trust Fund[267] at Seattle First National Bank for

> the raising of funds for the purpose of facilitating the study and research through medical, sociological, psychological, or any other means of the causes, prevention, cure, and amelioration of mental deficiency....

> Four "broad objects" of the Fund were listed. Although not limiting the Trustees in their wisdom, four points "among the purposes within the broad objects" of the Fund were offered as advice:

> 1.   To provide funds for grants-in-aid, fellowships, professorships and scholarships to students of medicine, sociology and psychiatry and to other qualified persons to study, survey or conduct research and fact finding studies in the field of mental retardation, such as:

> (a) Causes, prevention and amelioration of birth injury. (b) Endogenous factors of eugenics. (c)

> Communicable diseases of pregnant women. (d) Diseases or injury of children resulting in mental deficiency, not included in part (a) hereof.

> 2.   To provide funds for interns, graduate students, physicians, surgeons and others similarly engaged in the field to permit them to study and to perform laboratory work, including the formulation of case histories at custodial schools or elsewhere.

> 3.   To cause to be published, disseminated and otherwise made available such findings as may be developed by the research sponsored hereby, or otherwise and elsewhere in this field, through pamphlets, books, or publications for the education of the general public, and for the scientific knowledge of the professional field as well.

> 4.   To encourage through the use of these trust

funds a continuing study of the mentally retarded, to improve their well-being physically, mentally and socially.

The Trust Fund charter had been devised to include support by community leaders. Among the trustees would be nominees of the deans of the University of Washington Schools of Medicine and Law (early on, the deans themselves), and a nominee of the state banking association. Leavitt announced the designated nominees at the 1950 CBL convention and presented a check for $1500 from the King County Memorial Fund to be applied to the Trust Fund.[268]

Norman Clein, M.D., then announced that a third-year resident would do specialized work in mental retardation. The University of Washington would provide the facilities and a team of fifteen specialists to advise the resident. Monetary assistance would come from the Trust Fund.

In 1951, Edgar A. Doll, Ph.D., formerly director of the Vineland (NJ) Training Center but now a Washington resident, was given a grant to establish a research clinic for children with developmental disabilities in the Bellingham Public Schools. In 1956, H. C. Thuline, M.D., was awarded a grant to investigate "Metabolic abnormalities in mentally retarded children" at Children's Orthopedic Hospital in Seattle.[269]

To date, the Arc of Washington Research Trust Fund has awarded $1,000,000 in grant funds to researchers and graduate students. But for several reasons the Trust Fund struggled from inadequate revenues in its early years. First, King county parents were always the Trust Fund's primary supporter. Most other local chapters were less committed to the project. Most important, NARC's Research Fund began to solicit contributions, and by the 1960s every local chapter in Washington state had a local NARC Research Committee and made donations to its research efforts. The medical approach to mental retardation was popular with the public as well. In 1959, the Jaycees' Wives' Clubs, affiliated with the Auxiliary of the Washington Junior Chamber of Commerce, donated $5,500 to WARC to be used for medical research (HOPE, January 1960).[270]

Nationally, in 1956 NARC acknowledged the first federal funding of research by the previous Congress, but argued that, at $150,000, it was embarrassingly small compared to funding for research on far less common handicaps.[271] But with even limited funds, some important grants were made by WARC's Research Trust Fund during this early period. For example, Gerald LaVeck conducted a Down syndrome chromosome study at Rainier School with funds provided in 1959-60. He received most of the $5,500 that the Jaycee Wives had collected. When federal government support for research accelerated under the Kennedy administration, WARC members were elated that Gerald LaVeck could continue his chromosome work at Rainier School. In 1961 the National Institutes of Health awarded LaVeck a grant of $63,792 to study "DNA duplication by human chromosomes" which focused on Down syndrome. Washington's grant had proven its value as seed money.

University-Affiliated Programs. In 1962, the President's Panel on Mental Retardation visited the University of Washington and heard about the proposed "Children's Center on Research and Training in Mental Retardation," to be constructed on the campus. The center had been recommended by the state government report *Everybody's Child.* When Eunice and Sargent Shriver visited a year later, the Child Development and Mental Retardation Center (CDMRC) had been created by the state legislature with combined state bonds and construction funds.[272]

That was the same year that President John F. Kennedy gave his "mental retardation" speech to Congress in which he announced federal funds would be made available for the construction of "inpatient clinical units as an integral part of university-associated hospitals in which specialists on mental retardation would serve."[273]

Federal funding was provided by PL 88-164, the Mental Retardation Facilities and Community Mental Health Centers Construction Act of 1963, signed just weeks before the assassination of the president. When fully developed, the center would include four units, specializing in medical research, behavioral sciences, clinical research, and educational research (HOPE, July 1965).[274]

Today the re-named U.W. Center on Human Development and Disability provides expert diagnosis in developmental disabilities, the lack of which was once so lamented by WARC members. The first step in this process was the 1955 recommendation by the Health and Welfare Council of Seattle and King County, of which the King county WARC chapter was a part, that a diagnostic and parent-counseling service be established in Seattle (HOPE, April 1955). Parents were often uncertain what was "wrong with my child" and many primary physicians either could not or did not wish to tell them. The objective of the clinic, as approved by the WARC board in August, was:

> To establish or confirm or reject a diagnosis of mental
> retardation in children under the age of 14 years, and to
> provide such counseling and guidance services to the
> families as will assist them in adjusting to and accepting
> not only the diagnosis but also the prognosis, and in help-

ing the family assist the children to realize their fullest development and use of faculties.

By October, plans for the WARC Clinic to be opened at Children's Orthopedic Hospital, were nearing completion. The Retarded Children's Clinic would be financed through the Seattle Chapter of WARC at an estimated $10,000 to $12,000 per year. The clinic would employ a social worker, a secretary, and a part-time psychologist. Referrals to the clinic would be made by the patients' physicians, by public health and other social agencies, by WARC, or by other concerned organizations. Fees charged would be based on the family's ability to pay for services. Additional sources of funds for the WARC clinic included the Junior League, the WARC Guilds, the State Health Department, and other WARC chapters (HOPE, April 1959). Eventually the hospital was persuaded to adopt the clinic as its own responsibility, and the WARC name was dropped from the title.

A diagnostic clinic also opened in Tacoma in the summer of 1957, and WARC reported that clinics in Clallam and Snohomish counties were being developed. Spokane, Lewis, and Whatcom counties had expressed their interest as well (HOPE, January 1958). As medical personnel, special education teachers, and other professionals became more knowledgeable about intellectual disabilities, the need for these specialized centers declined.

Prevention

WARC members also supported the prevention of mental retardation through legislation. In 1966 WARC recommended that funds be appropriated from the Department of Health to set up nine additional diagnostic clinics and to expand pre- and post-natal care in Tacoma and Spokane to reduce the incidence of retardation among children born to high-risk mothers. Larger legislative campaigns were undertaken with regard to measles and phenylketonuria (PKU). In 1966 Frank Skerbeck, M.D., chairman of the Health Committee, sought state support for the distribution of measles vaccine to insure that all children in the state received inoculations. WARC specifically recommended that the Department of Health make measles vaccine available at all local public health clinics and that the Washington Medical Association should promote a widespread measles vaccination program. National attention on measles mirrored state concern, as illustrated by an article in WARC's newsletter (HOPE, July 1966):

The U.S. Public Health Service and the National Association for Retarded Children are urging all parents to have their children vaccinated NOW. More than half of the four million children who have measles suffer some form of brain involvement, as indicated by abnormal electroencephalographs taken during the course of the disease.

The 1967 legislature authorized $100,000 for a rubella (German measles) immunization program to help prevent mental retardation, and an official "End Measles Campaign" was begun on May 23, 1967 led by Governor Daniel J. Evans. Evans was photographed with representatives of the campaign's prime sponsors, WARC's Frank Skerbeck, the director of the Department of Health, and the president of the state medical association. Although the vaccination drives were conducted on children, the aim was to prevent their mothers from contracting the disease during pregnancy, because up to one quarter of the babies in such cases had significant birth defects.

The first effective screening device for phenylketonuria (PKU), an inborn metabolic error, was discovered by Robert Guthrie under a research grant from NARC. PKU is relatively rare (occurring in only 7 per 100,000 births). With early detection, diet, and treatment, mental retardation can usually be avoided. In the 1976 legislature, WARC's Prevention Committee, chaired by non-parent nurse Kate Roden, successfully pushed for legislation to mandate that all newborns be screened.

During the 1950s, research efforts were viewed quite optimistically. Certainly, many persons knew the course would be long and hard, but many did not. The excitement over medical research died down by the mid-sixties when it became apparent that there would be no Salk vaccine for persons with mental retardation.

Guardianship and Planning for the Future

Guardianship, religion, and recreation are all long-standing parent interests, each requiring its own form of advocacy. As early as the 1950s, concern about "what happens after I'm gone" led WARC to pursue parental successor laws and other legal arrangements to provide continuing care for their sons and daughters who were institutionalized.

Some parents thought that a special organization should be formed to insure that personal care and attention was provided after their own deaths. In response to this need, the Foundation for the Handicapped was formed in 1962. Harold Watkins, past WARC president, had pleaded at a WARC board meeting to revitalize the potential of the Trust Fund, which had been languishing, and Van R. Hinkle was asked to comment. Hinkle felt two significant needs were going unaddressed and might be added to the Trust's activities. First, provision for visitations to institutional residents after their parents' death or disability was being provided elsewhere but not in Washington. For example, in Massachusetts, the "MARC Retardate Trust" provided funds for such services. Second, Hinkle felt there was a need for a private care facility whereby parents could provide for their child's care through a bequest at death. Such a facility would provide an alternative to state facilities and their waiting lists and uncertainties.

Hinkle recommended that WARC establish a committee to determine if the Trust Fund could provide such services. Alternatively, a new corporate entity might be established for these two purposes. As it happened, John Hauberg announced the creation of the separately incorporated Foundation for Handicapped Children at the December 1962 board meeting, calling it an arm of WARC.[275] Thus the Foundation, now called Lifetime Advocacy Plus, became a totally independent organization that grew out of the committee's decision not to expand the mission of the WARC Trust Fund to include direct services.

But the old statutes on guardianship, not drafted with any sophisticated understanding of mental retardation, were still in force. In 1975, after months of work by the WARC Guardianship Committee, chaired by Grace Gould, a bill written by Legal Committee co-chair Bill Dussault was introduced to address the guardianship issue. Under the leadership of Kathleen Barnett, who chaired the Governmental Affairs Committee, the bill was successfully lobbied through to enactment.

The law has been highly regarded as a pioneering, model piece of legislation. Among its positive features are provisions insuring that the control exercised by the guardian over the affected individual can be limited to what is needed in a particular case and then revised further as the individual's personal development warrants. For example, a particular guardian might retain the rights to authorize medical treatment and to contract for a purchase of more than fifty dollars. Below this amount, a disabled individual would be free to exercise absolute discretion. Dussault took the idea of an individually tailored approach from the new field of special education law and applied it almost immediately to the guardianship statute.

Religion

When the push for schools and other community services began in the early 1950s, some parents requested religious education as well. In 1952-53 the Spokane WARC persuaded the school district to release children from public schools to attend simplified religious education programs at nearby Protestant churches (HOPE, July 1953). The classes were sponsored by the Spokane Council of Churches. But this program was discontinued after subsequent U.S. Supreme Court decisions, and the indirect assistance provided by public school officials was effectively ended.

Parents were behind other early efforts for religious services. Through their efforts, for example, the Greater Seattle Council of Churches began offering special services at the Lutheran Church of the Good Shepherd in 1960, and the first Catholic masses were held at Rainier and Fircrest schools that same year (HOPE, July 1960).

Parents have continued to be the primary force behind the provision of religious services, given the prohibition on state funding and the unavailability of United Way funds. Although new efforts have been made by the larger denominations in recent years, and although religious education programs have been implemented in a number of communities across the state, the results have not been widely successful. Unlike governmental programs, there has been no central point for advocates to apply pressure, nor any data collection point for assessing progress. It seems that churches and synagogues have lagged perhaps two decades behind other major institutions in providing equal access and inclusive services to persons with intellectual disabilities, though recent years have seen improvements.

Recreation and Physical Fitness

In the early 1950s, the first specialized recreational programs were formed as "parent cooperative playgroups." These mother-run enterprises were described as an opportunity for disabled children to engage in non-threatening learning with their peers with similar disabilities. Like kindergartens, these cooperative playgroups were justified in terms of preparing children for schoolwork.

In Washington summer camping programs had been a popular recreational option for older children without disabilities since the 1920s. Thus, it is not surprising that early recreational services for children with mental disabilities frequently took this form. For example, in 1958 the King county chapter of WARC established a summer residence program at Camp Waskowitz. Many other chapters eventually provided overnight programs, which often served both adolescents and adults.

Before Special Olympics, the early specialized athletic efforts that have been identified in the state include the Game of the Year basketball game for several years, discussed above. It also included "Weight Training for the Mentally Retarded at the Primary [School] Level,"[276] a program developed by physical education staff at Western Washington State University, in which young children lifted weights of seven, ten, and fifteen pound toy animals with buckshot in them. The children learned to do arm curls and bench presses. "This was no longer beanbag toss," but an indication of developing ideas of striving. In 1967 the program was publicized in *Challenge*, a special physical education journal backed by Eunice Kennedy Shriver and the Kennedy foundation. The journal played a key role in building up to the idea of a Special Olympics.[277]

With the financial and symbolic backing of the Kennedy Foundation, the first International Special Olympics in Chicago in July 1968 was soon followed with state and local programs and events designed to increase the physical well-being of children and adults through athletics. The February 1970 issue of HOPE announced the appointment of Patricia L. Karrasch as Washington's director of Special Olympics. Originally, the state Special Olympics meet had been sponsored by the King County Parks Department. But in 1970 WARC adopted Special Olympics as one of its projects.

Several chapters quickly moved to make Special Olympics a part of their local programming. A "state meet" was held in Longview in 1971 under the supervision of WARC activist Grace Gould. The following year, the state meet was held at the University of Washington with WARC funding. Additional funds were obtained by Lud Kramer, Secretary of State and chair of WARC's Ways and Means Committee, from a share of the proceeds from a New York Jets football game. With these funds and support from United and Air West Airlines, Washington Special Olympians competed in the International Special Olympics.

The Special Olympics remained in close relationship with WARC during 1973 and 1974. In 1974, Governor Daniel J. Evans proclaimed June 17-23 as "Washington Special Olympics Week." The Special Olympics coordinator reported to WARC board members that Special Olympics needed a year-round program. The ARC agreed and at its annual meeting in Richland, Special Olympics became a standing committee.

The WARC-Special Olympics relationship did not remain harmonious. In March 1975, the WARC board of directors discussed a communications problem which existed between the two organizations. The basic problem was WARC budget woes; it was simply unable to fund every project it favored. It was reported at the board meeting that Special Olympics definitely considered itself a separate organization under no obligation to keep WARC up to date on Special Olympics activities. But practically speaking, it still depended on the local ARC members to run a successful campaign. A committee was appointed by the board to resolve the problem. A board member suggested that WARC should withdraw funding for the Special Olympics if the differences could not be worked out. Budgetary constraints lent support to those board members who were beginning to question whether WARC's sponsorship of Special Olympics was compatible with its increasing adoption of the normalization principle. All ties between the two organizations at the state level were soon broken.[278]

Conclusion: Parents and Other Boosters

Between 1950 and 1975, a system of community services designed to address the needs of persons with intellectual disabilities emerged. Housing, employment, and other necessities of life in twentieth century America began to take shape. The long labors of families were paying off.

The particular advocacy role of parent as builder and as booster of local projects was new. Sheltered workshops, group homes, recreation and religious programs all provided opportunities for parents to exercise skills as promoters and then as de facto or actual owner-managers. Sometimes they were paid for their work, but more often parents, especially mothers, have been volunteers. Some parents have become so absorbed in the activity that they have become, as Farber points out, a Mr. or Mrs. Mental Retardation— with a finger in every pot in the area.[279] But, as his analysis implies, this dominance seems to have been a passing phase, appropriate when the times demanded a strong parent entrepreneur with ample charisma to lead dedicated followers to create local programs more or less from scratch.

As suggested earlier, a major reason why parent advocates are no longer dominant is precisely because they have worked themselves out of a job.[280] As the system of community services developed, federal, state, and local governmental officials began to assume more and more of the roles of advocate, innovator, and manager.

A case in point is Washington's 1975 Home Aid program, one of the early formal systems of family support in the nation. Families were supplied with therapy services and in-home or out-of-home respite care to reduce the stress of a continuing extraordinary level of care. Home Aid was conceived and enacted basically by the Division of Developmental Disabilities. It is true that parents had seen the need; Newland Reilly called for more in-home assistance at the 1941 state convention, as did Edith Stern at the 1950 annual meeting. And a persistent widow almost single-handedly persuaded her legislator to introduce a bill to provide periodic home visits by therapists and nurses as an alternative to institutions.[281] Although state officials heard parental complaints which demonstrated that a genuine need existed, neither WARC nor any other disability group began the push for Home Aid. The specific legislation is credited to Maurice A. "Buck" Harmon, director of the Bureau of Developmental Disabilities. Through the stories that filtered up from the front-line case workers, he learned the strains that many families faced and felt that addressing their needs would help the state achieve its goal of reducing institutionalization. As a result, Home Aid was born.[282]

Government officials continued to be innovators, but they were not the only agents of change. Service providers, as they became known, also increasingly played an influential role in the state legislature, with the public agencies, and in shaping current opinion in the field. Naturally, self-interest made the directors of sheltered workshops and group homes persistent lobbyists. A gradually increasing professionalism in such managers was possible, because of their full-time attention to the problem. It was rare to find a parent who could commit to such a high level of activity.

Many members engaged in building a community service system were more like the third category of allies who joined with them—volunteers. When the task to be accomplished is to open the first day program or clinic, to assist in athletics, or to provide transportation to specialized religious services, there are individuals of good will who can be counted on to join in. Naturally, the kind of volunteer differs depending on the nature of the task, from socially prominent members of the Junior League, Kiwanians, and teenaged camp counselors. Without such assistance, the facilities and programs might be *in* the community, but they would never be *of* it.

One such volunteer was Ralph Munro. As a college student in the late 1960s he first became involved in mental retardation through the Holiday Cruises program, which took people with disabilities on

Christmas cruises around the Seattle waterways in decorated boats. Later, as a volunteer at Fircrest School, he witnessed the unpleasantness of the lives of severely disabled persons. He decided to become the guardian of one of the residents and has remained so for years. As an aide to Governor Evans, Munro specialized in handling constituent requests concerning disabilities and became their advocate within the administration. He was active in WARC in two different counties, using his skills to help start group homes and other programs. He later joined the Foundation for the Handicapped as an executive and then took a leave of absence in 1979 to work full-time as the statewide coordinator for Referendum 37, a state bond issue for construction funds for facilities serving persons with disabilities and other needs. The successful passage of the referendum put Munro in a strong position to campaign for Secretary of State the following year. In his election to the new position, he continued to serve as a strong and accessible political ally of the disability community.

Ralph Munro started as a volunteer, and has remained a volunteer. And, not unlike some others, he has also moved into the other service-building roles as well. As guardian, he has become a de facto parent; as Evans' aide, he was a state official; and as a promoter of guardianship programs for the Foundation, he has been a service provider. As this chapter has shown, in the sixties and seventies the role of being a parent expanded and was no longer as distinctive. The parental advocate has often become service provider and sometimes a state official. State officials have served as WARC executives. A significant number of service providers started as volunteers, and some have become adoptive parents of those who were supposed to remain only clients. The only remaining advocacy role that had not yet emerged was about to – persons with intellectual disabilities, who were people first (and not their disabilities), began to speak for themselves.

Hawaiian Week raffle drawing 1978. Lou Day, Stan Baxter, Paul Dziedzic, Larry Jones, Connie Hilty, and Buck Harmon, head of DDD, drawing winning ticket

1979 WARC Mountain Trekkers celebrate reaching Anderson Pass, including Linda Rolfe (arms raised), Garry Reid (right with beard), and Andy Jones (center front)

Amburgey family celebrates Darren's attendance at Capital High School, Olympia, after Section 504 complaint in 1979

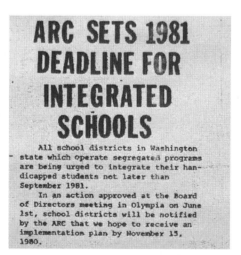

ARC SETS 1981 DEADLINE FOR INTEGRATED SCHOOLS

All school districts in Washington state which operate segregated programs are being urged to integrate their handicapped students not later than September 1981.

In an action approved at the Board of Directors meeting in Olympia on June 1st, school districts will be notified by the ARC that we hope to receive an implementation plan by November 15, 1980.

ARC announces actions to end segregated school buildings for students with disabilities

Bean Driscoll, Karen Woodsum, and Sue Scott watch Gov. Spellman sign the Arc's 1983 Program Options Act

Arc office in Olympia, 1980s

Bean Driscoll, longtime Arc staff, 1980-2010s

Gov. Lowry signs 1993 law barring death as penalty for criminals with low IQs, witnessed by Jerry Sheehan, ACLU, Lynne Darnell, The Arc, lobbyists for Catholic and Lutheran Churches, and Larry Jones, The Arc

**Gov. Gregoire and Kevin Britt, namesake of a 2007 law allow-
ing special education students to go through graduation
ceremonies at age 18, even if staying in school till 21 years**

**Gov. Gregoire & advocates at signing of SB6313 requiring
schools to recognize disability history month 2008**

Gov. Gregoire signs 2010 HB 2490 replacing "the R word" with "intellectual disability" in state law

Disability advocates on the steps of the capital

The Arc of Washington State staff in 2009: Cathy Davis, Bean Driscoll, Sue Elliott, Samantha Trotter, Heather Harper, Jackie Thomason, Patti Bell, and Emily Rogers. (Not shown: Susan Atkins and Diana Stadden)

CHAPTER SEVEN:
ADVOCATING FOR THE RIGHTS
OF CITIZENS

In the domain of Human Rights:
All people have fundamental moral and constitutional rights. These rights must not be abrogated merely because a person has a mental or physical disability.
Among these fundamental rights is the right to community living.
In the domain of Educational Programming and Human Service:
All people, as human beings, are inherently valuable. All people can grow and develop. All people are entitled to conditions which foster their development. Such conditions are optimally provided in community settings.
Therefore:
In fulfillment of fundamental human rights, and in securing optimum developmental opportunities, all people, regardless of the severity of their disabilities, are entitled to community living.

> "*The Community Imperative*," from the Center on
> Human Policy at Syracuse University (1979)

Three signs of the times from the 1970s show the new conviction of the ARC's leaders that its organizational mission was advocacy of "normalization." First, in 1974 the ARC filed papers to reserve an alternative corporate name, the "Washington Association for the Developmentally Disabled." Harry Carthum, of the Grays Harbor chapter, had cogently argued that the word "retarded" in the ARC name was not "normalizing," but instead stigmatized people with disabilities. The truth of the point was appreciated, although the suggestion was not chosen. In a compromise, the Washington Association for Retarded Children followed the national organization and changed its name to the Washington Association for Retarded *Citizens,* a name somewhat more normalized. (A few years later, Washington joined in the national change to "ARC," dropping the "R word" for which the initial had stood.[283])

The second event also involved a name. Usually struggling to expand the number of county units, the ARC was actually pleased to receive a letter of withdrawal from the Sunshine and Happiness ARC which represented rural Okanogan County. The state Board had written the unit asking it to revise its name in accordance with normalization principles and to broaden its activities beyond simply providing recreational activities. The state ARC had become convinced that any ARC unit worth its name could not simply provide direct services, such as recreation or housing. It must also serve as a general advocate for *all* the rights of persons with cognitive disabilities in its area. This movement away from direct services could threaten member support. But the ARC was prepared to accept this risk. When units refused to accept any responsibility for advocacy, they would be encouraged to withdraw. The Okanogan group refused to change and did withdraw from the ARC.

Third, in 1976 a national ARC bumper sticker commemorated the bicentennial of the country with the message, "Liberty and Justice for All Includes Retarded Citizens." The civil rights movements of blacks, other racial minorities, and women had set the stage for ARC leaders in Washington and elsewhere to campaign for the rights of persons with mental retardation. They did so with enthusiasm – a change that Elizabeth Boggs, the most important volunteer in first 50 years of The Arc, dated to 1968, when "we stopped talking about welfare and started talking about implementing rights."[284]

An ideology specifically tailored to persons with disabilities had emerged and it spread quickly through the ranks of parents and "direct consumer" advocacy groups of "persons with disabilities."

Professors and lawyers became role models for the day. Social criticism and litigation became common forms of advocacy. Thus, the parents' movement again evolved into a new stage, producing internal conflict, as well as external confrontations.

Normalization

Normalization, probably the central concept in the new ideology, was developed by Bengt Nirje, executive director of the Swedish Parents' Association for Mentally Retarded Citizens and popularized in America by Wolf Wolfensberger, who had been involved in the ARC in Nebraska.[285] Wolfensberger defined normalization as "the utilization of means which are as culturally normative as possible in order to establish and/or maintain personal behaviors which are as culturally normative as possible."[286] The concept was frequently linked with other terms: "least restriction," a phrase originating in the legal right to be free of unnecessary constraints on one's liberty and incorporated in federal education and rehabilitation regulations; "mainstreaming," which applies the idea of least restriction to education; and "deinstitutionalization," which does the same to residential services. Today "inclusion" is the term that means much the same and is most often used. All of these terms suggest that persons with disabilities should be incorporated far more into the ordinary rounds of everyday life than was commonly happening. Whenever individuals with intellectual disabilities were relegated to "special" separate activities or programs, alarm bells rang in the heads of these new advocates. This new generation of parents and others were fired up by the times. They believed that current social structures were in need of a thorough overhaul to stop the rampant dehumanization they were causing. Decisive actions were needed to be taken to obtain full human rights and equal dignity for all.

The second element in the ideology was "the developmental model," a term which was reinforced by the federal government's adoption of the funding category, "developmental disabilities." The developmental model was an idea applied to a system of services designed to help a disabled person grow toward greater independence and less control by others.[287] There may be little difference semantically in saying that a person's learning is "retarded" or that it is "developmentally delayed." But the former term places the accent on the slower learning rate, while "development" emphasizes the growth which takes place in everyone. According to the developmental model, every person can learn. Soon, advocates began to expect that all persons would become economically productive

212

adults and would assume far more responsibility and control over their own personal care.

Third, the new ideology treated the claims of disabled persons to services and opportunities as rights. According to this view, legislation and other public support for disabled persons should not be viewed as a social welfare hand-out geared to the "needs" of a particular interest group, but as an overdue recognition of rights which persons with disabilities had long been denied. Thus, if a school district had to cancel its high school athletics program in order to find the funds for appropriate programs for children with disabilities, so be it. This approach suggested that confrontational tactics were fully justified. Litigation and even direct, non-violent, protest actions might be just as appropriate, and perhaps as effective, as legislation.

Of course, the idea that Americans with disabilities have rights was not entirely new. Occasionally in the earlier decades, parents had demanded rights or justice, instead of appealing to motives of charity or fiscal prudence when they approached legislators or the public. For example, in 1936 the League argued that it was unjust that the State Custodial School received a lower per capita appropriation than all other institutions. In 1950, the convention keynoter Edith Stern had proclaimed that all persons had the right to a fulfilling life. Similarly, in 1953 NARC published an "Education Bill of Rights for the Retarded Child," arguing that every child had a right to education. But these claims to justice were voices crying in the wilderness.

What was new in the late 1970s and blossomed in the early 1980s and beyond was the rhetorical style and a least slightly more confrontational tactics of the civil rights movement.[288] How did parents come to adopt the ideas of rights, normalization, and the developmental model? Most ARC advocates learned about civil rights from the mass media, although a few personally participated in the movement for racial justice. But normalization, mainstreaming, and the developmental model could not be learned from Walter Cronkite, and these new ideas flowed through specialized channels. ARC conventions and special meetings at national, state, and local levels provided learning opportunities for families. These ARC sessions were supplemented by conferences sponsored by public agencies and other disability groups. Parents heard speakers explain successful lawsuits and describe prototype community residences on the developmental model run by the Eastern Nebraska Community Office of Retardation (ENCOR). Films like Marc Gold's "Try Another Way" dramatically demonstrated that far more individuals with multiple severe disabilities could be taught to assemble complicated bicycle brakes than had ever been conceived. Intensive multi-day workshops using Wolfensberger's "Program Analysis of Service Systems" (PASS) taught thousands of parents, persons with disabilities, service providers, state employees and others to apply normalization theory to particular settings in their local communities.

Of course, not every ARC member was enamored with these new ideas. Generally speaking, the opinion-leaders who adopted the new perspective were "cosmopolitans."[289] Those who "lagged behind", by contrast, were the "locals" who were oriented primarily to their local organization or program, be it group home, state institution, sheltered workshop, or recreation program. Cosmopolitans were more likely to read disability journals, attend conventions and workshops, and serve on state and national boards and committees. They saw themselves as "advocates," part of a national movement of persons with disabilities and their supporters.

Two additional variables also separated locals and cosmopolitans. The first was age. A generational conflict emerged within the ARC and similar groups, with younger activists reaching a consensus on the new ideology and tactics, while a significant fraction of older members were opposed. Parents whose experience had been formed before all children began to attend local schools in the 1970s were the core of the resistance.

Second, one's position within the movement was strongly correlated with one's beliefs. That is, the persons most likely to be in the vanguard of new ideas in the ARC were the ARC executive directors, followed by administrators of public and non-profit service programs. These people were the most cosmopolitan in their orientation—they were frequent readers of accounts of innovative programs and ideas, and they regularly attended state and national meetings. Parents were intermediate in their propensity to support the new directions for the ARC. Community volunteers were the least likely to favor the new ways. These men and women of good will were the most likely to be attached to the operation of a local program or to be absorbed in building and expanding the current service systems. On the whole, volunteers were unwilling to risk confrontation, because, unlike the parents, they had no personal self-interest to motivate the sacrifice. They did not internalize the feelings of injustice which began to propel the ARC to take stronger and more ideologically extreme positions. The Community Services Suit of 1978 was the primary example of the ARC's new militancy.[290]

The Community Services Suit

ARC leaders had become increasingly frustrated with the trend in residential services for persons with mental retardation. After a period in which the most able persons living in state schools had been deinstitutionalized, progress not only had halted, but seemed to be reversing direction. Because of Washington's entry into the Medicaid program, more and more dollars were going to institutions to comply with specific federal staffing and other requirements. Not only were there inadequate remaining dollars to fund a natural growth of community residences, but the actions taken by the Division of Developmental Disabilities and the legislature threatened to sustain an institutional system which the ARC leaders now thought was wrong.

The decision to advocate for total deinstitutionalization was based on several factors. Several ARC directors had children who had lived in institutions or had recently been institutionalized, although the parents preferred community placements which did not exist. They were powerful influences on the actions taken to change the status quo. Also, by the mid-1970s there were few parents whose children lived in institutions by choice in the ARC leadership at the state or county level. The president and other members of the state ARC board arranged with the state to tour all the institutional back wards, where the persons with the most medical problems and those with the most destructive behavior resided. What the Arc team saw was not good, for there was still plenty of neglect. They found none of residents had more medical or destructive behavior than individuals they knew who were living far better lives in the community. None had behavior that was impossible to improve by residing in an appropriately designed small home.

The legislature treated the ARC's lobbying for community services as just another plea by an interest group that could be balanced against other appropriations requests. But the ARC, filled with its new ideology, saw community services as a matter of fundamental justice which was being ignored. ARC leaders wondered about a lawsuit. Perhaps the courts, whose role it was to hear cases involving rights, would be more sympathetic. Washington state activists had heard about the favorable rulings in Alabama by Judge Frank Johnson in *Wyatt v. Stickney,* and in New York in the Willowbrook case, where the state agreed to move all but 250 of 5,400 persons to small-scale community settings over a six year period. But the immediate precipitant was federal Judge Raymond Broderick's December 1977 holding in *Halderman v. Pennhurst*

State School at the Pennsylvania institution's conditions were inhumane and that every resident should live in the community. The Pennsylvania ARC looked as if it would win another milestone case, one of equal importance with its celebrated education for all case in 1971. Washington did not want to be left behind in the race for full human rights for all persons with disabilities. Although, to be fair, it may have been only by accident that these were the same two states as contest the claim to have achieved special education for all first.

In January 1978, discussions were opened with Evergreen Legal Services, a tax-supported body for the legal rights of poor persons, some of whom had developmental disabilities. Evergreen provided legal counsel for the case. The next month Evergreen presented a plan for a lawsuit with the idea of winning improvements in both community resources and institutions, but the Executive Committee expressed displeasure with such an approach. In March, the full ARC board reviewed the proposal and authorized a task force to modify the nature of the suit. The revised version was mailed to the county chapters for discussion. By unanimous vote, on June 1, 1978, the twenty members of the state board voted to authorize the ARC's participation as a plaintiff against the state of Washington to gain a system of community services adequate to serve all persons regardless of disabilities. Since the suit included a claim that institutionalized persons were being unnecessarily and unconstitutionally deprived of their liberties, it called for the gradual closure of all five of the state schools as community services were developed. It was hoped that the era of institutions would be ended first in Washington, ironically the same state that parents had first fought to build them.

The lawsuit was filed on June 16, 1978 in the U.S. District Court for Eastern Washington as *WARC v. Thomas.*[291] In addition to WARC, the plaintiffs included the guardians of fourteen residents representing 2,800 residents, and many other persons who were at risk of being placed in the institutions because community services were not available for them. WARC expected institutional supporters to raise a public uproar. It was not disappointed. As Executive Director Stan Baxter put it, the organization had decided to risk controversy because "it had to be part of the action" on behalf of persons with developmental disabilities.

The Community Services Suit was described by WARC News (Aug./Sept. 1978) as "potentially the single most important thing WARC has done," with a full sense of the irony involved in the fact that forty years earlier the construction of Rainier State School had been its proudest achievement. Although the times had changed, the motives were similar. In the 1930s, a second state school meant that parents would be 200 miles closer to their sons and daughters. In the 1970s, the ARC saw that the remaining separation could be overcome as well—every disabled person could live in his or her home community.

In the court of public opinion. The board was soon advised by its Evergreen attorneys, led by Linda Potter, that class action lawsuits about institutions were frequently won not in the courts, but in the external political arena. Thus, it was important to counter the negative fear tactics employed by institutional parents' groups to attract media attention. The ARC established a task force to work toward winning the lawsuit in the realm of public opinion. In July, the ARC won the support of the Washington State Association of Group Homes for the suit, but additional endorsements proved hard to get.

In 1980 the King County ARC in Seattle withdrew from the state ARC in part due to its opposition to the lawsuit. Even those who supported the suit in principle—such as almost all other disability organizations—wanted to miss the flak that was soon filling the skies. The flak was provided by the parents clubs at the various state institutions. The Friends of Rainier, the Friends of Fircrest, Lakeland Village Associates, and the other groups retained Erik Froberg, a WARC leader in the 1950s, as their attorney. They were successful in gaining legal status as "interveners," or interested parties, in the suit. But the informal intervention of older parents *within* the ARC was also important.[292] Some of the institutional parents were still WARC members from previous decades when WARC had supported the "state schools." The rest had friends who were members. In effect, a strong coalition of senior citizens was mobilized by the suit.

Questions about the legality and propriety of the board's action in bringing the suit soon arose. Institutional parents claimed that the ARC did not represent institutionalized residents, whereas the parents clubs, with their nominal memberships of all parents of residents, could. It was further argued that the ARC had been "taken over" by the non-parents who were on the board, and that a parents' organization would never have filed the suit. The ARC was thrown into such a defensive posture that the state executive committee felt in need of some reassurance. An August telephone poll of the board confirmed that its members were still fully supportive of the suit. And at the September annual meeting the delegates unanimously voted to reaffirm participation in the suit. The association had spent

217

nearly three months determining that its own support for the lawsuit was secure. In the fall of 1978, the ARC was again able to try to win over the general public.

As part of a media campaign, a sixty-page press packet written by Linda Potter, Stan Baxter, board member Bill Wegeleben, and others, was printed and distributed. Baxter and others gained interviews on a few radio shows. Newspaper articles were also prepared. For example, an article in a newspaper in the state capital appeared. "Parents Want to Keep Retarded Children Home; Goal—To close state institutions" was ghostwritten by the author to support the lawsuit. The article featured interviews with three families of preschool children with severe disabilities. They offered reasons why "even the most severely handicapped child should be kept at home or in a homelike setting" —and could be, given proper state support. The article is more interesting for the positions adopted and the rhetoric used than as an example of how to win a media campaign. People in institutions were "locked up," while those families who recently chose out-of-home placements were "forced to send their children far away" by the state's current service system. The parents claimed that the Division of Developmental Disabilities could prevent such new placements by using its current discretionary authority, but was choosing not to. With only a few more services provided by the state, we could "bring everyone home."[293] The language of the article shows that the push for deinstitutionalization had taken on aspects of a crusade, complete with holy warriors and evil opponents.

Parent opponents of the lawsuit waged just as emotional a struggle, but struck different themes and emotions. Instead of liberation, the results would be rape and death for defenseless "children" who would be dumped onto city streets without protection. For example, in 1979 a hysterical letter writer to the *Bellingham Daily News* claimed that the lawsuit would result in wholesale dumping. An ARC board member and a local chapter president responded to the letter, pointing out that if the suit was successful, the court would order the state to "develop a plan that will first identify the service needs of all present and potential residents of the institutions and then develop the services needed to meet those needs." The ARC respondents admitted that there were instances in the past when residents had been moved from the institutions without having adequate community alternatives, but this was exactly what the suit intended to avoid through directing the state to develop an adequate community service system. The day after the ARC response, the editor ran another opposition letter as a rebuttal.

In a second example of responding to institutional attacks, a lone ARC director testified at a legislative hearing against a new bill designed to give resistant parents nearly absolute veto power over community placements through elaborate procedural devices. The voice of reason and moderation was overwhelmed by tales of rape and assault in the community. The fact that such offenses were also taking place in the institutions went ignored by the legislators, who enacted the bill (nicknamed the "Froberg law") despite objections from the executive branch. The new provision gave institutional parents a right to a hearing at which the state had to prove that it was appropriate to place a specific individual in the community. The state brought no hearings under the law. So if parents were opposed, their family member stayed in the institution. Thus the WARC lawsuit actually wound up strengthening the opposition.

The ARC did not win the suit in the court of public opinion. Perhaps it did not lose the battle either, since the greater part of the public remained ignorant of the struggle raging in the disability community. There proved to be several reasons involved in the inability of the ARC to overcome the institutional opposition. First, fear is a better motivator than hope. People will fight to avoid a loss quicker than to gain a better future. Second, the institutional camp had far more focus; they could meet at five places, rather than being scattered across the state. The suit's opponents were also more focused by an institution's inherent comprehensiveness and unity. By contrast, the advocates in the community had many different special interests —pre-schools, high schools, group homes, sheltered workshops, respite care—which spread their loyalties. Third, the opponents of the suit obtained assistance in publicity and organizing from the state employees whose jobs were at stake. When the ARC chose to enter into the lawsuit, it expected to gain additional weapons in the battle for more normalized living conditions—the law and lawyers. The leaders of the ARC did not fully face up to the fact that the organization would be required to increase its own efforts—persuading and educating the public and the legislators of the worthiness of its cause.

Taking a loss. After delays due to the death of the assigned judge and a change of venue from Spokane to Seattle, the Community Services suit was certified as a class action on May 22, 1980, by newly appointed Judge Donald Voorhees. The class action certification cleared the way for entering the discovery stage. From this point the case went downhill. Discovery, the process of collecting the evidence needed to present a suit, is governed by decisions which the judge lays down in each case. Judge Voorhees was very restrictive. When chief counsel Linda Potter brought in national authorities to survey the conditions in the institutions, they reported that they had never been denied such freedom of access to investigate conditions and expressed doubt whether they could collect enough quality evidence to enable the case to be won on a constitutional basis.

The outcome became dim indeed when the U. S. Supreme Court announced its decision in the *Pennhurst* appeal.[294] The Pennsylvania ARC and the other plaintiffs had contended that under the Developmental Disabilities Act of 1975 states were obligated to develop more community services rather than expand institutions (ARC News, June, 1981). But the Court held that Congress had only *recommended* that community services be given preference and had not made it mandatory. Thus, there was no statutory basis for deinstitutionalization and the state of Pennsylvania could maintain its facilities.

There were additional legal grounds for the remedies sought in *WARC v. Thomas* that were not decided in the Pennsylvania case. But the Supreme Court had turned conservative under the influence of its Nixon appointees, and thus the prospects of winning on any grounds were poor. Institutionalized developmentally disabled persons had no constitutional right to habilitation in a least restrictive environment, except to be trained, when possible, to defend themselves from assaults.

Given the similarities which did exist between the PARC and WARC cases, and the decisions on discovery made by the judge, Evergreen Legal Services was gradually convinced that a change had to be made. Even if there was a favorable decision in the lower court, the state had given every indication of willingness to appeal, and the Ninth Circuit looked tough. In addition, the continuing cost of the lawsuit became a matter of concern. In 1979, the state legislature had amended its appropriation of state funding for Evergreen Legal Services to eliminate funding for deinstitutionalization lawsuits. Although federal funds were still available, President Reagan made it one of his priorities to reduce, if not eliminate, federal appropriations to legal services programs; it was an effort in which he had great success. Thus, in December 1982 the lawsuit was voluntarily dismissed by the plaintiffs.

An out-of-court settlement had been reached with the state, providing some window dressing over a defeat. The settlement allowed the ARC leadership to present as good a face as possible to its members:

In exchange for dismissal of the suit, the State of Washington agreed to:

> increase the effectiveness of the Citizens Advisory
> Task Force now planning the future shape of develop-
> mental disabilities in the state; apply for a Title XIX
> waiver which will allow community programs, not just
> institutional ones; and make good faith efforts to seek to
> increase appropriations for long-term community support
> services for severely disabled persons by $1.5 million in
> the next biennium.
>
> (ARC News, February, 1983).

The ARC's first experience with litigation had not proven to be as painless or as effective as the advocates had hoped. By losing so early in the process, however, the ARC was not forced to learn the lesson that the "winners" who had sued over institutional conditions at Willowbrook in New York. For decades, they had problems gaining compliance with the judicial decree.[295]

Desegregating Schools

Filing a lawsuit to close the state's institutions for persons with mental disabilities was not enough for the happy warriors of the Washington ARC. Since there were other social systems which also demeaned and debased persons with mental disabilities by segrega-tion and neglect, the ARC leaped into action to challenge those systems soon after it was handed new leverage. The federal gov-ernment reluctantly provided that power. On April 28, 1977, after sit-ins by disability activists in San Francisco Bay-area government offices, Secretary Joseph Califano of the Department of Health, Education and Welfare finally issued the regulations implementing Section 504 of the Rehabilitation Act of 1973. Section 504 was the civil rights act for persons with disabilities until the passage of the Americans with Disabilities Act in 1990. Section 504 provided that no recipient of federal funds could deny equality of services and opportunities on the grounds of handicap. Accessibility and least restriction were included as part of the rights which the regulations mandated. Because federal government funding had by the 1970s become so pervasive, it is safe to generalize that persons with disabilities gained full rights in the public sector in 1977. It took thirteen more years before their rights were fully protected in law in "public accommodations," meaning most of the private sector, through the Americans with Disabilities Act (ADA).

In Washington, the story began in Olympia, where Jackie and Bill Amburgey had two teenage sons. One got to attend the newly-opened Capital High School, but the other son, Darren, had disabilities. He was housed across town in the old Administration Building. On the dingy top floor of that building, which in better days had once been a junior high school, were the classrooms for the most disabled students of junior high and high school age, including those who had trouble walking up the stairs, as Darren did. They were isolated from any contacts with other students. Jackie Amburgey had protested the inequality of facilities and equipment between the two settings at school board meetings in the fall of 1978, but, as newspaper stories recounted, her demands that Darren be allowed to attend school at Capital were treated as irrational behavior on her part.[296]

At that point, the local Thurston County ARC held its monthly program where the local president spoke on the subject of the new Section 504 regulations, explaining the rights granted and how to complain to the regional Office for Civil Rights in Seattle.[297] Amburgey could hardly believe her ears. She and her husband filed a complaint in short order. For the local ARC, it was the first time that it had ever been involved in confrontational advocacy, but it quickly endorsed the Amburgeys' action. After an immediate negative public reaction by the superintendent over being the object of a civil rights complaint, the school district decided it was indeed out of compliance with the regulations. It quickly made plans to move the students to a middle school and to Capital High, as Amburgey had requested.

The district took six months to implement the program and throughout that period a battle raged in the media with staff and volunteers at the segregated program decrying the move in newspaper articles and letters to the editor. The move would "destroy the special spirit" of the program and it would subject "our children" to the evil influences and abuse of the regular students. In fact, a majority of the parents of students in the program were persuaded by these sentiments, but the ARC and the Amburgeys were unmoved.

The program opened the following fall with wide publicity. By spring the newspaper carried a glowing account of the "success story" at the new high school. The superintendent even took credit for the move. The Amburgeys and the ARC were forgotten. Some of the same school staff quoted in opposition a year earlier were now among the most enthusiastic supporters.

The ARC's 504 Complaints. Given the unalloyed success of this first experience with Section 504, the state ARC also began to explore the use of such complaints. Two were filed in 1980. At the request of the local ARC, n the spring the state ARC filed a complaint against the Spokane School District alleging two violations of least restrictive education requirements. First, the ARC contended that the contract between the Spokane School District and the teachers' union discriminated against children with disabilities by treating every such child as the equivalent of two non-handicapped students—a practice the ARC feared would reward school districts for excluding children with disabilities from a regular classroom experience. If Spokane's contract provision stood, the ARC was afraid the practice would spread rapidly to other school districts. The ARC was also concerned about the educational placement of some Spokane children in segregated settings. The Office for Civil Rights conducted interviews with the ARC, the Spokane School District, and parents of the children involved. In early 1981 OCR found that the school district was indeed discriminating against the children. To ensure that the children would receive an appropriate education, the Office for Civil Rights obtained an agreement with the Spokane School District to renegotiate the teachers' contract and re-examine placement of affected children.

The second ARC complaint was not successful. It alleged that a three percent budget reduction in the state special education allocation was discriminatory, because only special education funds were affected, not basic education appropriations. But the Office for Civil Rights ruled that Governor Dixy Lee Ray and the Legislature were not "recipients" of federal funds in the sense covered by the Section 504 regulations.

Ending Segregated Schools Statewide. The ARC leaders enjoyed using their new-found leverage to increase the participation of students in integrated educational programs and moved optimistically to go statewide. On June 1, 1980, the board approved a plan to pressure all school districts in Washington to eliminate separate buildings for their students with disabilities by September 1981.

Under the federal Education for All Handicapped Children Act of 1975 each district was required to report how many children with a particular disability category, including mental retardation, were being educated in various settings: regular class, resource room, separate class, separate school and residential facility. It occurred to the ARC that this allowed it to easily compile a listing of Washington's best to worst districts in terms of how inclusive they were. A short research paper was produced and distributed in special education circles around the state. Some of the leading directors of special education used the tabulation to engage in friendly ribbing of their peers whose districts ranked embarrassingly further down the list. The Arc hoped that the ranking would be used to pressure districts into less segregated settings.

The Arc also identified all school districts operating segregated schools for children with mental retardation. The districts were notified by letter of the Arc's 1981 deadline and were asked for plans of compliance. The districts included Seattle, Bellingham, Lake Washington, Edmonds, Yakima, Ellensburg, Renton, South Kitsap, Kent, and Shelton.

In fact, the ARC's efforts were appreciated by some school officials. The special education director of one school district who had heard about the Section 504 complaint filed against the Olympia schools quietly called the Thurston county Arc president and asked that a Section 504 complaint be filed against his district. "I can't stop the superintendent," he said, from building additional segregated school buildings. The complaint was filed and the building stopped.

The ARC clearly implied that Section 504 complaints would be filed if good faith efforts to meet the timeline were not forthcoming. Members of the ARC Education Committee met with superintendents or special education directors in about twelve school districts, touring and challenging facilities that were the lineal descendants of the special education schools started by parents in the 1950s and 1960s and which had gradually been absorbed by the public school systems. Just as in the case of the Community Services Suit, the ARC was attacking the service system originally won by its parent members in earlier decades.

But the ARC's actions were not directly effective. Since the state ARC's actions were leading the advocacy efforts, the typical response by school district personnel was to accuse the Education Committee members of being outside agitators. Like white Southern segregationists during the civil rights movement, the districts claimed "our parents and handicaps" were happy with the status quo. Since the ARC had no active members in many areas, the charge of being outsiders was hard to rebut. The accusation was most telling where there were competing organized parent groups which opposed the closure move, such as the former King County chapter. Consequently, the board allowed its own deadline to pass without filing any complaints.

However, the ARC threats had precipitated broad discussion of the concept of least restriction in education within other state public and private groups concerned with special education. The ARC

Education Committee turned its attention to winning political support from these groups. Here success was forthcoming. Over the next two years, the ARC, acting directly or indirectly, won support for the elimination of separate buildings for students with disabilities from the state special education directors' association, the official Washington State Special Education Advisory Council, and the broad legislative Special Education Coalition. With the increased support, the ARC reasserted its monitoring function and found that many targeted districts had moved to close or reduce the population of students in segregated settings.[298]

On the other hand, certain districts defiantly rejected integration. As a consequence, the ARC filed Section 504 complaints against the Seattle School District, the Lewis county special education cooperative, and Grandview School, operated by the Kent school district and serving ten school districts in south King county. In each of these cases, the Office of Civil Rights found substantial non-compliance, and the districts negotiated plans of correction. For the ARC board, the victory in the Kent case was particularly sweet, because its special education director had boasted "there'll always be a Grandview." As in Olympia, by the time the implementation process was in full swing, the district leadership was taking credit for making the changes. Grandview is no more.

Washington's efforts had nationwide effects. In 1985-86, the Arc of the United States formed a Children's Issues Committee and compiled and published a similar ranking of the 50 states in terms of how integrated or segregated their schools were. According to Sharon Davis, then director of research at the national Arc, the ranking was widely used and when the Arc stopped putting out an updated ranking, TASH (originally named The Association for Persons with Severe Handicaps) took over the job.

Adult Education in Community Colleges

Immersed in advocacy for integrated settings for the education of children, the ARC gradually re-invented the idea that adults with mental disabilities would profit from generic educational opportunities. Just as the ARC in 1966 had suggested using community colleges to provide training, the ARC in 1983 took the logic of mainstreaming and applied it to adult education (ARC News, Feb. 1983). According to the announced ideal, adults with developmental disabilities should be educated and trained at the same sites and under the same supervision as nondisabled adults.

Unlike the situation in the 1960s, a survey of all community colleges in the state revealed that over half were already providing some services to adults with cognitive disabilities.[299] Even severely disabled persons were being educated. The August 1980 issue of *ARC News* asked readers to "Mark down this year in your diary as the first time profoundly retarded adults went to college in Washington State." Funded and operated by Spokane Falls Community College, the program was located at an institution, Interlake School. Burying its dissatisfaction with the program's location, the ARC congratulated Marjorie Rowe, Superintendent of Interlake School and Gerald L. Scaling, President of Spokane Falls Community College, for promoting this innovative program. The ARC was aware that such basic tactile stimulation, grasping and awareness programs needed by adults with mental disabilities might upset preconceived notions of what a college education consists of, but contended that since community colleges are designed to serve all adults regardless of previous skills, persons with mental disabilities should be among them (*ARC News,* August 1980).

Taking it to National. In 1983 the ARC of Washington submitted a successful resolution to the ARC national convention promoting community colleges and other mainstreamed educational settings for adults. The position statement that was adopted did not require, although it implied, that segregated adult training programs such as developmental centers and sheltered workshops should be phased out.[300]

Parent to Parent

Although mutual support between parents has been a major function of the ARC from the beginning, as the ARC grew, the commitments of its members spread out over a wide variety of programs. Sometimes veteran parents forgot the simple needs of families in the initial phase of surprise at an unexpected development. To meet that need, specialized programs have developed. At least as far back as the early 1970s, the ARC of Omaha had a "pilot parent" program in which a more experienced mother or father was matched with a beginner to offer personalized assistance through emotional support, knowledge, and contacts.[301] In Washington, a Parent to Parent project was first developed in the 1980s with the support of the ARC of King county. From there the idea of Parent to Parent spread across the state and has continued. Now there is both a national network of P2P programs, and a Washington state project based at the Arc of Washington state.

A persistent idea in the ARC during these decades of advocacy has been that it should develop innovative service programs when no one else will, and then "spin off" the services to another entity, so that the ARC can be free of conflict of interest when it might have to advocate against those services in the future. In theory this leaves the general advocacy role as the ARC's function. However, general advocacy has only been one of two goals that the ARC has served over the years, the other one being mutual support for parents. Thus, the idea of spinning off "parent-to-parent" as a function provided outside the ARC is particularly troublesome. (The same fundamental question must be given to the emergence of "parent coalitions," discussed below.)

Service System Advocacy and Monitoring

Legislatively, the ARC continued to spend much of its time on appropriations. But with the relative maturity of the special education system, less attention was focused on schools and more on obtaining adequate funding for community services. In this shift the ARC mirrored the larger disability community. Thus, the Special Education Coalition, which had grown to include several dozen organizations, was supplemented in 1980 by a new coalition called the Washington Assembly of Citizens with Disabilities. The Assembly was promoted by the tax-supported Washington State Developmental Disabilities Council.[302] The Assembly was an even larger alliance; its make-up included the ARC, institutional groups, representatives of every disability, but also many community service providers and their associations. More and more, such groups began to influence the direction of advocacy in the state, leaving a reduced role for the ARC to play. To a large extent, this was the inevitable by-product of the growth of services, and the ARC accepted it. The state ARC tried to distinguish itself by being in the vanguard of change.

In part, this was as simple as accenting the need for proportionately more funds for community services. For example, in 1979 Washington state government spent 73% of the developmental disabilities budget on institutional care, where a small minority of disabled persons lived, while respite care, group homes, and developmental centers were consistently underfunded. The ARC sought increased appropriations for the latter items. But to be a change agent, the ARC had to do more than simply lobby for more community service dollars. It did do more, in employment and training, in housing, and in criminal justice.

Employment. Employment and training programs for adults

with developmental disabilities were provided by sheltered work-shops and developmental centers. Founded in earlier decades, many of these workshops had grown to become the most visible programs for persons with disabilities in their local communities. Unfortunately, the ARC believed, such programs frequently presented a negative image of persons with disabilities as persons whose handicaps meant they needed our charity to survive. Facility names suggested that segregated institutions had been recreated in miniature: Northwest Center for the Retarded, New Hope, Exceptional Foresters, and even a name like Whitman County Epton Center. The accent was on enclosure and differentness and not on positive values like productivity.

The ARC decided to mail letters to every facility with a stigmatizing name, advising them of this fact, listing preferable alternative names, and offering further consultation on normalization theory. The letter attempted to avoid self-righteousness by noting that the "C" in "ARC" had once stood for children, now recognized as a demeaning term. The letter led to heated discussions among the governing boards at some facilities. Although the importance of the letter cannot be calculated directly, a number of facilities did change their names over the next several years.

The ARC was pleased with programs that confirmed some adults with severe disabilities could earn above minimum wages. One such success story was Seattle's Olympus Program, the first community replication of the specialized training program (STP) originated by Tom Bellamy at the University of Oregon. As a result of the project, a model was created for the necessary training. Workers with IQs below 40 were successfully trained to produce items needed by local industries. The program contracted with a number of industries, particularly those involved in the manufacture of electronics.

While adults with disabilities were gaining marketable skills if they were in good programs, the ARC began to identify a critical lack of preparation for employment in high school vocational programs. Thus, in 1984 ARC President Melba Grau asserted that young people were being relatively well served by special education programs because of strong gains in funding in the 1970s, but they faced the prospect of graduation with no particular place to go.

That was confirmed by excerpts from an article by Madeleine Will, Assistant Secretary of the federal Office of Special Education and Rehabilitative Services, that were reprinted in the *ARC News*. Will noted that while employment was an implied promise of the American school system, unemployment among youth with disabilities was high —from 50 to 80 percent of them were unemployed. Those youths who could not find jobs found long waiting lists for community services. Those who did find jobs were underpaid and were segregated from non-disabled workers. This problem of transition from school to work remains a priority of the ARC, although much progress has been made.

Supported Living

At the local level, ARC members assisted in the development of more normalized, higher quality housing in small group homes and apartments. At the state ARC level, a residential services policy statement was adopted which applied normalization ideas to concrete issues, for example, advocating privacy rights for the development of interpersonal intimacies. The opening sentences of the 1980 statement provided the general guidelines.

> Every person should be able to live in a comfortable setting which looks like, feels like, and is a valued home in the community. Each person should be enabled to choose where to live, with whom to live, and be enabled to control the conditions of his or her home environment. Every person should be enabled to individualize his or her home setting so that it truly becomes their own and provides a secure, stable haven within which to live and progress in their life goals.[303]

The ARC also lobbied for funding for progressive housing. For example, the ARC strongly backed funding for "tenant support," a program to assist renters. In the early 1980s the Department of Social and Health Services established funding for so-called tenant support projects. These were operated by local non-profit service providers such as the pioneering organizations founded in Yakima by Mary-Margaret Cornish and in Mount Vernon by John DeBlasio in 1980. Persons with mental disabilities lived in apartments or houses where they were assisted by live-in or drop-in aides. Assistance was gradually withdrawn as the tenants gained the experience necessary to become independent and responsible renters. A 1981 article on two developmentally disabled women living on their own—one of whom had spent 27 years in an institution—was given broad circulation by the ARC.

With more disabled persons moving into communities, the ARC recognized the need to educate persons with developmental disabilities on their legal rights and responsibilities in the area of housing. In cooperation with People First of Washington, the ARC used money from a "Law Day" fundraiser on May 1, 1982, to develop and publish a brochure which explained in simple language how to rent an apartment. Landlord and tenant rights and responsibilities were also outlined. A second brochure explained legal rights and responsibilities in the area of employment. The Disabilities Law Project of the University of Puget Sound School of Law provided the text for the two pamphlets.

Law and Justice: Offenders & Victims

The ARC's quest to secure fair treatment for persons with intellectual disabilities was now extended to the criminal justice system. In 1976 WARC formed a Law and Justice Committee and in December organized a meeting of various federal and state agencies to discuss whether there was a need for a comprehensive system for dealing with the relationship of offenders with disabilities and the criminal justice system. Not surprisingly, the agency representative said that it was already being adequately handled by the systems in place. In January 1977, WARC began a number of years of training police cadets at the Washington State Criminal Justice Training Commission.

Those facts and the material from a statewide survey were presented by a panel discussion at the WARC convention in August 1977. Tom Rolfs, president of the Mason County ARC, was an administrator at the Shelton Correctional Center. Rolfs was able to survey state prisons to determine the number of inmates with intellectual disabilities. The facts were startling (*ARC News*, August/September 1978):

> 77 retarded adults are locked up in Washington state prisons and work camps.
>
> Retarded persons who are locked up in jails and prisons are frequently victimized by other inmates—a retarded inmate at Walla Walla who resisted homosexual rape was murdered.
>
> Most prison officials do not know how to deal with retarded people, even though they would like to help.

Fortified by the survey results that confirmed its suspicions, the WARC Law and Justice Committee concentrated on getting all prisoners with developmental disabilities removed from victimizing situations to a more positive setting where they could be rehabilitated. The WARC board supported the concept of small regional correctional centers, with one specializing in offenders who had developmental disabilities.

On January 19, 1979, the WARC committee testified to the Human Resources Subcommittee of the House Appropriations Committee in favor of efforts to identify and transfer prisoners with disabilities to small specialized settings. It proposed coordinated actions by Corrections, the Division of Developmental Disabilities, and the Division of Mental Health. No specific budgetary item was proposed, but WARC did find sympathetic ears. The Law and Justice Committee also urged the Department of Corrections to make early work-release placements in secure group homes designed for disabled inmates. One such facility, Rap House, opened in Tacoma and lasted a few years. Another on Beacon Hill in Seattle ran into organizational problems before it opened and was abandoned.

In order to determine in a comprehensive manner how the community criminal justice system dealt with persons with mental retardation, an additional survey was undertaken. The Law and Justice Committee, in association with the Sociology Department of Saint Martin's College, obtained the consent of the Washington Association of Sheriffs and Chiefs of Police and the Washington Association of Prosecuting Attorneys. With their assistance, a three-page questionnaire was sent to every judge, police and sheriff department, prosecuting attorney, and public defender's office in the state. The survey revealed extensive experience with "mentally retarded" persons, especially among police departments. Estimates for the percentage of offenders with mental retardation ranged from 1-4%, representing 1,000-4,000 contacts per year by law enforcement agencies. The primary offenses involved were minor larcenies, trespassing, nuisances, and other non-violent crimes.

The primary needs identified by representatives of each type of agency were informational in nature: what program resources and alternatives to incarceration were available and what training was available for police officers. Hundreds of copies of a brochure summarizing the results, offering more information, and listing local contacts were mailed to all agencies. To address police officers' lack of knowledge about persons with mental retardation, the Law and Justice Committee began to provide pre-service and in-service training. A curriculum produced by the national ARC was used at the Washington State Criminal Justice Training Center in Lacey and at training sites in Seattle, Spokane, and Vancouver.

Officers were taught how to deal with disabled people as victims, offenders, and as citizens requesting services.

In November 1979, the ARC co-sponsored a Continuing Legal Education seminar on "The Rights of the Handicapped" with the ACLU. Held at Plymouth Congregational Church in Seattle, the symposium on criminal law was highlighted by a presentation from Miles Santamour of the President's Committee on Mental Retardation in Washington, D.C. He and the other speakers reviewed the law, current programs, and possible improvements. Bill Ehrlich from the WARC committee addressed ways in which police and attorneys could improve their ability to respond appropriately when faced with an offender with disabilities.

In 1980 the ARC also published and widely distributed a 100-page manual *How to Make the Law and Justice System Work for the Retarded Citizens of Washington State.*[304] The manual was intended to teach specialists in both criminal justice and mental retardation about the other field. A step-by-step description of the complexities of the adult and juvenile justice systems was provided for developmental disabilities specialists. More than a dozen past and present Washington state projects focused on offenders with mental retardation were described.[305]

Victims of Abuse

The ARC was also interested in addressing the problem of victims with intellectual disabilities. An examination of years of data from the state's confidential child abuse records revealed that sexual and physical abuse rates were much higher for persons who were listed as "mentally retarded."[306] The study demonstrated a special need for continuing to monitor teenagers and young adults for signs of abuse. Unlike other victims, the rates at which persons with mental retardation suffered abuse did not decline with age. The data on these increased risks was utilized by Seattle Rape Relief in obtaining funding for its nationally pioneering work with victims with disabilities.

Although the ARC's criminal justice efforts were worthwhile and accomplished some temporary improvements, it was clear to those involved that the problems of disabled offenders would continue. The people involved got lost in the intersection of two systems. Neither the developmental disabilities system nor the criminal justice system was set up to deal with the problem. Most of the Washington state projects were discontinued due to expiration of grants, changing federal and state priorities, and other factors.

Recently, some efforts have been revived, but the field remains a difficult one in which to make permanent gains.

Fighting Retrenchment and Moving Ahead

The election of President Reagan in the fall of 1980 was partly the result of and partly the cause of a conservative mood across the country. The President's call to cut human services was echoed in statehouses throughout America. In Washington, the 1981 legislative session was accurately predicted to be "the worst in recent memory for disabled persons." Budgetary cutbacks meant less money for support services in education; pupil-teacher ratios rose. Fewer dollars spelled fewer program hours in institutions and fewer monthly days of service at developmental centers. Cutbacks, inflation, and an increase in the number of persons needing services were expected to produce critical shortages in community residences within two years.

The Attack on P.L. 94-142. At the federal level, the Reagan administration proposed "block grants" in education and social services as a means to accomplish its goals. Block grants meant that federal funds for a wide variety of education and social services would come directly to the states without the specific rules that the federal government had adopted. In education, the ARC feared that such a move would result in special education funds being tossed in with other types of educational funds and distributed by state and local officials in such a manner that the substantial gains made for disabled persons over the past decade would be lost. The potential loss of the rules protecting children in P.L. 94-142, the Education for All Handicapped Children Act, caused real fear in the ARC. Parents would lose their guarantee of an individualized educational program for their children, their right to appeal what they considered an inappropriate placement, and other important procedures assured by P.L. 94-142.

In the June 1981 issue of *ARC News,* the proposed block grants were said to be creating "a desperate situation which requires persistent action from all of us who wish to prevent deterioration in the position of handicapped people." ARC members were urged to write their congressmen to preserve the rights and programs of disabled persons. In response to the Reagan administration's proposed budget cuts and block grant approach, the ARC and a coalition of other groups interested in developmental disabilities staged rallies on the steps of the nation's Capitol and in various states on May 7, 1981. In Washington, D.C., 4,000 disabled persons and their advocates assembled at an Independence Day for Disabled Persons to protest the Administration's plans. On the same day, the ARC of Washington and other groups held rallies on the street corners of federal buildings, and visited congressional offices in Seattle, Olympia, Spokane, Everett, and the Tri-Cities.

The rallies held across the nation, the letter-writing campaign by ARC members, and the effective lobbying of the ARC national Governmental Affairs Office were important factors in winning the fight with the Administration. P.L. 94-142, Vocational Rehabilitation, and Developmental Disabilities were taken out of the block grants.

In the fall of 1981 the ARC and its allies had reason to celebrate, but the celebration was short-lived, for the Administration made another vigorous effort to gut P.L. 94-142 by adopting new regulations. Again led by the national ARC Governmental Affairs Office, the state ARC worked hard to defeat the move, gaining the support of all but one member of the state's congressional delegation. The many hours of testifying at hearings and lobbying paid off when few of the proposed changes were adopted.

In 1982 the Administration also sought to reduce the effectiveness of Section 504 of the Rehabilitation Act of 1973. Two changes proposed by the Administration were of particular concern. According to the *ARC News*, June 1982:

> The special education protections would be largely withdrawn. These protections provide a back-up to those in P.L. 94-142.
>
> It is proposed to allow federal funding recipients to judge how productive a disabled person is likely to become before deciding whether they should make adjustments to allow the handicapped person to participate in the program. This change could effectively gut the whole section [504].

To commemorate the fifth anniversary of the Section 504 regulations and to show support for retaining Section 504 in its present form, June 3, 1982 was designated National 504 White Ribbon Day. Across the country disabled persons and organizations for disabled persons tied white ribbons on buildings and programs which were made accessible and available to people with disabilities over the past five years as a result of Section 504. Again the disabled community was largely successful in its fight with the Administration.

The Campaign for Senator Weicker

With the election of President Reagan in 1980, the Republicans took over the majority in the Senate. Coincidentally and fortunately for persons with intellectual disabilities, Senator Lowell Weicker (R, Connecticut) had recently had a son born with Down syndrome and had become interested in these issues. Since he was now in the majority party and was able to control these issues in committee, Weicker quickly proved to be the most powerful voice in the Congress protecting the integrity of the federal special education act, which everyone called simply "94-142." Weicker was up for re-election in 1982, and activists in the far-away ARC of Washington were determined to do what they could on his behalf to assist him in getting re-elected. They could do nothing officially on his behalf as the ARC or it might lose its tax-exempt status. But as individual Americans, they were moved to act – much as the founders of the CBL had been in the 1930s when they supported the election of the first president of the organization to the state senate.

A telephone consultation with his re-election staff dissuaded the activists from their original idea of forming a special political action committee (PAC), as the federal paperwork would prove to be too burdensome. Instead, the appeal was to "bundle" special contributions to Senator Weicker's own election organization "Weicker '82 Committee." The Arc activists would "bundle" the contributions they collected and mail them to Weicker's campaign.

With a little assistance from persons in the national ARC – who also had to be circumspect for IRS purposes –a number of national leaders were persuaded to join the appeal which listed those nationally prominent figures, along with eight Washington leaders. The national figures were Eleanor Elkin, Rosemary Dybwad, Gunnar Dybwad, Tom Nerney, Lou Brown, and Bob Perske.

The appeal proclaimed:

LET'S KEEP OUR STRONG ADVOCATE IN THE
U.S. SENATE. SUPPORT SENATOR LOWELL
WEICKER!
Dear Friends:
We owe Senator Lowell Weicker of Connecticut a
large debt. As much as any other Senator, he has led the
fight to preserve P.L. 94-142, the Education for All Handicapped Children Act. Without his powerful voice many
vital provisions of P.L. 94-142 would be gone today!

With recent court decisions and pending regulatory changes, we need his continuing leadership as chairman of the Senate Subcommittee on the Handicapped. We must not only hand onto what we have, but pass new legislation to regain what we thought we had won.

Now is the time to show our support. Senator Weicker needs our financial contributions for his tough re-election campaign this year.

The letter was mailed to identifiable disability leaders nationwide (over 100 to selected ARC officers) with a plea to copy it and pass it on to their friends. In the end, less than $25,000 was collected nationwide in this first ever national disability political fundraiser. But the Weicker staff member in charge of this effort stated that when he handed over the disability funds to Weicker, "frankly, it is the first time that I can remember that he was humbled. He really appreciated the efforts you made."

Baby Doe

Disability activists, including those in the ARC of Washington, applauded when Reagan used Section 504 of the Rehabilitation Act of 1973 to issue a controversial directive to hospitals on May 18, 1982. The "Baby Doe" case had attracted national attention in the spring of 1982. The parents and physicians of Baby Doe, an infant with Down syndrome, declined to operate to remove an obstruction so that food could be provided to the child. The infant later died. In response to the controversy surrounding the death of Baby Doe, the Administration issued a warning to hospitals that they may not "medically discriminate" by assisting parents in withholding treatment which would be provided to non-handicapped persons. Although the ARC nationally has no position on abortion, the association does assert that all children have a right to good medical treatment once they are born. The action taken by the Administration was commended by the ARC.

A compromise version of the Child Abuse Amendments of 1984, which contained Baby Doe protections, was adopted by the House and Senate in mid-September after several months' delay. The ARC/US as well as many medical organizations, pro-life groups, and disabilities rights advocates supported the compromise bill. The measure was signed into law by President Reagan at the Oval Office. Dee Everitt, ARC/US President, was among only three "public" guests invited to witness the signing of the bill. Her attendance at the White House ceremony signified the ARC's major role in the bill's passage.

Federal Funds for the Community: Waivers

In November 1982, the ARC of Washington held a workshop on families of persons with developmental disabilities.[307] The topics discussed included foster care, respite care, adoptions, and new community options. The new community options resulted from a 1981 change in Title XIX (Medicaid) of the Social Security Act. The change symbolized by the Katie Beckett case. Katie was an ill Iowa child who had been hospitalized. Her parents had average income, and thus were not eligible for Medicaid-funded community services, which were restricted to the poor. Katie's very expensive care was covered during her hospital stay, however, as is institutional care for persons with mental disabilities. President Reagan instructed the Secretary of Health and Human Services to "cut through the government's red tape" and allow Katie to go home and still receive home health services under Title XIX.

The Reagan Administration also drafted guidelines under which states would be allowed to submit requests called "Medicaid waivers" which would no longer consider parental income for institutionalized or hospitalized children and "waive" the requirement that the services be provided in a hospital or institution. The ARC considered this change to be one of the few good items for disabled persons enacted that year, but one that would become basic to the service system nationwide. The federal Omnibus Budget Reconciliation Act of 1981 (P.L. 97-35) gave states the option of providing community-based care by using Medicaid funds. Under the new Act, a special waiver became available to states for the following long-term care services, provided the total costs did not exceed the projected costs of maintaining current institutional programs:[308]

> Case management services
> Homemaker services
> Home health aide services
> Personal care services
> Adult day health services
> Habilitation services
> Respite care services
> Other services the state requests and the federal government approves, such as nursing care, medical equipment and supplies, physical and occupational ther-

237

apy, speech pathology and audiology.

Working with other advocates, the ARC convinced the State of Washington that the waiver would benefit persons with mental retardation and would also be a fiscally sound move. The first family to make use of the Medicaid waiver to create new community options was the Sue and Robert Scott family of Bellevue who were enabled to bring their teenage daughter home from Frances Haddon Morgan Center for Autistic Children. The family received extensive in-home support services on a permanent basis.

The Money Follows the Person in 1983

Although the concept has only recently and occasionally been enacted into federal statute, "the money follows the person" is now a popular theme in disability services. It means that the recipient of the services, individual or family, can autonomously decide how the support funds that are available will be used, not the public agency. In Washington, the ARC lobbied through such a statute in 1983.

The Program Options Act was an outcome of the 1982 Family Support Conference. A major accomplishment of the ARC of Washington in 1983, Program Options would be analogous to a Medicaid waiver for state-funded developmental disability services. House Bill 187, sponsored by Mike Kreidler (D-Olympia), received broad bipartisan support since it promised less expensive, but more appropriate, services.[309] The new law required that parents, guardians, and adults with developmental disabilities be notified annually of their right to propose any alternative system of services to meet their needs. The service would be support the person needed. The only restriction was that the proposed new program must not exceed the cost of currently utilized services.

The Program Options Act gave families the power to choose such individualized services as the following suggested in the *ARC News* of September 1983:

> A disabled adult attending a sheltered workshop could apply for tuition to attend a training program at a local community college or private business college.
> A severely mentally retarded person in a nursing home might move to an apartment with an in-home aide, and be transported to a day-training program.
> A resident of Rainier School might move to the community and be provided with the extensive behavioral

training program needed to make the placement work.

A child with nursing care needs might be able to come home to his or her family and receive the support needed there.

The parents of a handicapped child in an early childhood developmental center might be granted funds to place their child in an integrated regular day-care program instead.

A sheltered workshop might decide to place an extended sheltered employment client in an integrated work setting in industry, provide the employer with a subsidy, and be paid for follow-along monitoring of the case.

An overview of the newly enacted Program Options Act was presented at the 1983 ARC convention. Parents and service providers were told what the act would mean to them. "The Program Options Act: New Powers and Possibilities for Disabled Persons and Their Families" focused on the potential for substantial changes in the system of services provided to all people with developmental disabilities in Washington state. But all this depended on the continuing availability of the Medicaid waiver and other federal funding for community services. New legislation was needed before anyone could rest assured that these favorable innovations would remain guaranteed.

Attempted Medicaid Reform

In 1984, an historic bill was introduced in Congress by Senator John Chafee (R, RI). The Community and Family Living Amendments (CFLA) proposed to phase out federal Medicaid funding for institutions and transfer the savings to community services. Services included were respite care, habilitation, adaptive devices, personal attendant care, counseling, adult day services and a variety of other services needed to build a strong community services system.

Advocates called CFLA the most important legislation of the 1980's. Besides the ARC, Senate Bill 2053 was supported by TASH, the National Society for Autistic Children and Adults, the National Network of Parent Coalitions Representing Children with Disabilities, and People First International. A lobbying group, Washingtonians for Community Services, was organized by the ARC to promote support for S. 2053 in Washington state. Hearings were conducted during the summer of 1984, and S. 2053 gained supporters across the country.

239

It also gained opponents. Institutional parents groups mobilized to help stall the bill for the remainder of the Congressional session. As in the case of opposition to WARC's deinstitutionalization suit, it was easy to organize fearful older parents around the threat of institutional closures. Senator Chafee's office reported to the ARC of Washington that more letters in opposition were received from Washington than from any other state in the nation. Such a distinction testifies to the strength of WARC in the old days, strength unfortunately transferred to institutional groups now that the ARC was solidly pro-community.

Senator Chafee reintroduced CFLA in the next Congress (S. 873) with a modification providing that while Medicaid dollars for institutional facilities would be phased down, they would not be entirely withdrawn. In Washington, 25-33% of the current number of institutional residents could still receive Medicaid funding in institutions even after the year 2000, when the institutional phase-down would be fully in effect. A companion bill was introduced in the House by Rep. Florio (D-NJ). Although the ARC in Washington continued to work hard and although more support was obtained in Congress for the revised bill, it was not enough.

More Residential Options

Two new residential options were developed in Washington in the mid-1980s, both as part of the deinstitutionalization movement. State Operated Residential Alternatives (SOLAs) were developed by DDD which sought an alternative to ease the fears about deinstitutionalization held by many family members of institutional residents. One of their stated fears was the rapid turn-over of staff in many private community residences, due in part to the low wages paid. To address that fear, SOLAs are staffed by state employees, who are unionized, better paid, and have low turnover. This program even meant that in some cases a case worker could promise the family, "Your sister can move to a SOLA near you in Seattle and bring along Mary, the same DDD staff member who she and you have grown attached to over the past decade." Although they survive, SOLAs have not won over the opposition of many families tied to institutions, and so they have only been a small feature on the broad landscape of residential options. By virtue of their relatively small size and in acknowledgment that they were an attempt to deinstitutionalize persons, SOLAs did not attract the opposition from the ARC or other advocates like the "mini-institutions" — State Residential Training Centers —had in the 1970s.

Intensive Tenant Support, by contrast, was enthusiastically accepted by the ARC as a model for former residents of institutions.[310] Part of a broader movement discussed above called "tenant support" (now called "supported living"), it rejected the "continuum of services" model that had been the dominant model of the 1960s and 1970s. Really it was an idea that went back to the beginning of family advocacy in the 1930s. As some superintendents and others then proclaimed, while an institution would be the permanent residence of persons with the most severe disabilities, it would not be for those with lesser disabilities, who, with training that only the institution was designed to supply, would "graduate" and return to the community. But by the middle of 1980s the flaw in the concept had been identified. The model would deny persons with the most severe disabilities the right to ever live in the most valued settings, that is, in single family apartments or homes (or a close facsimile) in a regular neighborhood. The more severe the intellectual disability, the less a person can generalize from one setting to another; just because they have learned how to use appliances in one setting does not mean that they can carry those skills to a new, more normalized setting with different appliances. Under the Intensive Tenant Support program, persons would be placed from an institution right into an apartment and supplied 24-hour support as long as that proved necessary. Rather than the resident moving, the support program would change over time, hopefully requiring less staff time as the residents became comfortable taking over more of the day-to-day tasks.

Following National's Lead on a Medical Cure

When the ARC of Washington formed its Research Trust Fund in 1950, a "cure" for mental deficiency was one of its goals, not just prevention and treatment.[311] But that was a time of medical optimism due to the success of several vaccines and other medical discoveries. The intervening years showed how resistant brain damage was to treatment. Just as the national ARC's leadership on Medicaid waivers led to Washington's Program Options Act and other local efforts, once the national ARC began to talk of cures again, so did Washington state.

After thirty years, the national ARC revived the goal for medical cures of the various types of cognitive disabilities, organizing a 1980 conference titled "Mental Retardation: The Search for Cures." The conference was followed up with a campaign that lasted for the next few years. ARC members in Washington state joined the

241

national effort by speaking to the state and county ARC meetings, presenting and narrating a "slide show" from ARC National. But once again, ARC hopes were dashed, as the Search for Cures project was shelved after several years with no breakthroughs.

The Organizational Evolution of the ARC

The 1980s were not only a difficult time to make legislative progress; they were a difficult time for the ARC as an organization. Unemployment and high interest rates were national problems that affected Washington state. The ARC faced increased competition for funds as many previously publicly funded organizations turned to the private sector for financial support. The public, feeling the financial pinch, contributed less to organizations such as the ARC. Decreased fundraising and membership at both the national and state levels affected the strength of ARC.

As recently as the 1979 legislative session, the ARC had a major legislative presence. Timothy O'Sullivan had been hired as the ARC's first full-time lobbyist ("Administrative Assistant") before and during the session. Along with Executive Director Stan Baxter, Tim also had a hand in coordinating volunteer testimony and in the establishment of the first ARC Legislative Hotline, to which members could call for information on the approximately 100 bills covered. All ARC testimony was checked for consistency with established ARC policy and, lacking a policy, with President Lou Day or the Executive Committee.

But two years later, Executive Director Stan Baxter resigned his position to become director the Pierce County ARC in Tacoma which, unlike the state ARC, was in strong financial shape due to proceeds from a bingo operation. Because of the financial difficulties of the state ARC, it was not until 1983 that Judith A. Devine was hired as his replacement. Continuing financial problems led to a decade without an Executive Director beginning in 1986. Bean Driscoll, the state ARC secretary, provided office continuity throughout the period.

During some of the time that the state ARC was without an executive director, two "legislative consultants" were hired to assist the ARC's volunteer efforts in the capital. The first was Barbara Vanderkolk and the second was Michael Doctor, who took over beginning with the 1995 session. Each was a professional lobbyist with multiple clients. The contract for the lobbyist services totaled $9,000 in 1991. By 1996, the legislative consultant was being paid $17,500, which included preparatory work between sessions.

There were some financial successes in the 1980s. In 1980 the ARC purchased a house in Olympia and converted it to an office for the state organization. After thirty years of paying rent, the ARC began to accumulate equity. As noted earlier, the ARC was able to re-affiliate with ARC/US in 1979, although a past due debt to the national of $44,000 lingered for some time. Fortunately, the ARC/US revamped its system of assessing state and local units their financial obligations to the national organization. In a coordinated move, the ARC in Washington revised its assessments on local units. Both changes substantially decreased the financial obligations due from local to the state and from state to national, which had been weighing so heavily on the organization.

Decreased support from local units, however, demanded increased fundraising at the state level. New fundraising was a necessity, because the state ARC bingo operation in Tacoma collapsed in 1985 under competition from new unregulated Indian operations. The state ARC held its own "casino nights," benefit concerts and rodeos, and other events. The ARC's most distinctive fundraiser was the Mountain Trek, a pledge-raising "thon" for backpackers in the Cascade and Olympic mountain ranges. Begun by Stan Baxter and Murray Anderson in 1977, and later bossed by Steve Olson, the Treks continued for seven years.

Part of the weakness of the organization since 1980 was   due to the withdrawal that year of the ARC in King county, which held the Seattle metropolitan area, a third of the state's population and more of its wealth. The ARC decided that it could not continue to allow this omission to continue and began to do direct-marketing through telephone solicitors based in Seattle.

Letters from the national and state ARCs told the King county leaders that they could not use the ARC name. King county had changed its name to "Advocates for Retarded Citizens" when it disaffiliated and in 1986 changed it further to "Advocates, Resources, Counseling for Persons with Developmental Disabilities in King County." But it still referred to itself as the "ARC of King County," a name to which the state and national ARCs objected.

At the time, the national ARC had a nationwide contract to provide employment and training assistance, and it had an office in Seattle. In June 1988, the regional director wrote to the state ARC encouraging the formation of a new, replacement ARC in King County. The author, a Seattle resident, held two initial organizing meetings over the summer. In September, an attorney for "Advocates, Resources and Counseling" wrote two letters threatening legal action if the state ARC's telephone solicitors in Seattle did not immediately cease referring to themselves as "the ARC." On September 15, 1988, a summons, complaint, and temporary restraining order were delivered in the matter of

> Advocates, Resources, Counseling for Persons with Developmental Disabilities in King County, d/b/a ARC of King County, Plaintiff
>
> vs.
>
> Larry A. Jones, an individual, John Does I Through X and Jane Does I Through X doing business as ARC-King County, Defendants.[312]

The lawsuit named the regional NARC Employment program office as the site of the defendants. The crisis had a good outcome. It brought the parties together in mediation sessions in which an agreement was reached to have the county organization re-affiliate with the state and national ARCs under the decreased affiliation fees then imposed. Telephone solicitation operations were moved out of county.

Thrift Stores

The most financially profitable operation for the ARC came to be telephone solicitation of used goods. The sale of used goods at thrift shops operated by various charities is widespread across the country. But in this case, the ARC merely used its solicitors to telephone potential donors and send out its trucks to pick up the donations. The goods were in turn sold to a profit-making retailer, Value Village, a relationship that still has lasted since 1989. Originally one operation centered in Bellingham. After a few years a second Southwest Washington operation was established. Together the solicitation efforts continue to provide as an important component of the Arc's revenue. In 1989, Value Village profits were half of the state ARC's total budget of $99,233. (The fraction of revenues from memberships and the local Arc support had declined to 20%.)

By 1995-96, thrift store revenues provided 90% of the much larger $511,504 state Arc budget. And, in a bonus that surprised many disability activists, it often turned out that the public knew the Arc as a disability organization from its trucks and phone calls, rather than from the rest of its efforts.

Other Organizations and Alliances

As de Tocqueville noted, Americans are always forming associations and, partly because of a period of weakness in the Arc, new organizations were formed. In 1984, two linked organizations were founded, the Washington Assembly for Citizens with Disabilities and the Disabilities Research and Information Coalition. Led by Steve Schain, former director of the Developmental Disabilities Planning Council, the Assembly was designed as the political center for lobbying the legislature by the entire community of persons with disabilities.[313] Persons with sensory and physical disabilities joined with those in the developmental disabilities community with the hope of increased clout.[314] Because the Assembly was designed as a political instrument, it was not a 501(c) (3) public charity and was ineligible to receive government grants. The Disabilities Research and Information Coalition (D-ric or the Coalition) was formed for this purpose. For a few years, the Assembly was the largest and loudest center of advocacy, hosting well-attended conferences and heading up effective lobbying efforts. But although the two organizations lasted into the new century and the Assembly did some important lobbying, mostly the tutelage of legislators led by its president Mary Jo Wilcox, its strength declined.[315]

CHAPTER EIGHT:
THE NINETIES

The Nineties: a decade in which The Arc of Washington had become part of a progressive national consensus on what needed to be done to support, protect, and advocate for persons with cognitive disabilities. Sometimes playing a leadership role, the Arc was no longer acting alone. It was now often led by the ideas and experiences of its progeny and allies. It was a time in which there were often national trends that Washington State reflected and national efforts in which Washington joined.

Full Blossoming of Self-Advocacy

It is not typical for parents to continue to speak for their sons and daughters after they have become adults. Such a situation suggests that the parents do not trust their children to be able to choose or to find their own way in the world. Consequently, when a group of newly-labeled "self-advocates" with developmental disabilities sprung up in the neighboring state of Oregon, the Arc of Washington was quick to respond positively. In 1977 the Arc provided funding for Washington members to attend Oregon's People First Conference. By 1978 there were several chapters in Washington and Washington People First was looking forward to its first state convention. The Arc of Pierce County added a People First repre-

246

sentative to its board of directors and persuaded the state Arc to follow suit.

In the 1980s and 1990s self-advocates were added to the boards of many disability organizations. In the 1980s the Arc also began a tradition of picking up the costs of self-advocates who attended the annual Arc national federal legislative forum in Washington, D.C. Usually multiple self-advocates attended, some sponsored by the state Arc and others by various county Arcs. For example, 15 self-advocates from Washington state attended the 1995 national Arc forum. Self-advocates have proved important in lobbying the state's senators and representatives, and so the funds have been found to maintain that presence.

The Parent Coalitions

As noted earlier, Washington state has a mixed system of developmental disability services, meaning that the state offers or contracts for certain types of services (e.g., supported housing services) and the counties offer others (such as employment supports and some pre-school services). One component of that mixed system is that Washington not only has a state Developmental Disabilities Council made up of citizens who offer advice to the Governor and the executive branch of state government, but "county DD boards" made up of citizens who can advise their respective local governments.

In the 1980s, Ray Jensen was the director of the King County Developmental Disabilities Division and a supporter of the development of the statewide Coalition of County Boards. Jensen had the idea to form a Parent Coalition in King county to support each other with information and ideally find their way to the capitol to lobby. In 1990 Jensen hired Margaret-Lee Thompson to organize parent advocacy in the county, which she did promptly and effectively beyond all expectations. As the decade wore on, Parent Coalitions were formed in Clark, Pierce, Snohomish, and other counties with financial and other support of their respective county DD boards. In 1994 Thompson and the Parent Coalition came under the auspices of the Arc of King County where it has continued to flourish. Each November, it holds a Legislative Night which now boasts the regular attendance of dozens of state legislators, plus staff from the county's Congressional delegation. Throughout the legislative session, bills are monitored and volunteers mobilized to go to Olympia and testify. Some other Parent Coalitions are part of their respective county Arcs, while others are independent organizations. All of them are supported by funds from their respective counties.

President Harkin?

In 1992 the volunteer leaders of the Arc of Washington were faced with the question of whether they should again get directly involved in national politics, as they had for Senator Weicker a decade earlier. Senator Tom Harkin, D-Iowa, announced that he was running for President. More than any other presidential candidate before or since, Harkin made direct efforts to address the community of persons with disabilities and their families. He kept his promises, making attention to disability issues one of his hallmarks. To this day he continues that commitment and has many friends in the Arc.

But the voice of reason prevailed over emotion. Arc leaders in Seattle judged that Harkin had no reasonable chance of winning even his party's nomination. When the campaign came to Washington, it drew only nominal attention from the disability community.

Washington Voters for Disability Issues

The Arc of Washington leaders did want to get involved in political campaigns, just not those with poor prospects. Because the Arc would lose its tax exemption if it became involved in partisan politics, a separate organization was needed for the Arc activists to get involved. In 1992 a new organization called Washington Voters for Disability Issues was formed in which Arc activists joined with advocates with other disabilities to meet and raise funds for politicians who were sympathetic. However, the WVDI had to register with the Washington State Public Disclosure Commission and conform to its rules and regulations, which was somewhat burdensome. After two election cycles the WVDI was discontinued.

However, in 1997 disability advocates did put together fund-raising events for State Senator Adam Kline (D-Seattle), who was running for re-election to the state senate. Kline had proven himself a loyal and hard-working leader on disability issues and appreciated the support. The Arc leaders held a reception for him in a downtown law firm office. It raised a predictably modest amount, but adequately demonstrated the special appreciation that the disability community had for his work.

In 2004 King county Arc activists held a candidate's night and fund-raiser specifically supporting the re-election of powerful long-term Rep. Helen Sommers (D-Seattle), who was especially valued for her willingness to close Fircrest School in spite of union pressure on Democratic legislators.

Abolishing the Death Penalty

In *Penry v. Lynaugh*, 492 U.S.302 (1989), the United States Supreme Court ruled that applying the death penalty for persons with mental retardation was not barred by the constitutional ban on cruel and unusual punishment. In part, the decision said that "The prohibition against cruel and unusual punishments...recognizes the evolving standards of decency that mark the progress of a maturing society." But the court said, "In our view, the two state statutes prohibiting execution of the mentally retarded, even when added to the 14 States that have rejected capital punishment completely, do not provide sufficient evidence at present of a national consensus."

Advocates across the country took that sentence as a call to action. It was incumbent upon them to enact a ban in each state legislature where they could. Washington state was one of earliest to do. In 1992, the ARC met with the American Civil Liberties Union to strategize how to approach writing a bill. State Senator Marguerite Prentice was persuaded to be the prime sponsor of Senate Bill 6525, which in an amended form was enacted as Laws of 1993, Chap. 479 §1; RCW 10.95.030. The testimony of the ARC and the ACLU was supplemented by the testimony of Wendy Marlowe, a psychologist who testified on the reliability of intelligence testing for the Washington State Psychological Association. That, together with the testimony by author for the Arc and as president of the Washington State chapter of the American Association on Mental Retardation, seemed to relieve the worries of many legislators, who were concerned that enacting the bill might constitute a slippery slope that would suggest they opposed the death penalty across the board. The Washington State Catholic Conference was active in supporting the bill, as was the Lutheran Public Policy Office.

The opposition came only from the Washington Association of Prosecuting Attorneys. They argued that there were already sufficient protections to prevent such persons from being executed and that the bill was really just a stalking horse in the campaign to prohibit the death penalty altogether. The bill passed the House 70-28 and the Senate 38-3.

Ten years later that work paid off. On June 20, 2002, the Supreme Court issued a landmark ruling ending the execution of those with mental retardation. In *Atkins v. Virginia*, 536 U.S. 304 (2002) the Court held that it is a violation of the Eighth Amendment ban on cruel unusual punishment to execute death row inmates with mental retardation. The decision reflects the national consensus which has formed on this issue. Sixteen additional states had enacted such legislation, or roughly half of the 34 states who did not bar execution at the time of the first decision in *Penry*.

Moving to Close Institutions

In February 1993, the Arc testified before the House Human Services Committee in favor of HB 1552. The Arc and its allies had obtained sponsors of the legislation from committee members. The bill would have made it state policy for services for persons with developmental disabilities should be provided in the most normal, least restrictive, setting. Residents of Residential Habilitation Centers (RHCs) who were to be transferred to community settings could appeal the department's decision to transfer them, but their limited right to appeal would have been governed by the Administrative Procedures Act, chapter 34.05 RCW. The secretary of the Department of Social and Health Services would have been authorized to close RHCs if it is cost-effective to do so. As amended, it passed the House 66-31, but failed to pass the Senate, where state-employee labor unions were able to stop it.

Interlake School Closes. In 1994, Interlake School, an institution for children with medically fragile or severe disabilities, was closed. It was located on the grounds of Lakeland Village near Spokane, but operated as a separate facility. It was closed by DDD with the expected support of the Arc and all other advocates except the institutional parents' groups. The children were not simply transferred to other institutions, but provided enhanced funding for a life in the family home or another family-size community setting. Interlake remains the only DDD institution that has been closed.

Reaffirming Inclusion. Because of the continuing opposition by outsiders, the Arc felt a need to have its anti-institutional views reaffirmed as a Position Statement adopted at the annual membership meeting on September 1995. Titled "Where People Live," it emphasized the rights of persons to live in regular homes with their families or on their own with supports if they desire, and it declared that "large congregate facilities (institutions) are no longer appropriate for anyone, regardless of the type or severity of their disabilities."

Renewed Executive Leadership

In 1995 Sue Elliott, former head of the Washington state Division of Developmental Disabilities, was hired as the Arc's executive director. Seldom has the Arc made as brilliant a move. Elliott wanted a position where she could be a strong advocate and the long-vacant Arc position was a place where her talents could be used. In judging her impact (and taking nothing away from the skills and commitment of the intervening directors), no executive since Leo Lippman in the early years has been as effective in building the Arc and improving the lives of persons with intellectual disabilities in Washington state.

Because of her prior experience as a leading state official, Elliott understood how legislation got supported and gained a real chance at passage. As a result, the Arc got many of its initiatives enacted. Success bred success, and more advocates came to Olympia each following legislative session to be a part of a winning team.

Not only did Elliott's leadership make the Arc more successful in passing legislation, the breadth of legislative coverage reached a new peak. Janet Adams had begun working in the advocacy efforts for the Assembly in 1992. In that role she attempted to analyze and summarize all bills of interest to the disability community. When Sue Elliott became Arc Executive Director in 1995, she was able to recruit Janet to continue with her work, based at the Arc and mostly funded by the Developmental Disabilities Council.[316]

Beginning in the 1990s, technological innovations made it possible to send out electronic legislative action alerts to Arc members who signed up to be notified. Members may then immediately send email messages to their senators and representatives on the issues of interest, pro or con, as recommended by the Arc.

Elliott brought critical management experience, contacts and grant-writing skills to the organization. Over her next decade she attracted skilled staff members who raised the bar on what the Arc could accomplish. Under her leadership, advocacy grants were received from the state Superintendent of Public Instruction, the Developmental Disabilities Council, and the Division of Developmental Disabilities. Grant funding came to represent a third of the Arc's budget, although the Arc remained highly dependent upon fundraising activities. By 2008 only one percent of the state Arc's budget was derived from membership dues and assessments on local chapters. This made it much easier for local groups to stay in the state organization.

People First v. Rainier State School

The new prominence of persons with developmental disabilities and their own leadership abilities was manifest in Washington's second deinstitutionalization lawsuit filed in 1996 under the name *People First v. Rainier State School.* Whereas the first lawsuit had been filed as *WARC v. Thomas*, this one, filed under the Americans with Disabilities Act, had the self-advocates' organization People First as the lead plaintiff. Washington Protection and Advocacy supplied the attorneys for People First. The Arc of Washington was another litigant, happy to be superseded by People First. Filed in the U. S. District Court for Western Washington, the case was assigned to Judge Franklin Burgess. Unfortunately, the substantive issues were never addressed, because a year later, after institutional parents groups had appeared in opposition, Judge Burgess refused to certify a class. He concluded that People First could not serve as the symbolic representative of the class of persons at Rainier, because there was too much diversity in the population of persons with developmental disabilities who they claimed to represent. The court's decision was at odds with almost every deinstitutionalization lawsuit filed across the nation, which is perhaps testimony to the continued strength of institutional parents groups in Washington compared to other states.

The denial of certification meant that a successful lawsuit would only affect the rights of the several individual plaintiffs who wished to move from Rainier to the community. The efforts and expenses that would be involved were no longer justified and in 1998 the lawsuit was settled with community placement for the remaining individual plaintiffs.

Olmstead: Defending the Promise of the ADA

In 1998 the Arc learned that the U. S. Supreme Court had decided to review the circuit court's ruling in *Olmstead.* In that case, the State of Georgia argued that it should not be required by the Americans with Disabilities Act to expend the funds necessary to provide community placements for two women with both intellectual disabilities and mental illness. The state's own experts stated that the women could be appropriately released from the state psychiatric hospital to the community. So the issue of whether deinstitutionalization was required for some or all persons with disabilities was not necessarily before the court – unless it chose to make it so. Advocates for persons with developmental disabilities were worried that the Supreme Court, with its new conservative majority, would take away the very heart of the legislative achievements that advocates had struggled for over the decades. Alarm bells were clanking across the country.

In Washington state, advocates were even more dismayed (not to say outraged) to find that the state, through the action of Attorney General Christine Gregoire, had already signed Washington's name to an amicus brief filed in support of the state of Georgia by the National Governors Association! Quickly, the Arc and other advocates asked for a meeting with her. At the meeting, Governor Gary Locke, a notable ally for persons with developmental disabilities, dropped by. It quickly became clear that Gregoire wanted to support the state's authority to resist federal requirements and mandates. This assertion of "state's rights," which naturally appeals to governors and state elected officials, had once been anathema as the defense offered by white Southerners resisting demands for racial integration and equality. However, time had passed since then, and with a new more conservative federal executive branch and judiciary, moderates and liberals felt free to make the case. But on Gregoire's assertions of state's rights, the Arc answered that this was not the proper context in which to make such claims. The Arc suggested that this was a matter of basic civil rights, strenuously fought for over long years.

In a letter dated March 9, 1999, and directed to George Walker, chair of the official Developmental Disabilities Council, the Attorney General said in part,

> After careful consideration, we have decided to withdraw our state from the amicus brief. This has been a difficult decision as we have struggled to determine how to best fulfill our responsibility to protect the legal interests of the state and its citizens. What we have come to understand is the great symbolic importance many persons with disabilities place on this case. Our signature on this amicus was not intended to convey a message that the state is changing its direction toward providing broader choices and eliminating barriers for persons with disabilities. To the contrary, over the past few years the state has moved toward increased opportunities for community-based services for the disabled while seeking to preserve the option of quality residential care.
>
> The Governor and I have each affirmed our strong support for better services and choices for persons with

disabilities. We do not want our signature on this amicus brief to call that commitment into doubt and create unnecessary fear and anxiety.

The *Seattle Times* (March 10, 1999) reported the reversal as well:

State Pulls Out of Suit Challenging Disability Law

OLYMPIA - Bowing to pressure from the disabled community, state Attorney General Christine Gregoire has withdrawn Washington's support for a lawsuit, now before the U.S. Supreme Court, that advocates for the disabled fear might undermine the federal law intended to protect them from discrimination.

Gregoire sent a letter to advocates yesterday announcing the reversal. Gov. Gary Locke also supports the shift.

Gregoire's office last month filed a friend-of-the-court brief supporting the state of Georgia's challenge to the Americans with Disabilities Act. Georgia contends the act usurps a state's authority to decide how to distribute already limited resources to pay for the needs of disabled people.

"Our signature on this (brief) was not intended to convey a message that the state is changing its direction toward providing broader choices and eliminating barriers for persons with disabilities," Gregoire said in the letter.

Disabled community members and representatives from the American Civil Liberties Union barraged state offices with letters and phone calls, and then met with Gregoire and Locke to encourage the reversal.

"We came to understand the symbolic importance many disabled people have on this case," said Narda Pierce, solicitor general for Gregoire's office.

Pierce had authorized the friend-of-the-court brief and worked closely with the state's Department of Social and Health Services in determining that Washington should lend its support.

The state supported only a section of Georgia's case that challenges federal regulations the state considers unfunded federal mandates. Pierce had said her concern was that federal regulations are "taking the policy choices away from state legislators on how to serve the disabled community as a whole."

Advocates for the disabled said they were excited about the state's reversal.

"I understand the legal reasons for the brief," said state Sen. Darlene Fairley, D-Lake Forest Park, who uses crutches and lobbied heavily for the state to remove its name from the brief. "But when it comes to civil rights of any group of people, I think that's where there are more important reasons to consider."

Advocates were working not only in Washington state. Seventeen states that had previously signed on the amicus in support of Georgia were persuaded by advocates for persons with disabilities to remove their signatures. One wonders when, if ever, so many states have reversed their positions on an amicus brief to the U.S. Supreme Court. It certainly was a testimony to how important advocates thought the decision could be.

On June 22, 1999, the "Supreme Court Upholds ADA 'Integration Mandate' in Olmstead decision," as the AP headline put it. But though celebrated nationwide as a victory for persons with disabilities, and though it certainly was not as bad as some feared, was it really a victory? Ten years later, the decision[317] and its evaluation are still unclear. On the one hand, the court did uphold the symbolically central meaning of the ADA to Arc advocates, namely, the integration imperative as formulated and promulgated by the Department of Justice. It requires public agencies to provide services "in the most integrated setting appropriate to the needs of qualified individuals with disabilities." That certainly relieved many advocates. On the other hand, the court rejected the formulation of the both the district and the appellate court below and reduced the potential fiscal demands placed on the states. Writing for the court, Justice Ginsburg said that if the state demonstrates that it has a "comprehensive, effectively working plan for placing qualified persons with mental disabilities in less restrictive settings, and a waiting list that move[s] at a reasonable pace not controlled by the State's endeavors to keep its institutions fully populated," the state cannot be required to do more by way of deinstitutionalization.

Lawyers for persons with disabilities soon concluded that the decision effectively granted the states five years of inactivity. Any deinstitutionalization lawsuit would be dismissed by a federal court on the state's motion that it had to have a little more time to implement a plan that would meet the requirements of *Olmstead*. Over a decade later, it is only in the past year that the pace of Justice Department action to promote deinstitutionalization of persons with intellectual disabilities has picked up steam.

255

The same slow pace, but even worse, is true in Washington state. This was a disappointment to many. Washington is the only state in the nation where you are more likely to leave the institutions in a pine box than you are to be placed in the community.[318] Among its Pacific Northwest neighbor states, Washington has been the slowest to deinstitutionalize. In 1967 the number of Americans, and Washingtonians, with intellectual and developmental disabilities who were living in institutions reached its highest total ever. After an early lead, Washington state has fallen behind the nation in deinstitutionalizing. Washington has by far the highest percentage of segregated persons in the Pacific Northwest – 13 times as many as Oregon. Oregon has found community placements for 99% of its residents. Alaska no longer has any persons in state institutions. But forty years after its peak, Washington still has a quarter of that number in large, segregated settings—951 people, or 1.5 persons for every 10,000 state residents.[319]

Why is Washington among the slower states to deinstitutionalize? Various answers are commonly heard among advocates. First, and most powerful, is that Washington is a strongly unionized state, at least in its public sector, and it is state employees' jobs and their union dues that are at risk when state institutions are closed. The public employee unions are solidly Democratic. Thus, Arc leaders and others generally find Democrats more supportive of spending on human services and are more likely to see them as allies. But they find themselves getting a more sympathetic ear from Republicans for efforts to deinstitutionalize. Second, in an ironic twist to the Arc's early achievements in Washington state, some suggest that the polished political skills of institutional advocates honed inside the Arc in its glory years of the 1950s and 1960s aided the aging cohort advocates in mobilizing allies and erecting roadblocks against moves to deinstitutionalize in the 1970s and 1980s and these alliances and roadblocks remain today.[320] Another potential ironic answer, but one shared with other states and one which is thus better at explaining the persistence of institutions in every state, is that the institutional groups have only one, simple object of their attention each legislative session, namely, maintaining the institution as it is. By contrast, the Arc has at a *minimum* of three dozen bills demanding its attention in any given session, including issues as diverse as pre-schools, aversive techniques in public schools, "respectful language" in referring to persons with disabilities, establishing a "disability month" for public school students to celebrate, funding for job coaches, supported housing, etc. But slowly the average age of institutional residents increases and eventually the process will be completed by the deaths of some fraction sufficient to move the legislature to act.

Supported Employment after High School

In the past decade one of the proudest achievements of advocates, and indeed one of the few areas in which Washington has been praised in national surveys compared to other states, has been supported employment for young adults with developmental disabilities who have left high school. In the Seattle metropolitan area it is claimed that those workers, supported by job coaches, are averaging over $1000 per month.[321] Although these are still wages in the poverty level, they are many times greater than what such workers had earned in sheltered workshops just 20 years earlier.

Gary Locke, currently Secretary of Commerce under President Obama, played an important role in committing the state to try to support employment for every student with disabilities who could work. First elected to the Washington state legislature in 1982, he became chair of the House Appropriations Committee, where he first became a clear advocate of supported employment. In 1990 Margaret-Lee Thompson and Ray Jensen met with Rep. Locke to explain their frustration that there was no "transition funding." That is, the prevocational training that special education students had received through high school did not lead to any desired outcome once they graduated. There had to be a specific plan of support for the transition from school to work. With Locke's support a plan was funded for such services as employment analysts who can examine a particular job for an individual and job coaches to maintain a successful placement when the occasion demanded.

In 1993 Locke left the legislature and was elected executive of King County where he became even more acquainted with the fundamentals that served him well when he was elected governor in 1996. Year after year, until the Great Recession of 2007-09, the legislature has honored the commitments of Locke and his allies that they would provide funding sufficient to support employment for approximately 80% of the students with developmental disabilities who were leaving high school. And, after a one year hiatus to fix some related funding problems, in the spring 2010 the legislature provided the needed funding for all 1,400 high school graduates.

In 2004 the Division of Developmental Disabilities began a "Working Age Adult Policy" which committed the state to a policy of providing "supports to pursue and maintain gainful employment in integrated settings in the community shall be the primary service option for working age adults," regardless of the severity of the developmental disability. While the Arc had no problems with policy itself, and indeed could celebrate the day it was adopted, implementation has caused the Arc to object. People with the most severe disabilities in some counties suddenly found themselves with nothing to do during the day because the providers of their prior grouped sheltered "employment" no longer received funding for them and had decided to discontinue their services. DDD now states that even after the best efforts of its contractors, no gainful employment has been found for the 20% of its caseload with the most severe disabilities. They are said to be on "Pathways to Employment." This lack of high quality programming for those with the most severe disabilities is one of the biggest failures which the Arc and the state confront.

CHAPTER NINE: A NEW MILLENNIUM

The Smithsonian Calls the Arc of Washington

The new millennium started with a backward glance at history. In 1999 the Arc of Washington was pleased to be contacted by a representative of the Museum of American History at the Smithsonian Institution in Washington, D.C. The Museum was planning a tenth anniversary celebration of the enactment of the Americans with Disabilities Act. It wanted historical documents to represent early activities of organizations of family members advocating for persons with disabilities. The national Arc referred the Smithsonian to the Arc of Washington.

The Arc of Washington proudly mailed several original documents from the postwar era (*One out of Fifty*, *Children Limited* and several issues of the state newsletter from 1950). The Museum used the material as part of a traveling exhibit that toured the country during 2000 and also posted several of Washington's pieces online as part of a disability history website that remains partially accessible ten years later.

University of Alabama v. Garrett

Even though the anniversary of the Americans with Disabilities Act

259

was being celebrated, it did not mean that the ADA was safe, as advocates soon learned. *University of Alabama v. Garrett,* another U.S. Supreme Court case, again threatened the ADA. And again the Arc went to work to protect and promote the rights of persons with disabilities.

In the earlier *Olmstead* challenge to the ADA the court majority had decided that it would not address the question of whether the ADA was an unconstitutional infringement on the rights of the states, but merely interpret the statutory language that Congress had passed. In the *Garrett* case, the Alabama Attorney General argued that parts of the ADA violated states' rights. So the constitutional question was at stake. As noted on the Bazelon Center for Mental Health Law website,

> under the Supreme Court's current approach, the question of whether a particular civil rights statute exceeds Congress' power largely depends on two factors: (1) whether, when the statute was enacted, there was a significant problem of unconstitutional discrimination, and (2) whether the requirements of the statute are proportionate and reasonable responses to the problem that Congress sought to remedy.

In their briefs to the Supreme Court, lawyers for individuals with disabilities and friends of the court contended that states' history of discrimination based on disability was so egregious that Congress had the power to override state sovereignty.

A few years earlier in the *Olmstead* case, the Arc of Washington, like its allies in other states, had to persuade the state to remove its name from the amicus brief in support of Georgia. In supporting the national defense of the ADA in *Garrett,* the Arc's job was different; it had to gather instances of discrimination against persons with disabilities by state and local governments.[322] Because the discrimination had to occur around the time Congress passed the ADA in 1990, no evidence of the commonplace discrimination in earlier decades, like sterilization in the 1930s, or involuntary institutionalization, was relevant.

In July 2000, the Arc quickly prepared an analysis of recent discrimination in the State of Washington and sent it off to the national team of attorneys developing an amicus brief on behalf of the plaintiffs. Among the evidence of discrimination that the Arc uncovered were the following.

According to the state education agency, 396 complaints of discrimination by local school districts were filed by parents of children with disabilities between 1985-96. Of the 241 cases since 1996 (that is, about 60 cases per school year), the parents have prevailed in 64 cases and the district was found not to have discriminated in 60 cases. In 76 cases, there was a split decision, while 23 complaints were withdrawn, and 18 were still pending.

A second venue for filing a complaint against a school district is with the U.S. Department of Education. The Arc learned from the local Office of Civil Rights that a total of 1,477 civil rights complaints on the grounds of disability had been filed against local school districts in Washington state between1980 and 2000.

Like the Department of Education, the federal Department of Health and Human Services has an Office of Civil Rights which receives and investigates complaints of discrimination on the basis of disability by states and local governments. Although the Arc also requested a tabulation of recent complaints of discrimination, HHS was unable to do so within the short time frame. Instead it provided a few recent examples.

To the Arc's compilation of statistics, WPAS, the state protection and advocacy agency (now called Disability Rights Washington), added a list of individual cases in which it had been involved.

On Wednesday, February 21, 2001, the United States Supreme Court ruled 5-4 (531 U.S. 356 (2001) that suits in federal court by state employees with disabilities to recover *money damages* under Title I of the Americans with Disabilities Act *are* barred by the Eleventh Amendment. But it left untouched the constitutional basis for actions against state and local governments under Title II of the ADA for non-employment matters, the most important part of the law from the perspectives of many advocates.

The Arc v. Quasim: Demanding Medicaid Benefits

Over the last 25 years, Medicaid Home and Community-Based Services waivers have quickly expanded to become the foundation for most services for adults with developmental disabilities across the country. (They are called "waivers" because this program provides assistance while waiving the old requirement that a person had to be in a hospital or institution to get Medicaid.) Waiver services include supported housing, supported employment, therapies, and personal care attendants, in addition to paying for doctors, hospitals, and prescriptions.

The U.S. Court of Appeals for the Eleventh Circuit is at the geographic opposite end from Washington, with Florida among the states over which it has appellate jurisdiction. In February 1998, it issued *Doe v. Chiles*, a decision that found that Florida was wrongly withholding Medicaid benefits for persons with developmental disabilities due to inadequate state appropriations. The court ruled that such a delay was illegal. Medicaid is a contract between the state with the federal government, said the court, and when the state agreed to take the Medicaid funds, it had to provide the services for which persons were eligible, whether the legislature had appropriated adequate funds or not. Because almost every state, including Washington, had been limiting services to eligible persons with developmental disabilities based on the dollars available, this represented a new opportunity for advocacy.

The Arc of Washington quickly analyzed the opportunity. It eventually filed a class action lawsuit that was part of the activities that it had to balance with other opportunities throughout most of the first decade of the new century. But before filing, the Arc decided to inform the state of the new decision so that the state knew that the Arc had new leverage. Because Governor Gary Locke had already promised Arc advocates that he would obtain an additional $100 million from the next legislature, the Arc decided at its June 1998 board meeting to postpone filing a lawsuit. A year later, only 80 million in new dollars had been appropriated by the legislature. Unwilling to back down from its $100 million demand, which itself had been a compromise, the Arc board authorized the lawsuit.

The Arc v. Quasim was the lawsuit filed on behalf of the Arc of Washington and three named plaintiffs in November 1999. (*The Arc of Washington State, et al v. Lyle Quasim, et al.*, U.S. District Court for Western Washington, Cause Number 99-5577FDB). The lawsuit asked the court to order that people who have requested Medicaid-funded services and been found eligible, be given those services with reasonable promptness.

There were many twists and turns in the lawsuit. Eventually an appeal to the Ninth Circuit was required, which reversed Judge Burgess's dismissal of the case. A class action on behalf of all persons with developmental disabilities was originally certified by the court, but later decertified. An initial settlement with the state would have provided $100 million dollars in new Medicaid services annually for persons with developmental disabilities but only paid out $6 million before the court refused to approve the settlement. Sometime allies and would-be interveners at Columbia Legal Services and the state Protection and Advocacy Agency decided to go their own way. They filed a separate lawsuit and settled that lawsuit with the state for no additional funds but various guarantees of due process for persons applying for Medicaid or receiving it. That settlement was framed in a way that precluded the Arc from its continuing quest for more Medicaid services for persons with developmental disabilities.

Litigation Gains or Losses?

The case cost the Arc little in out of pocket funds, but did occupy many hours of the time of its executive director Sue Elliott over the decade. What was the result of the litigation? Some persons with developmental disabilities got Medicaid services or additional services, such as supported employment or housing. The total value of the settlement would need to calculate that new dollar level carried forward into the subsequent state budgets. This is because for persons with developmental disabilities, it is usually difficult, and often politically impossible, to withdraw public supports once they have been supplied. Thus, perhaps the $100 million originally promised was eventually attained. On the other hand, the state revised its Medicaid waiver program with the federal government so as to reduce its potential exposure to future escalating costs. It did so by replacing its single waiver, which had granted full Medicaid benefits to all, with four targeted waivers that allowed the state to grant some, but not all, services to its younger clients, especially children who would no longer leave school at age 21 with automatic entitlement to services supporting employment and housing.

Did the Arc lawsuit stop or reverse the use of federal Medicaid funding in Washington state? During 2002-2007, when the lawsuit was being litigated, the State of Washington had the worst trend in the nation in terms of declining waiver services, that is, federally matched community services for persons with developmental disabilities.[323] Over that five year period, only three states showed declines in the number of persons receiving waiver services. People with developmental disabilities in Washington suffered the largest percentage decline. From 2002 to 2007, Washington's waiver recipients fell by 17%, from 11,173 to 9,317. Georgia fell from 9,826 to 9,194 (6%) and Michigan fell from 8,550 to 7,714 (10%).

Perhaps the State was cynically letting the waiver population decline as persons died, moved, or no longer needed the services, in order to appear to offer in settlement a larger increase over where they were at the time to impress the Arc and its allies, and afterwards the court, than if the State had continued to fill the waiver slots with new persons while the litigation progressed.[324]

263

Nation's Only Tax-Matched Special Needs Trust

Margaret-Lee Thompson had for some time been the head of the King County Parent Coalition, a program of the Arc of King County. In 1998 she drew together various advocates to discuss the possible creation of a tax-matched special needs trust for persons with developmental disabilities. The first formal meeting was held under the auspices of Senator Dan McDonald (R, Bellevue) who was her senator and part of the majority in the state senate. As the idea was discussed with a group of advocates, it was seen as a way to motivate families of young children with developmental disabilities to enter into a public-private partnership to fund services for their children when they became adults. The rationale for Senate Bill 5693, which the legislature enacted in the 1999 session after heavy Arc lobbying, was equity for persons with disabilities. Like most states at the time, Washington had plans that provided financial incentives for families to start saving for the tuition needs of their children or grandchildren at public colleges and universities. Thompson proposed to Senator McDonald a new program for families whose children might not be able to seek a university degree.

Now called the Life Opportunities Trust of the Washington State Developmental Disabilities Endowment Fund, it is the nation's first tax-matched special needs trust. Contributions to the Fund up to $31,000 are matched at a 25% rate. As long as assets are in a properly drawn trust to address the special needs of a person with disabilities, eligibility for Medicaid-funded programs is protected. Thus, grandparents, for example, could make a gift of $25,000 on behalf of a five year old with Down syndrome and see that investment grow for the next twenty years and have their contribution matched by 25% in state tax funds.[325] The State Investment Board, which handles billions of dollars of state investments, manages the Endowment investments and the Arc of Washington currently holds the state contract for managing applications and disbursements.[326]

Special Education Funding

Over a decade after the last intensive discussions over the state's funding of special education, in 2004 the Washington State Special Education Coalition held meetings with the Arc and other advocacy organizations and school districts. Proponents of new litigation, like the very successful earlier lawsuits in front of Judge Doran, argued that the school districts were still not being reimbursed for the true extra costs of special education.[327] However, the school districts were divided over the wisdom of additional litigation, as were the advocacy groups. The Arc decided not to support a lawsuit, but the Special Education Coalition did. The districts and their allies were unsuccessful in the suit.

Claiming Institutional Savings for the Community

In 2005 state government faced a projected $2.2 billion deficit, foreclosing advocacy efforts to authorize new major programs that required funding. The Arc did manage to lobby through 2SHB 1791 which created a community developmental disabilities trust account (aka the Dan Thompson Memorial Trust Account).[328] The Community Services Trust Fund directs that the proceeds from any property that the state declares surplus at Rainier School, Lakeland Village, or Frances Haddon Morgan shall be directed to the budget for expanded community services for persons with developmental disabilities.

Funding Genetic Studies in the Era of Biotech

In the Nineties, hopes for cures for the various intellectual disabilities had been muted among Arc leaders and members in Washington state and nationally. This was true even though—in apparent imitation of the Arc's "Search for a Cure" a decade earlier—in 1990 President George W. Bush declared the Nineties the "Decade of the Brain" and the National Institute of Mental Health conducted a decade long funding effort to implement the campaign. But there were no clear breakthroughs that the public could appreciate.

This was true even though by 2006 the National Institutes of Health's annual budget for medical research totaled $18 billion, of which a sizable fraction was being spent on the brain. And the private sector ("Big Pharma") invested heavily in neurological problems like Alzheimer's disease. The total funds involved in research on the brain become almost beyond measure. Add to that the constant media stream of stories announcing genetic discoveries and a basis for a third wave of renewed optimism about cures, even partial ones, seemed there.

But there was little that ordinary Arc members in Washington state could do. At least the Arc of Washington Research Trust Fund was there. With its small funding, it nonetheless did support several new genetic studies, the results of which might suggest new underlying causes of disability and even treatment. When the first dramatic breakthrough in treating brain disorders occurred, there would be plenty of opportunity for renewed efforts to support a search for cures.

The End is the Beginning

The 2008 Annual Report of the Arc of Washington State provides a fitting end to this story of its past and its hopes for the future.

> The backbone of The Arc of Washington State is grassroots advocacy by individuals with developmental disabilities and their families. In order to ensure that their needs, interests and values drive public policies, we work with parent and self-advocacy groups throughout the state to inform and educate individuals about the legislative process and current developmental disabilities issues.

Two grants from the Developmental Disabilities Council to the Arc provided the funding for major advocacy projects.

> For persons with disabilities, the Self-Advocacy Initiative Project supports training and assistance in the legislative process, regional self-advocacy coordinators across the state, workshops, and support for Self-Advocates in Leadership (SAIL), a statewide self-advocacy coalition. Since 2004 SAIL has counted eight legislative victories, including respectful language that eliminated "the R word" in state law, and replaced it, when needed, with intellectual disability, a law allowing special education students to participate in graduation ceremonies, even though the school districts continued to provide training for their transition to employment until age 21, and a law requiring school districts to mark disability history month in October each year. (www.sailcoalition.org)

For families, friends, and other allies, funding went to the Arc's Advocacy Partnership Project, which provided information and assistance on state and federal legislative issues, sends out On-line

Action Alerts, and hosted Advocacy Day which brings self-advocates and families to the state capitol to observe and lobby each Wednesday during the legislative session.

And with its statewide support and coordination based at the Arc of Washington, Parent to Parent programs, some of them part of local Arcs, some independent, continue to provide "new parents" with the same personalized support that the first families provided to each other 75 years ago.

POSTSCRIPT:
LESSONS FOR ADVOCATES

Welcome. I salute your efforts. Here are a few thoughts about your task. They are not new ideas. Lessons about the wisdom necessary to be a great advocate have ancient roots. Aristotle called it "practical wisdom."[329] It is that intellectual quality which can guide and control action from one fight to the next. Wise men and women reflect on their actions and can give rational justifications for their behavior. Thus, it is also true that you, an advocate for persons with intellectual disabilities, can benefit by reflecting on patterns that recur and which, if ignored, can effectively control the course and outcome of your efforts.

Part of practical wisdom is coming to the understanding that no two situations which we face are entirely alike. Human behavior is a response to a broad range of features in the environment, each of which can carry meaning and each of these meanings can modify the significance of the other. Second, human beings can take account of any previous generalization about their behavior in what they do next. Thus, often at some cost, you can sometimes manage to be an exception to the general patterns recognized as social scientific generalizations. Finally, since people differ in what they judge to be proper, and try to act in accord with their differing judgments, regularities of behavior are reduced by human freedom and rationality.

But if the rules of human action could be broken easily, there could be no wisdom about human affairs worth passing along. This is not the case. Some of what have been variously called social scientific laws, theories, and hypotheses identify regularities based on factors which are powerful constraints on "ordinary" behavior. Unless heroic efforts are made, the generalizations will apply in your case. No statistical probabilities for the validity of the following rules of advocacy can be specified, but parents and others activists may find them of use. These practical hypotheses are derived in part from reflection on seventy-five years experience of the Arc, and in part from the experience of the author. These rules are directed to the activist, the agitator, the organizer, the advocate, and the leader, and to those who hope to be.[330] Those readers who wish to study these ideas at greater length are directed to the works in the References section under the authors credited in parentheses.

Volunteers

Personality, sex and age roles, social status, official position, organizational environment, and other factors interact to determine the type of advocacy an individual will be willing and able to undertake. Wise leaders will take account of this fact and structure opportunities according to the character of the membership. (Alinsky)

"If you want something done, give it to a busy person." This aphorism represents the truth that many advocacy assignments require special skills and persons who have more developed skills are often busy and have already learned how to perform tasks quickly. Developing latent talents in new members is an imperative which must be balanced against getting necessary jobs done on time.

Different types of advocacy are appropriate at different times and the passage of time can render certain models obsolete. For example, the rise of female labor force participation has reduced the supply of inexpensive volunteer labor, and, as a result, parent groups have been permanently changed.

The relationship between objective conditions and subjective response is complex. Good times may breed satisfaction and apathy, while hard times may breed despair. But if a period which threatens past achievements arises, those bad times may see renewed dedication to the cause (as when the Reagan administration threatened to abolish a federal role in disability services).

Advocacy is probably most likely when there is a revolution of rising expectations. If after a time in which no gains were made, a few gains begin to be made, men and women may sense that the time is ripe for major strides forward. These times demand boldness, for opportunity abounds. As Lenin said about conditions in Russia in 1917, "power was lying in the streets, and we picked it up."

As the status of two groups becomes more equal, remaining inequities seem all the more unjust and unbearable (De Tocqueville). This applies to races, genders, and other inequalities. Thus, the increased militancy and stridency of persons with disabilities and their advocates came just as large advances toward full and equal citizenship were finally being made. No one demands normalized services when none at all exist. Similarly, the achievement of justice in one sector leads to increased demand for equity in other sectors.

Volunteer leadership depends upon personal charisma, tends to use symbolic rewards, and waxes and wanes continuously. Deeds of heroic magnitude and periods of apathy should both be expected. Appeals to rededicate oneself to the cause, and jeremiads bemoaning the loss of commitment, are a regular feature of voluntary organizations (Etzioni).

Interaction processes within groups produces instrumental, task-oriented and socio-emotional expressive leaders; these styles tend to complement each other (Bales).

Instrumental leaders value "getting the job done" above all else; socio-emotional leaders moderate such drives with concern for the feelings of the diverse individuals who are a part of the team. Traditionally, men tended to be instrumental leaders and women tended to be expressive leaders.

Parent movements run in part off the emotional energy generated in the reaction to the birth of a child with disabilities (Menolascino). When the parent becomes adjusted to the problem, solves it, or the problem goes away when the child dies, activity tends to decline.

Membership in a parents' organization dealing with devalued members will be disproportionately composed of those who cannot disavow the stigma (Goffman). Thus, in the field of developmental disabilities, parents of children with Down syndrome and of children with severe disabilities will be over-represented among members, since their children have more visible stigmata.

A historical progression of advocacy functions from "providing," through "obtaining," and on to "monitoring," services is, on the whole, a useful schema (Wolfensberger, 1973). It risks becoming an over-simplification about a "bad past," however, since efforts to obtain and monitor public services were present from the beginnings of parent advocacy.

Furthermore, the typology needs to be viewed additively and in light of a progressive differentiation of functions. That is, the provision of services was not abandoned by parent groups when they began to demand and obtain public services, but the latter function was added to the former. Provision of services may become a specialized activity of some, rather than all organizational members. Generally speaking, direct services are more likely to be provided by persons whose time is deemed less valuable. Thus, young persons are typical service providers.

Professionals

Paid staff members of parent advocacy organizations bring a rational-legal or bureaucratic orientation to such groups (Weber). The level of activity and the quality of the performance becomes far more dependable. Since staff requires remuneration, budgetary concerns loom larger, and goal succession and displacement tend to occur (Sills). That is, more time is spent finding the money to keep the organization running; less, and, at worst, little time is spent directly attacking the identified problem.

Professional advocacy, by Arc staff and now by federally funded protection and advocacy staff, has had a negative effect on volunteer efforts by parents. However, "citizen advocacy" (in which members of the public at large are trained to become friends and advocates for persons with disabilities) and self-advocacy groups, such as People First, have not, because the latter are, so far, largely volunteer efforts.

The professionalization of advocacy may be nearly inevitable and essential to achievement of group goals. Without the persistence which hired guns bring to the task, opposition bureaucrats will often win through a war of attrition (cf. Bardach). Few part-time volunteers will stick with the effort in season and out.

The same historical succession of advocacy functions which Wolfensberger pointed out in parents' movements—providing, obtaining, and monitoring—tends to apply to non-parent professional advocacy as well.

Watch where the money goes! Organizations are made up of people and people want money. Apparently complex and distant relationships often make sense by focusing on the resource allocation system and who benefits from the arrangement.

271

The Effects of Size on Advocacy

Assuming an organization which divides itself on a geographical basis, where a large population base exists, a parent organization is more likely to exist. But if it does exist, a parent group serving an area with a smaller population has more chance of achieving fleeting glory.

One is more likely to find an advocacy group in a county, city, or school district of 100,000 persons than in one of 1,000. However, a less well-known statistical regularity is that, year after year, membership rates and per capita fundraising tend to be lower in larger areas than in smaller ones. It is also true that the groups with the most ideologically correct programs will be smaller.

This is not a paradox. Rather, the larger the population base, the greater the likelihood of bureaucratization or institutionalization of unit efforts in a staff. The larger base will guarantee the continual existence of an organization, but a small organization, which runs on the commitment to self-sacrifice of a committed band of warrior-advocates, has an easier time achieving brilliance. However, such an area may well be found without any group at all five or ten years later.

The so-called "star system," in which a local parent becomes Mrs. or Mr. Mental Retardation (Farber), is more likely in less populous areas and in areas where the total system of disability services is small. In larger areas, and where there is more money and power in the system, no one player is likely to control all the action. Rather than a star who controls everything by the force of his or her personality, various "empire builders" emerge and organizations are more likely to become the monopolists.

Ideas and Action

Leadership positions develop a "cosmopolitan" orientation to abstract ideals (e.g., normalization theory), while ordinary members remain "localistic" in their commitments (e.g., to a particular program or facility) (Gouldner). The primary loyalty of cosmopolitans are to the ideas or faith they believe in (like inclusion), which few, if any, programs ever measure up to. Locals, on the other hand, see the issue as one of supporting the particular programs they know, and can fall into a simple "boosterism." Cosmopolitans labor for humanity, locals for their family members and friends.

This conflict between these types of loyalties among disability advocates has been particularly evident in recent years, as proponents of normalization have attacked the expansion, and even the existence, of many current service systems, suggesting they do more evil than good. Locals have responded by charging the ideologues with a willingness to sacrifice real people to abstractions.

Bricks and mortar and direct service programs are easier to sell to members and the public than abstractions like advocacy. Thus, non-service-providing parent groups face continual threats to survival. Those who advocate ideological purity have an obligation to make clear its price, or to make other provision for its toll.

The good is the enemy of the better. Frequently, critics of the status quo face the retort that what exists is so much better than what went before that it should not be tampered with. Advocates should not expect that those who labored hard in the past to build the present will eagerly accept a different future.

The inertia of society is so stubborn that no one will move against it, if he cannot believe that it can be more easily overcome than is actually the case. And no one will suffer the perils and pains involved in the process of radical social change, if he cannot believe in the possibility of a purer and fairer society than will ever be established. These illusions are dangerous because they justify fanaticism; but their abandonment is perilous because it inclines to inertia (Niebuhr).

Organizations need action as an individual needs oxygen. It is impossible to maintain constant action on a single issue. Therefore, a single issue is a fatal strait jacket that will stifle the life of an organization. Many issues mean many members (Alinsky).

Coalitions and Alliances

A "fragmentation of efforts" in advocacy is inevitable and has many causes. De Tocqueville celebrated the peculiar ability of Americans to spawn associations. And one can expect that new groups will always be forming, as long as the system is expanding, which is, in turn, a function of the richness of the environment in which the parties contend. In part, this is a differentiation of groups, with general purpose advocacy organizations succeeded by groups with narrower, more specialized interests (Parsons). The newer groups are able to focus on single issues and tasks and may make more progress. Currently, the growth of groups devoted to autism, one of the developmental disabilities, has been most dramatic, but that they are merely the latest parent groups formed differentiating themselves from the Arc. At one time, for example, new Down syndrome groups were the most prominent special-interest groups.

Established groups may feel betrayed and angry as the usurpers capture newly developed funding sources or other resources. But in America the knowledge and entrepreneurial skills required to start and run organizations is widespread and those who demonstrate such qualities are admired, so there is constant pressure to form new groups. Thus, in field of disabilities each newly identified syndrome soon has its own family organization.

The smaller the organization, the higher the percentage of persons who can gain the personal rewards associated with leadership. To flourish, large organizations must take heed of the personal element in advocacy and provide ample opportunity for its expression.

Coalitions seem like motherhood and apple pie, since cooperation is deemed a virtue, and combined efforts are repeatedly justified by rhetorical appeals that "we're really all working for the same thing." Yet coalitions need to be approached with care. It has been said that "everybody wants to coordinate, but nobody wants to be coordinated" (Chu and Trotter).

Coalitions provide occasions for both gaining and losing power. Alliances are most valuable for their weaker members, which could otherwise not hope to achieve shared objectives. Large groups are the least likely to join in voluntary cooperation. Units representing the largest city or county in the state, and the largest state in the nation, are the most likely to "go their own way" and secede from a union.

Personal ambitions are another factor which can be masked by the language of cooperation. Those who control "coordinating councils" or their analogues are individuals with personal agendas, just like the leaders of the separate groups.

Power and Conflict

Power need not be a zero-sum game. When parents are locked in a struggle with school administrators over the form or content of special education, it usually seems to both sides as if either the one or the other has the power and control, and to the extent one gains new power, the other has lost it. Game-theorists refer to this as a zero-sum paradigm.

But over the last fifty years, parents, service providers, and persons with disabilities have all gained power. Thus, as resources are mobilized through conflicts, and by other means, there is the potential for progress by all parties toward their partially shared, but also

274

partially antagonistic, goals and interests. The character of advocacy should reflect this reality and avoid a sense that the players are animals locked in a life and death struggle over the last bone.

It is difficult to operate a service and be its monitor at the same time (Wolfensberger, 1973). Mistrust of authority is as American as the Constitution and the national experience is reflected in the experience of the disability community. A separation of powers allows some control over the inevitable narrowness of perspective which forms around each of us. Strong and confident advocates look for, and sustain, independent sources of criticism.

Conflict is inevitable and often a functional feature of organizational life. Among other effects, conflict can bind groups together, provide a safety valve for the release of tensions, clarify ideas and dreams, and build alliances with other groups (Coser). At one level, avoiding conflict may appear to be the peace-loving alternative, but it is not without its price.

In conflicts, reason and be open to reasoning; yield to principle, not pressure (Fisher). Negotiation has become an entire field of study by itself. Students of the process have found that negotiation need not mean either "playing hardball" or playing "nice guy" by caving in to the other side. Effective advocacy can get beyond restricted options and move creatively toward shareable solutions.

Appendix 1:
The Arc of Washington Presidents

1936-39 Monty Percival, Tacoma
1940-42 Roy Fowler, Bellingham
1942-44 Harold A. Isenhath, Seattle/Tacoma
1944-46 W. Newland Reilly, Spokane
1946-48 Alan H. Sampson, Seattle
1948-49 Marvin P. Nolden, Spokane
1949-51 Herbert N. Clifton, Seattle
1951-53 Olaf E. Caskin, Seattle
1953-55 Harold Watkins, Kalama
1955-59 Edward H. Riviere, Tacoma
1959-61 Mae Wise, Hoquiam
1961-65 Raymond Howell, Everett
1965-67 Elise Chadwick, Spokane
1967-69 Frank J. Skerbeck, Port Angeles
1969-71 Omer L. Carey, Pullman
1971-73 Harold E. Little, Richland
1973-75 Lou W. Healy, Walla Walla
1975-76 David Foscue, Aberdeen
1976-79 Lou Day, Puyallup
1979-81 Connie Hilty, Richland
1981-83 Larry A. Jones, Olympia, Seattle
1983-85 Melba Grau, Puyallup
1985-87 James Marick, Vancouver
1987-89 Joy Isham, Bremerton
1989-91 Linda Clark, Spokane
1991-93 Susan Roberts, Lake Stevens
1993-95 Sharon York, Longview
1995-96 Al Lewis, Spokane
1997-99 Bill Sellars, Seattle
1999-01 Doug Cook, Seattle
2001-03 Tim Hornbecker, Seattle
2003-05 Sue Scott, Yakima
2005-09 Sharon York, Longview
2009-   Kathleen Watson, Seattle

Appendix 2:
The Arc of Washington Executives

1952-62   Leopold Lippman, began as Executive Secretary
(1954   Robert L. Hillock Acting Executive Secretary for four months while Lippman was on loan to NARC.)

1963-65   Van R. Hinkle
1965-68   Michael Kreider
1969-71   David S. Alkins
1971-74   Perry J. Liljestrand
1975-76   Patricia K. Wilkins
1977-81   Stanley L. Baxter
1981-83   Vacant
1983-85   Judith A. Devine
1985-95   Vacant. Bean Driscoll, Executive Secretary
1995-   Sue Elliott

Appendix 3:
Annual Meetings of the Arc

1. 6-27-1936 Chamber of Commerce Building, Yakima
2. 8- 7-1937 Site of the future school, Buckley
3. 8-27-1938 New Washington Hotel, Seattle
4. 8-26-1939 Hotel Winthrop, Tacoma
5. 8-24-1940 Leopold Hotel, Bellingham
6. 8- 2-1941 Rainier State School, Buckley
7. 8- 2-1942 Rainier State School, Buckley
8. 8- 7-1943 Gowman Hotel, Seattle (gas rationing)
9. 8- 6-1944 Gowman Hotel, Seattle (")
10. 8- 5-1945 Gowman Hotel, Seattle (")
11. 8- 3-1946 Masonic Temple, Spokane
12. 8-16-1947 Civic Recreational Center, Bremerton
13. 8- 6-1948 Commercial Hotel, Yakima
14. 8- 6-1949 Carpenters' Hall, Vancouver
15. 8- 4-1950 Edmond Meany Hotel, Seattle
16. 8-10-1951 Spokane Hotel, Spokane
17. 8- 8-1952 Edmond Meany Hotel, Seattle
18. 8- 7-1953 Spokane Hotel, Spokane
19. 8-14-1954 Leopold Hotel, Bellingham
20. 8-11-1955 Morck Hotel, Aberdeen
21. 10-28-1956 Olympic Hotel, Seattle
22. 8-23-1957 Columbian Hotel, Wenatchee
23. 8-21-1958 Marcus Whitman Hotel, Walla Walla
24. 8-20-1959 Winthrop Hotel, Tacoma
25. 8-18-1960 Hotel Monticello, Longview
26. 8-17-1961 Hotel Davenport, Spokane
27. 8-23-1962 University of Washington, Seattle
28. 8-22-1963 Chinook Tower and Motel, Yakima
29. 8-20-1964 Elks Lodge, Everett
30. 8-21-1965 Desert Inn & Community Center, Richland
31. 8-20-1966 Peninsula Community College, Port Angeles
32. 10-21-1967 St. Paul's Lutheran Church, Vancouver
33. 9-28-1968 Haddon Hall, Bremerton
34. 9-26-1969 Tacoma Motor Inn, Tacoma
35. 9-20-1970 Ridpath Hotel, Spokane
36. 9-10-1971 Hyatt House, Seattle
37. 9-17-1972 Quay Inn, Vancouver
38. 9-21-1973 Ridpath Hotel, Spokane
39. 9-27-1974 Hanford House, Richland
40. 8-17-1975 Chinook Tower and Motel, Yakima
41. 8-20-1976 Quay Inn, Vancouver
42. 8-19-1977 Tyee Motor Inn, Tumwater
43. 9-15-1978 Ocean Shores Inn, Ocean Shores
44. 9-29-1979 Sheraton Hotel, Spokane

45. 9-20-1980   Thunderbird Hotel, Wenatchee
46. 9-19-1981   Quay Inn, Vancouver
47. 6-26-1982   Executive Inn, Tacoma
48. 9-24-1983   Ridpath Hotel, Spokane
49. 9-22-1984   Bayview Inn, Bremerton
50. 9-14-1985   Sheraton Inn, Tacoma
51. 9-20-1986   Central Washington University, Ellensburg
52. 9-19-1987   Executive Inn, Fife
53. 9-24-1988   Nendel's Inn, Everett
54. 9-23-1989   Mark 205 Inn, Vancouver
55. 9-29-1990   Cavanaugh's River Inn, Spokane
56. 9- 7- 1991   Tyee Hotel, Tumwater
57. 9-12-1992   Red Lion Hotel, Bellevue
58. 9-11-1993   Silverdale on the Bay Hotel, Silverdale
59. 9-17-1994   Arc of Cowlitz County office, Longview
60. 9-30-1995   Cavanaugh's River Inn, Spokane
61. 9-21-1996   Quality Inn Baron Suites, Bellingham
62. 9-13-1997   Arc of Kitsap-Jefferson Retreat, Lake Leland
63. 9-12-1998   Arc of Snohomish County, Everett
64. 9-11-1999   Cavanaugh's Inn, Yakima
65. 9-16-2000   Marriott Hotel, SeaTac
66. 9- 8-2001   Marriott Hotel, SeaTac
67. 9-28-2002   Marriott Hotel, SeaTac
68. 9-20-2003   Marriott Hotel, SeaTac
69. 9-18-2004   Wyndham Gardens Motel, SeaTac
70. 9-10-2005   Radisson Hotel, SeaTac
71. 9-16-2006   Radisson Hotel, SeaTac
72. 9-15-2007   Marriott Hotel, SeaTac
73. 9-13-2008   Radisson Hotel, SeaTac
74. 9-26-2009   Radisson Hotel, SeaTac
75. 9-25-2010   Radisson Hotel, SeaTac

NOTES

[1] For example, years before JFK became president, a news story titled "Kennedy Foundation Gives $1,250,000 to Aid Chicago Home for Retarded Boys," *New York Times*, February 21, 1952, makes no mention of a sister with disabilities. Instead, in the story Eunice Kennedy speaks of the way the gift will honor their brother Joseph who was killed in the war.

[2] In the 1940s some groups formed in other states, like Iowa and Utah, called themselves Children's Benevolent Leagues, too, following Washington's lead. Such names largely disappeared after the national organization NARC was founded in 1950.

[3] Cone, Inc., the public relations firm that published the *Cone 100 Nonprofit Power* Brand (2009), also calls The Arc "the nonprofit power brand no one's ever heard of." It reported that the Arc in 2007 had $2.4 billion in the sale of inventory and $678 million from government funding, in addition to direct consumer charitable gifts.

[4] Upon inquiry, leaders of the International Association for the Scientific Study of Intellectual Disabilities were unable to identify an older organization of family members outside the United States.

[5] A July 20, 1935 letter from Superintendent Parker acknowledges Oakley's letter, thanks him for his efforts in spreading news of "the proposed plan," and promises to meet him the next time he is in Seattle.

[6] *Catholic Northwest Progress*, October 18, 1935, p. 5. A shorter article appeared in the *Seattle Post-Intelligencer*, October 18, 1935, p. 16.

[7] Catholic Order of Foresters

[8] James Luther Adams, quoted in Stackhouse, Max L. "James Luther Adams: A biographical and intellectual sketch." In D. B. Robertson, ed., *Voluntary Associations: A Study of Groups in Free Societies.* Richmond, VA: John Knox Press, 1966, 333-57.

[9] Children's Benevolent League, Clark county unit, Minutes, April 4, 1936.

[10] Wolfensberger, Wolf . *The Third Stage in the Evolution of Voluntary Associations for the Mentally Retarded.* Toronto, Canada: National Institute on Mental Retardation. 1973: 25-28

[11] Clark County unit, Children's Benevolent League, *Minutes* April 4, 1936.

[12] Shorter *The Kennedy Family and the Story of Mental Retardation.* Temple University Press, 2000, p. 21.

[13] As reported in the *Yakima Daily Republic.*

[14] Ibid.

[15] *Cf.* James W. Trent *Inventing the Feeble Mind. A History of Mental Retardation in America.* Berkeley: U of California Press, 1994.

[16] U.S. Census available online.

[17] State Custodial School file, Papers of Governor Martin, State Archives, Olympia, Washington.

[18] Minutes of the Clark County unit.

[19] This is based on comparing the 1930 census of Chelan County with the census of the Custodial School at Medical Lake. Four of the leaders were married women, one of whose maiden name might have matched and revealed a sibling at the School. The men's occupations were Episcopal clergyman, normal school teacher, fruit dealer and shipper, railroad engineer, and barber.

[20] $5,500,000 in 2010 dollars.

[21] Indeed, in 1941 Newland Reilly, CBL leader from the east side of the mountains, implied that Percival's own fortunes, political and otherwise, were his motive, as noted below.

[22] Braddock, David *Federal Spending for Mental Retardation and Developmental Disabilities.* Baltimore: Paul H. Brookes. 1986.

[23] According to the minutes of the Clark County unit, 1937.

[24] Lash had been director of adult education for the Works Progress Administration in Washington state. His dissertation was a historical survey of education in the Seattle Public Schools, including special education.

[25] Minutes of Kitsap county unit, CBL, October 10, 1940.

[26] Minutes of the Kitsap county unit, CBL, March 9, 1938.

[27] In 1939 the King county unit of the CBL met monthly on Olive Street in downtown Seattle,—memorably, above a doughnut factory. Alan Sampson interview, February 11, 1982.

[28] Minutes, Kitsap county unit, CBL, April 13, 1938.

[29] Minutes, Kitsap county unit, CBL, Sept. 14, 1938.

[30] Letters of Charles Parker, Olaf Olsen, and others. Washington State Archives, Olympia, filed under "Institutions, General,

1939-43."

[31] The image of the daily lives of the Custodial School residents reminds us that persons with relatively mild disabilities were being institutionalized. Trent (1994) argues that institutions, and the whole concept of "the feeble-minded" was used in the first part of the twentieth century to control troublesome members of disadvantaged social groups, who were viewed as a threat to social order.

[32]Letters of Charles Parker, Olaf Olsen, and others. Washington State Archives, Olympia, filed under "Institutions, General, 1939-43."

[33] Obituary for Miriam Cassill Naundorf. *Spokane Chronicle.* May 21, 1971.

[34] See Reilly's address to the AAMD for more heated rhetoric – and an apology for it. Reilly's letter and Naundorf's telegram are in Governor Martin's papers at Washington State University Libraries.

[35] Vineland, perhaps the most famous American institution at the time, was founded in 1888. It was famous both for its early use of intelligence tests and later for its publication of the Vineland Adaptive Behavior Scale. Edgar Doll, a former Vineland superintendent, moved to Washington in the 1950s and became a consultant for WARC.

[36] Note how similar this phrasing is to the original name of the national organization formed in 1950.

[37] Louis Musso 'Less Children from the Unfit': Eugenic Sterilization in Washington State, 1909-1980. M.A. thesis, Central Washington State University, 1993. Reviewed in *Seattle Times*, May 9, 1993.

[38] "School Doctor's Ouster is Hit," *Seattle Times*, March 21, 1941.

[39] It is striking that a parent advocate could say that conditions were "ideal." By contrast, it is also notable how the most sensational complaints about institutions remain the same 50 years later. Hopefully, the additional real dollars poured into institutions have improved conditions. However, a basic fact remains: vulnerable persons will be victimized.

[40] "Buckley School Investigated; Dr. Lash OK'd," *Seattle Times*, March 23, 1941.

[41] *Seattle Times*, March 24, 1941.

[42] Smith, Stevenson (1912-21). Miscellaneous correspondence.

Filed with the Charles R. Strother Papers, University of Washington Archives, Seattle. Cole, Thomas R. (1925). Superintendent's letter to Seattle School Board, including a report from Nellie A. Goodhue, May 29. Seattle School District archives, Seattle, Washington. She was a statewide education leader as well. In 1914, she was president of the Study of Defective Children Section of the Washington Education Association

[43] American Red Cross, Seattle Chapter, Special Research Committee. *Feeblemindedness in Washington* (1924). The committee consisted of Goodhue, a deputy prosecuting attorney, a Seattle physician, and a former school principal of a Minnesota institution.

[44] But this analysis, if dominant, was not the sole voice at the time. In 1911 Lilburn Merrill, M.D., best known as the young author of an earlier popular book *Winning the Boy*, was appointed Diagnostician of the Seattle Juvenile Court. In 1914 Merrill reported his diagnosis of 421 consecutive juvenile boys whom he saw at Seattle Juvenile Court. Contrary to the overblown claims of eugenicists, only 6.8% were "feebleminded", and those of almost normal intelligence. Instead of the feebleminded, Merrill found that 81.5% were delinquency cases attributable to environmental and physical causes, and thus were amenable to eradication through social betterment and physical hygiene. *Medical Review of Reviews* (1914).

[45] That is, in an age where contraceptive means were limited and little known, it was widely believed that the feebleminded would naturally be unable to control their sexual desires, as well as proper, middle-class families could.

[46] Those same ideas justified the sterilization measures in this country and in Washington state.

[47] Emphases here and below in the original.

[48] *Ibid.*

[49] Smith, Stevenson. "Provision for feebleminded in Washington." *Addresses and Proceedings of the Thirtieth Annual Session.* Seattle: Washington Educational Association, 1916, 170.

[50] Walsted, Mary B. "Should diagnosis determine school training?" *Addresses and Proceedings of the Thirty-First Annual Session.* Seattle: Washington Educational Association, 1917.

[51] E.g., Cooper, Frank B. Superintendent's letter to Seattle School Board, February 14. 1917. Seattle School District archives,

Seattle, Washington.

[52]Cooper, Frank B. Superintendent's letter to Seattle School Board, October 2, 1919. Seattle School District archives, Seattle, Washington.

[53]Nelson, Bryce E. *Good Schools: The Development of Public Schooling in Seattle, 1901-22.* Unpublished doctoral dissertation. Seattle: University of Washington, 1981.

[54] Jones, Susan Delanty. *Progressivism and the Election of 1920 in Washington State.* Unpublished Master of Arts thesis, University of Chicago, Chicago, IL, 1969.

[55] LeWarne, Charles P. *Utopias on Puget Sound, 1885-1915.* Seattle: University of Washington, 1975.

[56] Later the American Association on Mental Retardation. Recently it became the American Association on Intellectual and Developmental Disabilities.

[57] Sloan, William and Harvey A. Stevens. *A Century of Concern.* Washington, D.C.: American Association on Mental Deficiency, 1976.

[58]E.g., Scheerenberger, R. C.. *A History of Mental Retardation.* Baltimore: Brookes, 1983, p.229.

[59] That was the same year that Gunnar Dybwad, later the executive of the NARC during early critical years, joined the association. He was made the AAMD's liaison to the Delinquency & Corrections Association; up to that point, his professional career had focused on juvenile justice, not intellectual disabilities.

[60] Original AAMD certificate dated June 1, 1946 to Ada L. Percival-Nelson is in the possession of The Arc of Washington State. She wed Otto Nelson, another CBL leader, after the death of her husband Monty Percival.

[61] A 1986 review of the AAMD membership records from the 1940s, which included the members' occupations, reveal no others, although some superintendent, psychologist or other professional could have had a child with a disability. Indeed, it seems likely. But no member except Percival was identified solely as a parent.

[62] W Newland Reilly, "Let the Parent Live Again." *American Journal on Mental Deficiency* 46 (1941): 409-13.

[63] Six years later Alan Sampson rallied opinion at the AAMD national convention in a speech that is credited with an important role in creating a national parents' organization. Sampson was an

insurance salesman.

[64] To be sure, Reilly also raked himself and other parents over the coals. He admitted his early personal arrogance had led him to avoid associating with other parents whom he had thought were inferior. He implies that an unnamed Monty Percival was just using the CBL to advance his own political career to the detriment of the Pierce county chapter. (It is certainly true that the Percivals profited from Monty's CBL work, encouraging the use of the *Buckley News,* of which he was part-owner, as the CBL newsletter.) Reilly also claimed that "a state officer of our league" had given false grand jury testimony against Superintendent Parker in a failed attempt to become superintendent. Hardly a pretty picture of parents.

[65] W Newland Reilly, "Let the Parent Live Again." *American Journal on Mental Deficiency*, at 13.

[66] In the 1940s the word "retarded" had acquired no stigmatizing meaning. It was not a swear word on school playgrounds. Alan Sampson said that they adopted the word "retarded" because the then-current words of imbecile and feeble-minded were then the stigmatizing words. Washington State Dept of Social and Health Services, *Alan Hungate Sampson: Association for Retarded Children,* 1991, p. 34.

[67] As noted in the Postscript below, Saul Alinsky, a famed community organizer in the 1960s said something similar. Organizations need action as an individual needs oxygen. It is impossible to maintain constant action on a single issue. Many issues mean many members.

[68] Stevenson Smith's daughter says that he ran a free clinic for children. Letter from Bradford Smith Mattson, February 11, 1992. He also worked with adults, for example, recognizing an eye-blink as an indicator of the intelligence of a paralyzed man, who was then taught to read.

[69] Reilly, W. Newland *For the Happiness of Children.* Children's Benevolent League of Washington: Spokane, Washington. 1945.

[70] Sampson, Alan H. "Developing and maintaining good relations with parents of mentally deficient children." *American Journal of Mental Deficiency 52*: 187-94, 190 (1947).

[71]Bair, Barbara. "The Parents Council for Retarded Children and social change in Rhode Island, 1951-1970." *Rhode Island*

History 40: 144-159 (1981). Dybwad reaffirmed his perspective in a note to the author June 6, 1986, which was before the discovery of Newland Reilly's 1941 speech to the AAMD. Whether that discovery would have made a difference is unknown. At the time he wrote, "I think your experience with the Chn's Benevolent League was an isolated instance rather then the beginning of a development, there was just too long of an intervening hiatus." In saying "too long an interval" Dybwad probably was thinking of the gap between the 1936 founding of the CBL and the 1947 speech by Sampson at the AAMD convention. Now that gap has been filled in with a number of interstate overtures. In addition, one must assess the effect of his own experience on alternative explanations. As a member of a family that had fled Nazi Germany, Dybwad might naturally accent such a factor, seemingly more than it deserves here as a purely domestic American social movement with neither ideological nor global claims. Of course the gift of Gunnar and Rosemary's international experience and allegiance did wonders for the growth of advocacy organizations worldwide, but that should not blind us to the trivial role that such human rights perspectives had on the growth of the first American parents' groups.

[72] Rosemary Dybwad's book, *Perspectives on a Parent Movement. The Revolt of Parents of Children with Intellectual Limitations* (1990), is a collection of her speeches to parents' groups around the globe and does not try to explain the origins of the "revolt."

[73] Pelka, Fred. *The ABC-CLIO Companion to the Disability Rights Movement.* (1997) at 240.

[74] Farber, Bernard. *Mental Retardation: Its Social Context and Social Consequences.* Boston: Houghton Miflin, 1968, pp. 126-27.

[75] Thomson, Mildred. *Prologue.* Minneapolis: Gilbert Publishing, 1963, pp. 145-46.

[76] Some thirty conscientious objectors from the Church of the Brethren, a pacifist denomination, were assigned to wartime duty at Rainier (Trent, 1994:298).

[77] Reilly, W. Newland. *For the Happiness of Children.* Children's Benevolent League of Washington: Spokane, Washington, 1945.

[78] Parker, Charles L. "State Custodial School." Pp. 158-63 in *Department of Finance, Budget, and Business, Biennial Report,*

1934-36. Olympia: State of Washington, 1937.

[79] W. Newland Reilly. *For the Happiness of Children. This is the Story of the Children's Benevolent League of Washington, Incorporated.* Spokane, p.13.

[80] From the perspective of the 21st century, it is notable that things had not evolved far enough so that the objects of the benevolent acts of the members, namely, persons with disabilities, were conceived as being able to contribute as members themselves.

[81] As noted, the parent-to-parent support has always been an important Arc function and continues to be. This is a different issue than whether anything else is accomplished. Leavitt clearly said, not before us. Alan Sampson said that Auerswald, one of the founders, got mad at the younger leaders and withdrew.

[82] There was no family connection between the CBL leaders, Newland Reilly and Phil Reilly, from different sides of the state. Bob Leavitt says that, after recognizing Phil's speaking and writing ability, he blackmailed him into joining. Leavitt, a social worker, claimed that he could get Phil's son Larry into Rainier School if Phil gave Bob $5,000. Leavitt soon made it clear that he meant, if Phil would give $5,000 in volunteer time. But even if it was a joke, it presumably was initially plausible because "pull" often did get one's child "placed" in Washington state. As noted below, Edith Stern, a national figure, said that she had never seen that elsewhere. But it did in New York, see below.

[83] It all boiled to do "just gifts for the kids or public awareness," with Alan Sampson and allies clearly committed to educating the public. Interview February 11, 1982.

[84] Clifton, H. N. Personal interview. Seattle, Washington, March 27, 1986.

[85] Cunningham, Ross. "Long fight can only bring harm to Rainier School." *Seattle Times*, October 24, 1949 p. 4.

[86] Years later Clifton reported that by accident he and Governor Langlie were in Providence Hospital in Seattle for hemorrhoids at the same time and he was able to eavesdrop on Langlie's secrets, which Clifton was then able to exploit in an unsuccessful attempt to save Lash's job.

[87] It is a further mark of the prominence and power of the parents' organization that the state's largest newspaper would find it worthy of editorializing against it in the 1940s.

[88] Although Depner's resume and references were acceptable to the CBL, when he arrived in "a Derby hat, overshoes, and steel-rimmed spectacles," his supporters began to melt away. Soon he was popular with no one and he resigned the post, according to Clifton (1986). He lasted perhaps ten months.

[89] There is an apt comparison with the loss of support from King and other chapters in the late 1970s and early 1980s as the state ARC moved to challenge the existence of institutions and of patronizing practices of employment providers.

[90] Elizabeth Boggs later became NARC's fourth president and in fact became the most important single Arc leader of the 20th century. Her decades of legislative leadership were only the most important of many roles.

[91] Thomson, Mildred (1963). *Prologue*. Minneapolis: Gilbert Publishing, p.151.

[92] Of course, virtues can be vices seen from another perspective. If Sampson's speech was far more diplomatic than Newland Reilly's, and no cause could be found to object to it, that was the same trait that another CBL state president, H. N. Clifton, remembered as a defect: "Sampson would never talk on controversial issues, that S.O.B." Clifton remembered that he always fought Sampson "on everything." According to Clifton, Sampson wanted praise, wanted to be accepted as the father of the group; and without the recognition he would not work. By contrast, Clifton claimed that Harold Isenhath, "Kash" Kasminski and he were the real work-horses in the Seattle unit who got things done by long hours of work. Interview March 27, 1986.

[93] Presumably the "unorganized" Cleveland group was the Council for the Retarded Child. After his leadership in Washington state special education, Ross Hamilton became the first executive director of the Cuyahoga County (Cleveland) Association for Retarded Children.

[94] According to *Parallels in Time*, a history of developmental disabilities and policy, on the website of the Minnesota Developmental Disabilities Council, accessed 2009.

[95] Newland Reilly had joined the AAMD in 1941. Other Washingtonians who became members were: in 1946, Jacqueline Barr, Alan Sampson, and Marceline Turner (the state CBL Secretary); in 1947 R P Cunningham, Otto Nelson, Robert Leavitt, and Warren

Mattson; in 1948, Phil Reilly; and in 1949, Harold Watkins and H N Clifton. The AAMD records were examined April 3, 1986 at its office.

[96] According to a 1986 search of the AAMD records of the 644 members in 1939-40 there were twelve members without a stated professional position whom online Google and census searches in 2009 were unable to eliminate as possible earlier family members.

[97]Sloan, William and Harvey A. Stevens. *A Century of Concern*. Washington, D.C.: American Association on Mental Deficiency, 1976, p. 207; cf. Farber, Bernard. *Mental Retardation: Its Social Context and Social Consequences*. Boston: Houghton Miflin, 1968, p.132.

[98]Scheerenberger, R. C. *A History of Mental Retardation*. Baltimore: Brookes, 1983, p.229. Hay, a New Yorker and author-editor of an insurance treatise, was killed in a Chicago traffic accident soon after his election as NARC president and perhaps while on NARC business. At least, a school for children with disabilities in the Shoreline suburb of Seattle was named for him and later the Woodhull Hay chapter of WARC was formed around that school's parents.

[99]Coser, Lewis *The Functions of Social Conflict*. New York: Free Press, 1964, p. 154.

[100] Compare Shorter's account of the three persons contending to get the credit to be the founder of the Special Olympics.

[101]Bill Hay had been asked to write an article on parents groups for the *Encyclopedia Americana* (1952) by Richard Hungerford, president of the AAMD. Hay was the secretary of the steering committee which was to become the NARC, where he became its first secretary. The resulting article is "Associations for Parents of Mental Retardates." Woodhull Hay, Secretary, National Association of Parents and Friends of Mentally Retarded Children.

[102] Available at the Braddock archives, University of Colorado. There is also a June 20, 1950 letter to Hay from Alan Sampson citing Hungerford's role.

[103]It would be interesting to know exactly what and how its early work was. Was the Council, like the League, political from its very beginning, even if it lost the initial battle?

[104] *Board of Education of Cleveland Heights v. State ex rel. Goldman*, 47 Ohio.App. 417, 191 NE 914 (1934).

[105] The terminology of "opportunity classes" was nationwide and deserves further study.

[106] 1930 US census, available online at www.ancestry.com.

[107] If the higher scores had been accepted, one imagines that the Goldmans would never have incorporated the Council for the Retarded Child.

[108] The latter provision is guaranteed by the constitution of Washington state, and it is fair to imagine that most, if not all, of the state supreme courts would find that to be true.

[109] Sally Schmidt, 1970, p.vi.

[110] A February 13, 1953 letter from NARC secretary Dorothy Moss mentions that Schmidt had resigned from the NARC board of directors because she believed that the NARC leaders discriminated against non-parents. Letter at Braddock Library, Coleman Institute, University of Colorado.

[111] Schmidt, Sally Nowak. *The Birth of the Ohio Association for Retarded Children.* Cleveland, Ohio: Council for the Retarded Child, 1976, p. 13. Cf. Rothman, David J. and Sheila M. Rothman. *The Willowbrook Wars.* New York: Harper, 1984 p.60. Whatever happened in Columbus, four months later at the NARC organizing meeting in Minneapolis, Schmidt and Weingold served together on the Constitution and Bylaws Committee that he chaired, and she seconded Weingold's nominee to appoint the chair of the committee in charge of liaison with the AAMD. It is true that Weingold's undiplomatic manner continued. An NARC memo of May 15, 1953 by Eugene Gramm, editor of the Association for Help of Retarded Children in New York newsletter, noted that "I think of a bright, astute fellow like Jerry Weingold in New York City with a Mongoloid youngster he keeps at home. He and Mrs. W rush off to work in the morning while a nursemaid takes over. In fact, practically their total relationship with the youngster is in the luxury of tucking him and kissing him at night. Yes, in his capacity as Executive Director Mr. Weingold speaks with such vigor about the 'crime and stupidity' of doctors who suggest institutionalization for the Mongoloid. Result: Weingold's brash generalizations alienate the professionals, and fill with alarm, self-doubt, and aching guilt those parents who have already taken the 'fatal step' of institutionalizing their child." Letter of Gramm to Bea Bemis in Braddock/Coleman Institute archive.

[112]David Goode. *And Now Let's Make a Better World: The Story of the Association for the Help of Retarded Children, 1948-98.* New York: AHRC New York City 1998, p.16.

[113] See Weingold's forward in Lerner, Herbert J. *State Association for Retarded Children and New York State Government, 1948-1968.* New York: New York State Association for Retarded Children, 1972.

[114] Goode, *And Now Let's Make a Better World.*

[115] Weingold was clearly involved. Whether his proposed constitution and agenda were important has not been analyzed. He was a lawyer, but Washington state already had 15 years of living with a constitution of a parents group. *Changing the World for Our Children. A 60 Year Journey.* NYSARC, New York, NY, 2009, p. 11. This repeated claims from Weingold reported in David Goode's earlier 50 year history. *And Now Let's Make a Better World: The Story of the Association for the Help of Retarded Children, 1948-98.* New York: AHRC New York City.

[116]Rothman, David J. and Sheila M. Rothman. *The Willowbrook Wars.* New York: Harper, 1984, p.61.

[117]Segal, Robert M. *Mental Retardation and Social Action. A Study of the Associations for Retarded Children as a Force for Social Change.* Springfield, Illinois: Charles C. Thomas, 1970, p. 45.

[118] *Changing the World for Our Children. A 60 Year Journey.* NYSARC, New York, NY, 2009, p. 5.

[119] Segal, Robert M.. *Mental Retardation and Social Action. A Study of the Associations for Retarded Children as a Force for Social Change.* Springfield, Illinois: Charles C. Thomas.,1970, p.24

[120]Thomson, Mildred. *Prologue.* Minneapolis: Gilbert Publishing, 1963, p. 164; Boggs, Elizabeth. Personal interview, Washington, D.C., April 21, 1986.

[121]"St Paulites Aid to Retarded Pupils to be Told at Meet" *St Paul Dispatch,* September 27, 1950.

[122]Thomson, Mildred. *Prologue.* Minneapolis: Gilbert Publishing, 1963, p.166.

[123]By that time NARC headquarters was in New York City. Alan Sampson said that, earlier, during his term as first president of the NARC, he typed all his own correspondence on a typewriter in his Seattle basement, which was the first "office" that NARC had.

Washington State Dept of Social and Health Services, *Alan Hungate Sampson: Association for Retarded Children*, Olympia, 1991, p. 43.

[124] Alan H. Sampson, "The Development of the National Association of Parents and Friends of Mentally Retarded Children." *Training School Bulletin* 48:120-22 (October 1951).

[125] *Ibid.*, p.122.

[126] Sampson's untitled speech is found on the front page of the national newsletter.

[127] Niebuhr, Reinhold (1932). *Moral Man and Immoral Society*. New York: Scribner's.

[128] This brainstorm suggests why Reilly excelled as an advertising executive. Obituary, *Seattle Times,* July 25, 1998. Note also that Janice Leavitt says that King county parents had been dreaming of a national parents' newsletter since 1944.

[129] Blumenfeld was primarily employed at University Publishing Company which was owned by the father-in-law of Phil Reilly.

[130] Bob Leavitt claimed that he wrote 80% of the text. Interview September 8, 1985.

[131] The imagery was effective, too. The author's 10 year old son was troubled when he saw the image, asking "Why is that boy half in the dark?"

[132] Epton, Kathryn. (1992) *The Gift of Inspiration from a Little Boy in Prison*. Olympia: Washington State Department of Social & Health Services, 104.

[133] In January 1946 the CBL unit in Pierce county (Tacoma) began publishing a glossy newsletter, *CBL Bulletin*, although how long it lasted is unknown.

[134] Wolfensberger, Wolf. "The Origin and Nature of Our Institutional Models." Pp. 35-82 in Robert B. Kugel and Ann Shearer, eds. *Changing Patterns in Residential Services for the Mentally Retarded*. Rev. ed., Washington, D.C.: President's Committee on Mental Retardation, 1976.

[135] According to *HOPE*, July 1959, the film also circulated to Sweden and Alaska. There may have been earlier films. In the 1930s CBL leaders had talked of filming at the State Custodial School and showing those films to parents on Puget Sound who were unable to travel to see their children, and perhaps did so. At the first NARC convention in Minneapolis in 1950 delegates were

shown a film of the "Beta Parents Group" of St Paul.

[136] NYSARC says that in September 1949 Buck spoke to the parents of the AHRC, whose initials for many years stood for Association for the Help of Retarded Children. *Changing the World for Our Children*, p. 10.

[137] Woodbine House ed., 1992, p. 47.

[138] Pp.27f.

[139] Pp. 43f.

[140] P. 50.

[141] *HOPE for Retarded Children*, January 1959.

[142]*Angel Unaware*. Fleming H Revell Publishers, 1953, pp.14-15.

[143] Page 52.

[144] Page 59.

[145] Jackson, it is widely accepted, was Kennedy's first choice as vice-president until a deal had to be made with Lyndon Johnson in a successful effort to (narrowly) carry Texas. It is interesting to speculate whether President Jackson would have done more or less than President Johnson for persons with intellectual disabilities.

[146] Early NARC leaders like Elizabeth Boggs counted the response they elicited from Rep. John Fogarty (D-RI) as being their first important victory.

[147] Before this, the CBL presidents had always given their home addresses for official correspondence. Tucker's primary job was as a secretary to Clifton's business affairs. She was paid $20 per month by the CBL, or about $200, adjusted for inflation.

[148] Lippman, Leopold. *Attitudes Toward the Handicapped*. Springfield, Ill.: Charles C. Thomas, 1972.

[149]Etzioni, Amitai (1961). *A Comparative Analysis of Complex Organizations*. New York: Free Press.

[150] Parkinson, C. Northcote. *Parkinson's Law*. New York: Ballantine, 1964, p.16.

[151] O'Connor, Harvey. *Revolution in Seattle*. New York: Monthly Review, 1964.

[152] Lippman, Leopold. "The public." Pp. 95-103 in Robert B. Kugel and Ann Shearer, eds. *Changing Patterns in Residential Services for the Mentally Retarded*. Washington, D.C.: President's Committee on Mental Retardation, 1976, p.97.

[153] Alan Sampson's wife Louise wrote the by-laws for that

Guild. It was regarded a major milestone in achieving interest by outsiders, without a family member with mental disabilities. Personal interview February 11, 1982.

[154] Nonetheless, as the rhetoric of civil rights spread increasingly over all aspects of American society, local Arcs receiving United Way funds have been able to carry out some type of advocacy without concern, especially when labeled "information and referral."

[155] *HOPE for Retarded Children,* April 1958.

[156] *HOPE for Retarded Children,* July 1958.

[157] *HOPE for Retarded Children,* April 1959. Today there is an IRS dependency exemption for permanently disabled children who live with their parents who provide over half of the support. There are now federal agencies whose mission is the welfare of persons with disabilities. It is unknown if Tollefson's bills contributed to either of these achievements.

[158] *HOPE for Retarded Children,* April 1959.

[159] *HOPE for Retarded Children,* April 1960.

[160] *HOPE for Retarded Children,* July 1960.

[161] An Illinois group with the same name was formed in 1969, but no connection is known. It is now known as the Family Resource Center on Disabilities. Like the Washington group, professionals were actively involved in the Council, not just parents.

[162] Chu, Franklin and Sharland Trotter. *The Madness Establishment.* New York: Grossman, 1974.

[163] Relations between the Arc and United Cerebral Palsy continue nationally to this day. Their lobbying activities are jointly run through the Disability Policy Collaboration.

[164] Cuta, Frank. "Early life at the School for the Blind and other memories." *Newsline.* Second Quarter, 1985: 10-11. Published by United Blind of Washington State.

[165] Swift, 1937.

[166] Wooden, 1980.

[167] Robinson, 1985.

[168] Thomas, Orlando. Interview, Seattle, Washington, July 21, 1986.

[169] In fact, years later Orlando Thomas felt it had been a mistake for the Woodhull Hay group to join the CBL. The leadership

was just too focused on institutions. "They wanted us to place children who we thought were our own people." Interview, July 21, 1986.

[170] In 1962 the Kennedy family recruited Aldrich from the University of Washington Medical School to become the first director of what is now called the Eunice Kennedy Shriver Institute of Child Health and Human Development, part of the National Institutes of Health. After leaving the NICHD, Aldrich returned to the University where he remained for many years.

[171] Any voluntary organization connected to a stigmatizing condition will be disproportionately made up of members who cannot disavow the stigma. Thus, parents of children with severe disabilities or recognizable ones, like Down syndrome, have always been over-represented among Arc activists.

[172] Cf. Katz, Alfred H. *Parents of the Handicapped.* Springfield, IL: Thomas, 1961.

[173] Farber, Bernard. *Mental Retardation: Its Social Context and Social Consequences.* Boston: Houghton Miflin, 1968.

[174] The relative strength of public institutions in this state probably also had another salutary effect. Washington never built many large community residential facilities, profit or nonprofit. To oversimplify, it went straight from institutions to small apartments and houses as the preferred residential settings. Charlie Lakin, a University of Minnesota scholar of national trends in disability services, recently told the author that Washington's residential profile is unusually "bipolar."

[175] It is unclear if, at this late date, a study could even validly examine those who made the choice to institutionalize and what factors motivated them, beyond the anecdotes that appear in the literature.

[176] Goffman, Erving. *Asylums.* Garden City, New York: Doubleday, 1961; Wolfensberger, Wolf."The Origin and Nature of Our Institutional Models." Pp. 35-82 in Robert B. Kugel and Ann Shearer, eds. *Changing Patterns in Residential Services for the Mentally Retarded.* Rev. ed. Washington, D.C.: President's Committee on Mental Retardation, 1976; cf. Edgerton, Robert. *The Cloak of Competence.* Berkeley: University of California, 1967.

[177] Sykes, Gresham (1958). *The Society of Captives.* Princeton, N.J.: Princeton University Press.

[178] The Center should be compared to Gresham Sykes' analysis of the "center" in a maximum security prison, 1958.

[179] Stern herself had herself only made a conversion from a pro-institutional viewpoint about 1950. Her most famous book, *Mental Illness: A Guide for the Family* (1942), suggested no way to avoid hospitals.

[180] In 1955 Rainier School got a new superintendent, Wesley White, Ph.D., who had been head of training at Southbury and was later president of the AAMD. Burton Blatt, author of the institutional expose *Christmas in Purgatory*, lauded White for advocating that everyone, regardless of the severity of disability, can learn and for turning from institutions to community services. Blatt, *Am J. of Mental Deficiency* (1978) 83:101-03.

[181] Actually, New York leader Jerry Weingold used similar clout to overcome waiting lists and facilitate the admission of Eugene Gramm's son to Letchworth Village in the early 1950s after Gramm's wife had a "nervous breakdown." Goode, *And Now Let's Build a Better World: The Story of the Association for the Help of Retarded Children, 1948-1998.* NY: AHRC, 1998, page 25. Cf. Gramm's 1953 evaluation of Jerry Weingold's situation, footnoted above.

[182]Froberg, Erik. Personal interview, Seattle, April 23, 1985.

[183] Governor Albert D. Rosellini. "Welcoming Address." Northwest Regional Meeting, American Association on Mental Deficiency, Rainier School, Buckley, Washington, October 17, 1958.

[184] The irony of strait jackets being used in 1966 after the CBL had proudly proclaiming their end under Superintendent Parker in 1936 is a heavy one.

[185] Thomas, Joseph K. *Dedicated to Serving the Disabled.* Olympia: Washington State DSHS, 1991, 115.

[186] Thomas. *Dedicated to Serving the Disabled*, 110.

[187] In 1946, for example, the superintendents' request to the legislature was 60% salaries and 40% for all other operational expenses, in addition to the separately-budgeted capital improvements.

[188] *Tacoma News Tribune*, October 9, 1966.

[189] *Seattle Times*, October 24, 1966.

[190] Hinkle himself had a son with intellectual disabilities. He

was later the first president of the National Association of State Mental Retardation Program directors. Interview August 13, 1985.

[191] According to Alan Sampson, in 1947 the CBL had invited Doll to visit Washington state and advise them on best practices. It was his first visit to Washington and upon retirement from the Vineland School, he moved to Bellingham where he was a consultant on special education to the local schools.

[192] According to H. N. Clifton, another president, it was really Riviere's dedicated and talented wife who got done most of the work accomplished during his presidency.

[193] *Mental Health and Retardation Politics: The Mind Lobbies in* Congress (1975).

[194] Epton, Kathryn. (1992) *The Gift of Inspiration from a Little Boy in Prison.* Olympia: Washington State Department of Social & Health Services, 109. In the 1980's it was calculated that senior citizens had become the most powerful human services lobby, followed by developmental disabilities.

[195]Executive Committee Minutes, January 8 and 9, 1966.

[196] In 1985 the legislature directed the Department of Social and Health Services, which included the Division of Developmental Disabilities, to conduct a "financial responsibility study" to identify possible new sources of revenue from service recipients and agreed-upon principles for such a unified plan. The Arc representative was part of a 30-person "oversight committee." In 1998 DSHS issued its Final Report on the project, which recommended assessing parents for the costs of services provided to their children on a sliding scale based on income. The Arc representative dissented in a Minority Report. No such legislation was enacted.

[197] According to H. N. Clifton, in the twenty years after the CBL lobbied for the creation of Rainier State School, the thinking of the CBL had shifted from seeking a safe, secluded, secure place, to one near the University of Washington, so that diagnoses and clinical interventions would be easily available. Interview, April 1, 1986.

[198] Her mother was also a State Senator, the Lulu Haddon who played a key role in the legislation authorizing Rainier School in 1937. Frances said that the birth of a grandchild with Down syndrome in 1958 made her run for the legislature, despite the onerous duties of a legislator that she knew first hand having a mother there.

[199] Rich, Chester L *The Progress of Humane Legislation in Washington.* Doctoral dissertation. Seattle: University of Washington, 1921, p.104.

[200] Laing, James M. *A History of the Provision for Mentally Retarded Children in the State of Washington.* Unpublished doctoral dissertation. Seattle: University of Washington, 1955, p.96.

[201] Bixler, Earl G. Superintendent's Report on the State Custodial School. Second Biennial Report of the Department of Business Control. Olympia: State of Washington, 1924.

[202] Edward Shorter *The Kennedy Family and the Story of Mental Retardation*, p.18. As Shorter points out, this is very close to the arguments made against educating slaves in the antebellum South.

[203] Woodruff, Samuel C. *Superintendent's Report on the State Institution for the Feeble-Minded.* Twentieth Biennial Report of the Superintendent of Public Instruction. Olympia, Washington, 1910. It is of note that the report is from the state department of education.

[204] Woodruff, Samuel C. *Superintendent's Report on the State Institution for the Feeble-Minded.* Twenty-second Biennial Report of the Superintendent of Public Instruction. Olympia: State of Washington, 1914.

[205] Landsburg, Leona. Personal interview, Aberdeen, Washington, 1975.

[206] Hoquiam School Board, 1909; Woodruff, 1910: 170. Hoquiam School District (1909). Minutes of the School Board. May 5.

[207] Conley, Mary Jo. *The History of the Development of Care for the Mentally Deficient Child in the State of Washington, 1854-1938.* Unpublished Master of Science in social work dissertation. Washington, D.C.: Catholic University, 1939. Cf. Lash, Frederick M. (1934). *An Historical and Functional Study of Public Education in Seattle, Washington.* Unpublished doctoral dissertation. Seattle: University of Washington.

[208] Conley, Mary Jo. *The History of the Development of Care for the Mentally Deficient Child in the State of Washington, 1854-1938.* Unpublished Master of Science in social work dissertation. Washington, D.C.: Catholic University, 1939, pp. 28-40. Cf. Laing, James M. *A History of the Provision for Mentally Retarded Children in the State of Washington.* Unpublished doctoral dissertation. Seattle: University of Washington, 1955.

[209] Conley, Mary Jo. *The History of the Development of Care*

for the Mentally Deficient Child in the State of Washington, 1854-1938. Unpublished Master of Science in social work dissertation. Washington, D.C.: Catholic University, 1939, pp. 34-5.

[210] This was eight years before the national Council for Exceptional Children was formed (Wooden, 1980).

[211] Laing, James M. *A History of the Provision for Mentally Retarded Children in the State of Washington.* Unpublished doctoral dissertation. Seattle: University of Washington, 1955, p.221.

[212]Quigley, E. G. Letter of superintendent to the Seattle School Board, December 7. Seattle School District archives, Seattle, Washington, 1915.

[213]Cooper, Frank B. Superintendent's letter to Seattle School Board, February 14. Seattle School District archives, Seattle, Washington., 1917

[214]Nelson, Bryce E. *Good Schools: The Development of Public Schooling in Seattle, 1901-22.* Unpublished doctoral dissertation. Seattle: University of Washington, 1981. Pp. 162-63.

[215]Kirk, Margaret L. *The Social Utility of the Curriculum in the Special Rooms of Tacoma, Washington.* Unpublished Master of Arts thesis. Seattle: University of Washington, 1939. The special education program was judged a success, with most of the former male students employed and the women married; only one person had been incarcerated for a criminal offense.

[216] Conley, Mary Jo. *The History of the Development of Care for the Mentally Deficient Child in the State of Washington, 1854-1938.* Unpublished Master of Science in social work dissertation. Washington, D.C.: Catholic University, 1939.

[217]Williams, Mae F. "Together again." quoted by Lillian Hill, *"News letter of the Pacific Coast Region, AAMD."* American Journal of Mental Deficiency. 48:122 (1943).

[218] Wanamaker, Pearl A. *Thirty-seventh Biennial Report of the Superintendent of Public Instruction.* Olympia: State of Washington, 1944.

[219] Wanamaker, Pearl A. *Thirty-eighth Biennial Report of the Superintendent of Public Instruction.* Olympia: State of Washington, 1948, p.24. "Seattle's Honored Mother." Seattle Times, May 6, 1956.

[220] Strayer, George D. *Public Education in Washington.* Olympia: State of Washington, 1946.

299

[221] Four, because, besides her own, Magnuson had foster children.

[222] Magnuson, Anna. Personal interview, Kirkland, Washington, August 12, 1985.

[223] Clifton, H. N. Personal interview, Seattle, Washington, March 27, 1986.

[224] Magnuson reported that at least one CBL leader, Phil Reilly, was a great help, providing much-needed moral support. She got her primary training in how to lobby not from the experienced CBL leaders, but from Arthur Dunbar, legislative chair of the organization of the blind. Interview August 12, 1985.

[225] Magnuson swore the author to secrecy on the identity of the professor. Interview August 12, 1985.

[226] In 1955 Washington districts reported a total of 5,647 identified children with mental disabilities of whom they were serving 2,305. Cf. Charles Coffey. *A Study of the Provisions for Mentally Retarded Children in Selected Public Schools in the State of Washington.* Dissertation, School of Education, University of Washington, 1955. The NARC official who quoted these statistics in a November 11, 1959 letter to Leo Lippman, WARC executive secretary, said that that compared favorably to other states.

[227] Interview with Orlando and Jean Thomas, Seattle, July 21, 1986.

[228] Epton, Kathryn. (1992) *The Gift of Inspiration from a Little Boy in Prison.* Olympia: Washington State Department of Social & Health Services, 100.

[229] Letter in Braddock archives, Coleman Institute, University of Colorado.

[230] This was the first of a long line of Ellensburg conferences spanning the decades that provided education and training for practitioners and activists in education, employment, and other matters.

[231] See Susan Schwartzenberg. *Becoming Citizens: Family Life and the Politics of Disability* (2005).

According to Dolan, it was Newt Buker, who declared "What you need is a mandatory education law." Dolan, Kathleen (1991). *We Lived in the Ghetto of Mental Retardation.* Olympia: State of Washington Department of Social and Health Services, 158. Lindquist says it was Ralph Munro.

[232] According to Orlando and Jean Thomas, Katie Dolan got the idea for a school from the Woodhull Hay experience. Jean introduced Katie to Ross Hamilton, state director of special education, who was very helpful.

[233] Unexpectedly, the *Catholic Northwest Progress* editorialized against the bill, perhaps in part because it was viewed as a threat to parochial school practice. Dolan and Taggart met with a diocesan administrator and talked to him, without concrete result. Dolan, Kathleen (1991). *We Lived in the Ghetto of Mental Retardation*, 237-38.

[234] Chapman, Evelyn. Personal interview, Seattle, Washington, 1986.

[235] Levine, Erwin L. and Elizabeth M. Wexler *PL 94-142: An Act of Congress*. New York: Macmillan 1981.

[236] Chapman, Evelyn. Personal interview, Seattle, Washington, 1986

[237] George Breck claims that the only contribution for which he is entitled special credit is the phrase "education for all." Interview Seattle-Winslow ferry July 17, 2009.

[238] In what can be viewed as yet another case of "Success Has a Hundred Fathers," other states also claimed to have achieved universal education early or first. In 1961 NARC surveyed the states and listed those whose laws included mandatory education for "trainable" mentally retarded children (i.e., those with intelligence too low to be "educable"): Massachusetts (1954), New Jersey (1954), Rhode Island (1955), Pennsylvania (1956), Kentucky (1956), Connecticut (1959), Missouri (1960) and New York (1960).

[239] *Washington State Special Education Coalition v. State of Washington*, Thurston County Superior Court Cause #85-2-00543-8. By this time Judge Doran had become the expert with all education cases brought before him and the state not choosing to appeal when it lost in front of Judge Doran.

[240] "Officials split on need for Fort Worden school for retarded." *Seattle Times*. January 24, 1956.

[241] "Mrs. Epton seeks post of state representative." June 8, 1954. *Spokane Valley Herald*.

[242] Katz, Alfred H. *Parents of the Handicapped*. Springfield, IL: Thomas, 1981, p.30.

[243] Sampson, Alan H. Special Bulletin, April 23. National As-

sociation of Parents and Friends of Mentally Retarded Children, 1951.

[244] NARC asked for an appropriation of over $6,000,000. "Proposals on a Federal Program of Action in 1956-57 for America's Mentally Retarded Children and Adults." 50pp. Braddock Archives and Library on Disability, University of Colorado.

[245] Braddock, David *Federal Spending for Mental Retardation and Developmental Disabilities.* Baltimore: Paul H. Brookes, 1986.

[246] Braddock, *Federal Spending for Mental Retardation and Developmental Disabilities.* Baltimore: Paul H. Brookes, 1986, 17-18.

[247] Bardach, Eugene. *The Implementation Game.* Cambridge, Mass.: MIT Press, 1977.

[248] Braddock, David *Federal Spending for Mental Retardation and Developmental Disabilities.* Baltimore: Paul H. Brookes, 1986, 60

[249] Braddock, David *Federal Spending for Mental Retardation and Developmental Disabilities.* Baltimore: Paul H. Brookes, 1986, 11, 61.

[250] This claim is disputed by NYSARC, which claims "the first workshop for people with developmental disabilities in the United States" in Brooklyn. *Changing the World for Our Children*, p.8.

[251] Lindley, James H. *This is Exceptional Foresters.* Shelton, WA: Exceptional Foresters, 1982.

[252] Remmerde, Barbara. *Seattle's Epton Schools. A Developmental Process.* University of Washington, School of Education, B.A. thesis, 1966, for Prof. Charles Strother, special education. In possession of Northwest Center Industries, 1986.

[253] $73 is the equivalent of $359 in 2010 values, according to the Federal Reserve Bank.

[254] Despite many improvements, however, the transition between schools and adult employment or training programs is still often uncertain even today.

[255] Preferential treatment in state settings has been around since at least 1936 when blind adults were granted vending operations rights in federal and state government buildings.

[256] State of Washington. Annual School Census Reports of Defective Youth 1930. Copy in State Archives, Olympia, Washington.

[257] Looking back years later Epton did not like the effects of the

302

bill, which she considered opened the door to operators who were not responsive to parental efforts to maintain high quality. Epton, Kathryn. (1992) *The Gift of Inspiration from a Little Boy in Prison*. Olympia: Washington State Department of Social & Health Services.

[258] The criteria are also notable for at least nominally including the resident's own preference as a component in the placement process, a principle which could conflict with the continuum model and a principal which has become primary in recent years.

[259] Recently DSHS was reorganized with developmental disabilities paired with senior citizens programs in the Aging and Disability Services Administration, which again has alarmed advocates.

[260] Compared to some other states, in Washington only a small fraction of persons with developmental disabilities ever resided in nursing homes.

[261] Governor's Budget Request. *Biennial request for the fiscal years 1973-75*. Olympia: State of Washington, 1972.

[262] Rolfe later directed the state Division of Developmental Disabilities.

[263] Looking backward, the judgment is less clear-cut, because receiving federal matching funds for institutional care has sustained the large state-operated institutions which otherwise might have closed, as the ARC came to desire.

[264] Epton, Kathryn. *The Gift of Inspiration from a Little Boy in Prison*. Olympia: DSHS, State of Washington, 1992, 44.

[265] Ibid.

[266] Edward Shorter. *The Kennedy Family and the Story of Mental Retardation*. Philadelphia: Temple University Press, 2000, pages 50, 75. Before beginning to fund research, the foundation had made several grants to support Catholic residential schools (institutions) for children with mental retardation, at the urging of Cardinal Richard Cushing of Boston, according to Shorter. The percentage of the foundation's grants made to mental retardation rose from 17% in 1957 to 66% in 1960.

[267] The Research Trust Fund had a separate board which has evolved somewhat independently of its mother organization. By design, only a minority of the board is selected by the parents group.

[268] Equal to $13,500 in 2010 dollars.

[269] Thuline was the director of laboratories at Rainier State School.

[270] Over $40,000 in 2010 dollars.

[271] "Proposals on a Federal Program of Action in 1956-57 for America's Mentally Retarded Children and Adults." 50pp. Braddock Archives and Library on Disability, University of Colorado.

[272] In the 1950s John Hauberg, a wealthy patron of the arts, gave the first funding for a "pilot school" for children with developmental disabilities, which became one of the foundations of the CDMRC, the UW's research hospital. In the 1960s he chaired Gov. Evans' Task Force on Mental Retardation. Obituary, *Seattle Post-Intelligencer*, April 6, 2002. According to Van Hinkle, Hauberg gave the first $50,000 for the CDMRC with the Shrivers in attendance. Hinkle interview, August 13, 1985. WARC and Hauberg must be credited with one of original impulses leading to the creation of the nationwide system of University Affiliated Programs that receive federal funding for research and training in developmental disabilities. According to Charles Strother, director, they were astounded that after all the enthusiasm that the Shrivers showed for the new work being done at the University clinic, their proposal was not funded by the Kennedy Foundation, which, as far as they could tell, had only to do with Sargent Shriver's run for U S Senate in Illinois, which dictated that all the available funding went to the University of Chicago in a major well-publicized affair. Strother, Charles. (1992) *Child Development and Mental Retardation Center*. Olympia: State of Washington, Department of Social and Health Services.

[273] JFK speech February 5, 1963. Shorter, *The Kennedy Family and the Story of Mental Retardation*, 102.

[274] LaVeck went on to become director of National Institute on Child Health and Human Development.

[275] Its articles of incorporation were filed November 27, 1963.

[276] James Lounsberry, *Challenge*, May 1967, pp. 1, 4.

[277] Shorter, p. 121. Writing in 2000, Shorter tells the story of three still plausible contenders for the origin of the idea of what became Special Olympics – Canadian fitness expert Frank Hayden, a Chicago Parks and Recreation leader Anne McGlone-Burke, and Eunice Kennedy Shriver.

[278] In recent years the national leaders of Special Olympics have promoted much more integrated, inclusive athletics.

[279]Farber, Bernard. *Mental Retardation: Its Social Context and Social Consequences.* Boston: Houghton Miflin, 1968, p. 137.

[280]Also, women have *gotten* jobs. With the dramatic increase in female participation in the labor force, gone are the days when the day-to-day work of the Arc and many other organizations could rely on countless hours of volunteering by mothers.

[281]"Handicapped children may get assist in state bill." February 2, 1959. *Tri-City Herald.* Pasco, Washington.

[282] Harmon said that the Home Aid program was recognized as a commendable innovation by the U. S. Department of Education and Welfare. Interview, September 10, 1986.

[283] In a similar move the AARP is no longer the American Association for Retired Persons, but simply the AARP. The NAACP came close to a similar amendment of its name, but decided to honor tradition by retaining the full word behind the initial C. But "colored" was no longer in common use as a pejorative, as "retarded" still is.

[284] Shorter *The Kennedy Family and the Story of Mental Retardation,* p. 162.

[285] This has distressed a minority of eloquent parents, most prominently Elizabeth Boggs, who was president of the Arc US and also a sophisticated critic of normalization theory. Boggs, Elizabeth (1985). "Whose Head is in the Clouds?" H R Turnbull & Ann Turnbull, eds., *Parents Speak Out. Then and Now.* 2nd ed. Cleveland: Merrill 1985.

[286] Wolfensberger, 1972: 28.

[287]Lensink, Brian. "ENCOR, Nebraska." Pp. 277-96. In Robert B. Kugel and Ann Shearer, eds., *Changing Patterns in Residential Services for the Mentally Retarded,* rev. ed. Washington, DC: President's Committee on Mental Retardation, 1976.

[288] Biklen, Douglas. *Let Our Children Go: An Organizing Manual for Advocates and Parents.* Syracuse: Human Policy Press, 1974.

[289] Gouldner, Alvin. "Cosmopolitans and locals." *Administrative Science Quarterly.* 2: 281-306, 444-80, 1957-58.

[290] The national landmark for deinstitutionalization is called "The Community Imperative: A Refutation of All Arguments in

Support of Institutionalizing Anybody Because of Mental Retardation" was issued by the Center on Human Policy, Syracuse University in 1979. Its backers launched a nationwide campaign for signatures to the Community Imperative petition. It did not get much play in Washington, because the ARC had already filed the Community Services Suit on the same grounds and the author had already given a speech with a notably similar title to the Region I conference of the American Association on Mental Retardation at Portland, Oregon in 1978 "Deinstitutionalization for all: A review of the literature and a new defense."

[291] Gerald Thomas was the acting secretary of the Department of Social and Health Services.

[292] Phil Reilly was one of the leaders in the 1950s. He was an intervener on behalf of his son who still lived at Rainier.

[293] Jones, Larry A. "Parents want to keep retarded children home." *Lacey Leader.* October 18, 1978. Published under the pseudonym "Sue Ballard."

[294] *Pennhurst State School & Hospital v. Halderman* 451 US 1 (1981).

[295] Rothman, David J. and Sheila M. Rothman. *The Willowbrook Wars.* New York: Harper, 1984. Cf. Burt, Robert. "Pennhurst: A parable." Pp. 265-363 in Robert H. Mnookin, ed. *In the Interest of Children: Advocacy, Law Reform, and Public Policy.* New York: Freeman, 1985.

[296] A minority had long advocated that "exceptional" children should be integrated with other children in order to prepare for an integrated and productive adulthood. On balance, that was seemingly the judgment that Mae Williams, Tacoma teacher quoted above, came to in her description of the involuntary mainstreaming of her special education students during to the wartime shortages in 1943. That was the argument of L. C. Ruff, a local school district superintendent from California who gave a talk "Integration Rather Than Segregation" at the 4th NARC convention in Chicago in 1953. Proceedings, pp. 85-87. At Braddock Archives, Coleman Institute.

[297] At the state's first Section 504 training conference that Bob Thurston, who used a wheelchair, and the author had organized at the state college in Olympia, the activists were allowed to address affected public agencies on what Section 504 meant, because the regional Office of Civil Rights staff had not yet received official

instructions from Washington, D.C.

[298] In 1985-86 Lake Washington School District was pressured about its separate Gordon Hauck school and Northshore School District was pressured about its separate C. O. Sorensen School. Letters were written to the superintendents and to the state Office of Superintendent of Public Instruction.

[299] Jones, Larry A. and Randi Moe. "College education for mentally retarded adults." *Mental Retardation* (1987) 18: 59-62.

[300] Actually there were several resolutions offered by the ARC of Washington in those years urging the closure of institutions and the adaptation of integrated, inclusive service models. Similar resolutions were offered by the ARC of Colorado, the other state with which Washington competed to see who was most progressive. The resolutions usually lost but may have had educational value as they were debated on the convention floor.

[301] F. Menolascino and R. Coleman. "The Pilot Parent Program: Helping Handicapped Children Through their Parents." *Child Psychiatry and Human Development.* 11:41-48 (1980). When a group of Nebraska staff in developmental disability programs moved to Arizona, they took the idea for pilot parents with them and replicated it. Gene Edgar, a professor of special education at the University of Washington who was on the Arc King County board of directors, knew of the Arizona program and played an important role in its development here.

[302] These councils in every state were created by federal legislation that the national ARC had lobbied through to monitor the provision of federally-funded state disability services. It is a good example of ARC advocacy, because it provided tax-supported rivals to the ARCs as advocates in the respective states. The ARC wisely believed that more advocacy was needed, even if it weakened the ARC itself. The author felt the conflict directly when about 1981 the executive director of the council asked him to abandon the ARC with the statement that "the ARC is dead, come to the Assembly where things are happening." That was at a time that the ARC was weak, perhaps due to its advocacy style. State finances were so inadequate that, for the first time in 30 years, there was no executive director. But later the Assembly was gone. The Arc survives.

[303] This was a quote from part of the normalization theory as formulated by Wolf Wolfensberger.

[304] Lorelei Thompson and Larry A. Jones, eds. *How to Make the Law and Justice System Work for the Retarded Citizens of Washington State.* Olympia: Washington ARC, 1980.

[305] There have been more efforts in Washington and elsewhere since then, highlighted nationally by the years of efforts by Bob Perske to rescue men wrongly convicted from death row and other lengthy incarcerations, frequently on the basis of confessions falsely given to please their interrogators.

[306] Jones, L. A. & Shelan, N. "Abuse and Neglect of Mentally Retarded Children. Washington's Central Registry Statistics 1974-79." A paper delivered at the 25th Annual Conference of the Region I, American Association on Mental Retardation Yakima, WA October 13, 1980 and distributed by the ARC of Washington.

[307] Part of the background was a September 1982 ARC report by the state president who, accompanied by Ray Jensen of the King County Developmental Disabilities Division, visited Wisconsin to learn about several of its innovative ways of using Medicaid funds to support community services. The trip was funded by the Washington State Developmental Disabilities Planning Council.

[308] There are several reasons why the conservative Reagan administration favored waivers. Waiver expenditures had to cost less per person than the current institutional services. Second, the number of persons receiving these services was limited to the number that the state decided to serve, unlike the institutional services that are open to all who qualify for them. Third, institutional staff are unionized public employees and unions support Democrats. By contrast, most community service providers are not unionized.

[309] Kreidler, who later was a Congressman, is now Washington State's Insurance Commissioner. When the ARC of Thurston County (Olympia) learned that their first term representative in the state House had had a child with spina bifida, they soon sprang into action. Considering him a natural ally, the young men of the Arc county chapter volunteered to help in his re-election campaign and put up most of his signs in the next two elections.

[310] In Washington, unlike some other states, the Arc has never been a major operator of community residential facilities. Only a few of the local chapters have operated any residential programs. Instead the dominant model has been for independent non-profits to operate these programs (sometimes composed of Arc leaders, it is

308

true). Now there are more profit-making ventures, but so far these are small in size. The same is true of employment support programs.

[311] The Trust Fund is dedicated to "the raising of funds for the purpose of facilitating the study and research through medical, sociological, psychological, or any other means of the causes, prevention, *cure*, and amelioration of mental deficiency..."

[312] King County Superior Court Cause #88-2-17277-3.

[313] To some of its founders and backers, the Assembly was perceived as a broader group that would mirror the success some saw in the Washington State Special Education Coalition, which was incorporated in 1980. The Special Education Coalition was a place where parents, teachers, administrators, and others met and searched for unified efforts to press for increased funding and increased quality of special education.

[314] Another organization, the Alliance of People with Disabilities, formerly the Washington Coalition of Persons with Disabilities, survives today.

[315] For example, by 1995 Jeff Larsen, who had earlier been the paid professional lobbyist for the Assembly, was a lobbyist for residential providers opposing a bill that the Assembly supported.

[316] When Linda Rolfe became director of the Division of Developmental Disabilities in 2000, she recruited Janet Adams away and the Arc's survey of pending legislation was turned over to others, especially Grier Jewell. Not that this was the first session in which the Arc surveyed all legislation. For example, in December 1977 Kathleen Barnett, co-chair of the Arc's Governmental Affairs Committee, told the board of directors that there were 50-60 bills that the committee was following. The full board discussed and formulated an Arc position (or neutrality) on 25 bills.

[317] *Olmstead v. L.C.*, 527 U.S. 581 (1999).

[318] Interview with Charlie Lakin (2001), a University of Minnesota professor and authority on state-by-state comparisons of developmental disability programs.

[319] Naomi Scott, K. Charlie Lakin, Sheryl A. Larson. "The 40th Anniversary of Deinstitutionalization in the United States: Decreasing State Institutional Populations, 1967–2007." *Intellectual and Developmental Disabilities* 46: 402-05, 2008.

[320] One roadblock is the Froberg law, discussed above, requir-

ing hearings, if requested, before any community placement. The unions as allies were suspected of subsidizing attorneys who opposed the two lawsuits seeking to close all institutions, *WARC v. Thomas* and *People First v. Rainier.*

[321] With the Recession of 2007-09 there have been job losses among supported employees as well as those in the larger economy.

[322] This time, Attorney General Gregoire signed onto an amicus brief supporting the ADA against attack in the *Garrett* case.

[323]K Charlie Lakin, et al., "Twenty-Five Years of Medicaid and Home and Community Based Services (HCBS)," *Intellectual and Developmental Disabilities*, 46:325-28. August 2008.

[324] Also, after the court was persuaded to disapprove the original settlement, the State was free to use the savings accrued from natural attrition to fund the continuing cost of the promised increases already in force.

[325] Not surprisingly in the severe economic downturn of 2009 advocates were unable to obtain funding from the legislature to allow contributions from new applicants to be matched.

[326] Advocates succeeded in locating the Endowment Fund in the Commerce and Economic Development department of state government, not in the Division of Developmental Disabilities of DSHS. They did this to hopefully deter future DSHS budget officers – and legislators – from not making appropriations from the general fund for developmental disabilities by the amount generated by the Endowment Fund. That is, they sought to ensure that Endowment Fund dollars would supplement, not supplant, regular appropriations.

[327] Judge Doran retired in 1993.

[328] The idea of diverting the savings reduced institutional expenditures to fund expanded community services had been around since at least November 1994 when Janet Adams, Advocacy Coordinator for the Washington Assembly for Citizens with Disabilities proposed a bill using the model of a New York statute enacted the prior year.

[329] Joachim, 1951.

[330] Of course, these same lessons were favorites of President Obama when he was a community organizer in Chicago, especially those from Niebuhr and Alinsky.

REFERENCES

Alinsky, Saul (1972). *Rules for Radicals*. New York: Vintage.

American Association on Mental Deficiency (n.d.) *List of Officers, Committees, and Members, 1939-40*. AAMD: n.p.

American Red Cross (1924), Seattle Chapter, Special Research Committee. *Feeblemindedness in Washington*. Seattle.

Bair, Barbara (1981). "The Parents Council for Retarded Children and social change in Rhode Island, 1951-1970." *Rhode Island History* 40: 144-159.

Bales, Robert F. (1955). "Role differentiation in small decision-making groups." Pp. 259-306 in Talcott Parsons and Robert F. Bales, et al., eds. *Family, Socialization, and Interaction Process*. Glencoe, IL: Free Press.

Bardach, Eugene (1977). *The Implementation Game*. Cambridge, Mass.: MIT Press.

Berger, Peter L. (1961). *The Noise of Solemn Assemblies*.

Garden City, N.J.: Doubleday.

Biklen, Douglas (1974). *Let Our Children Go: An Organizing Manual for Advocates and Parents.* Syracuse: Human Policy Press.

Bixler, Earl G. (1924). *Superintendent's Report on the State Custodial School. Second Biennial Report of the Department of Business Control.* Olympia: State of Washington.

Blatt, Burton and Fred Kaplan (1974). *Christmas in Purgatory.* Syracuse, N.Y.: Human Policy Press.

Boggs, Elizabeth (1971). "Federal legislation." Pp. 103-27 in Joseph Wortis, ed., *Mental Retardation: An Annual Review.* New York: Grune and Stratton.

Boggs, Elizabeth (1985). "Whose Head is in the Clouds?" H R Turnbull & Ann Turnbull, eds., *Parents Speak Out. Then and Now.* 2nd ed. Cleveland: Merrill 1985.

Boggs, Elizabeth (1986). Personal interview, Washington, D.C., April 21.

Braddock, David (1986a). *Federal Spending for Mental Retardation and Developmental Disabilities.* Baltimore: Paul H. Brookes.

Braddock, David (1986b). "From Roosevelt to Reagan: Federal spending for mental retardation and developmental disabilities." *American Journal of Mental Deficiency.* 90:479-89.

Burt, Robert (1985). "Pennhurst: A parable." Pp. 265-363 in Robert H. Mnookin, ed. *In the Interest of Children: Advocacy, Law Reform, and Public Policy.* New York: Freeman.

Census of Defective Youth (1930). *Annual School Census Reports of Defective Youth.* Copy in State Archives, Olympia, Washington.

Center on Human Policy (1969). *The community imperative: A refutation of all arguments in support of institutionalizing anybody because of mental retardation.* Syracuse, NY.

Chapman, Evelyn (1986). Personal interview, Seattle, Washington.

Chu, Franklin and Sharland Trotter (1974). *The Madness Establishment.* New York: Grossman.

Clark (1937). *Minute Book.* Children's Benevolent League, Clark County Chapter, Vancouver, Washington.

Clifton, H. N. (1986). Personal interview, Seattle, Washington, March 27.

Cole, Thomas R. (1925). *Superintendent's letter to Seattle*

School Board, including a report from Nellie A. Goodhue, May 29. Seattle S c h o o l District archives, Seattle, Washington.

Conley, Mary Jo (1939). *The History of the Development of Care for the Mentally Deficient C h i l d i n the State of Washington, 1854-1938.* Unpublished master of science in social work dissertation. Washington, D.C.: Catholic University.

Cooper, Frank B. (1917). *Superintendent's letter to Seattle S c h o o l Board, February 14.* Seattle School District archives, Seattle, Washington.

Cooper, Frank B. (1919). *Superintendent's letter to Seattle S c h o o l Board, October 2.* Seattle School District archives, Seattle, Washington.

Coser, Lewis (1964). *The Functions of Social Conflict.* New York: Free Press.

Cunningham, Ross (1949). "Long fight can only bring harm to Rainier School." *Seattle Times*, October 24, p. 4.

Cuta, Frank (1985). "Early life at the School for the Blind and other memories." *Newsline.* Second Quarter, 1985: 10-11. Published by United Blind of Washington State.

De Tocqueville, Alexis (1969). *Democracy in America.* Garden City, NY: Doubleday Anchor.

DiMichael, Salvatore (1950). *Vocational Rehabilitation of the Mentally Retarded.* Washington, DC: U. S. Government Printing Office.

Dolan, Kathleen (1991). *We Lived in the Ghetto of Mental Retardation.* Olympia: State of Washington Department of Social and Health Services.

Dybwad, Gunnar.(1994) "From Feeble-Mindedness to Self-Advocacy. A Half Century of Growth and Self-Fulfillment." Speech to 1994 AAMR Convention. Available online at the Minnesota Developmental Disability Council's website.

Dybwad, Rosemary. (1990). *Perspectives on a Parent Movement. The Revolt of Parents of Children with Intellectual Limitations.* N.p.: Brookline Books.

Edgerton, Robert. (1967). *The Cloak of Competence.* Berkeley: University of California.

Epton, Kathryn.(1992) *The Gift of Inspiration from a Little Boy in Prison.* Oral transcript. Olympia: Washington State Department of Social & Health Services.

Etzioni, Amitai (1961). *A Comparative Analysis of Complex*

Organizations. New York: Free Press.

Farber, Bernard (1968). *Mental Retardation: Its Social Context and Social Consequences*. Boston: Houghton Miflin.

Felicetti, Daniel. (1975). *Mental Health and Mental Retardation Politics: The Mind Lobbies in Congress*. New York: Praeger.

Fisher, Roger and William Ury (1983). *Getting to Yes: Negotiating Agreement Without Giving In*. Baltimore: Penguin.

FOCUS (1964). Vol.1, No. 6, August 13. Washington Association for Retarded Children.

Froberg, Erik (1985). Personal interview, Seattle, April 23.

Goffman, Erving {1961). *Asylums*. Garden City, New York: Doubleday.

Goffman, Erving (1963). *Stigma*. Englewood Cliffs, NJ: Prentice-Hall.

Goode, David. (1998). *And Now Let's Make a Better World: The Story of the Association for the Help of Retarded Children, 1948-98*. New York: AHRC New York City. Available online.

Gouldner, Alvin (1957-58). "Cosmopolitans and locals." *Administrative Science Quarterly*. 2: 281-306, 444-80.

Governor's Budget Request (1972). *Biennial request for the fiscal years 1973-75*. Olympia: State of Washington.

Hoquiam School District (1909). *Minutes of the School Board*. May 5.

Institutions (1939-43). Letters of Charles Parker, Olaf Olsen, and others. Washington State Archives, Olympia, filed under "Institutions, General, 1939-43."

Joachim, H. H. (1951). *The Nichomachean Ethics*. D. A. Rees, ed. London: Oxford University Press.

Jones, Larry A. (1978). "Parents want to keep retarded children home." *Lacey Leader*. October 18. Published under the pseudonym "Sue Ballard."

Jones, Larry A. and Norma J. Shelan (1980). "Abuse and neglect of mentally retarded children: Washington's Central Registry statistics for 1974-79." Paper delivered at American Association on Mental Deficiency Region I convention, Yakima, Washington.

Jones, Larry A. and Randi Moe (1980). "College education for mentally retarded adults." *Mental Retardation* 18: 59-62.

Jones, Susan Delanty (1969). *Progressivism and the Election of*

1920 in Washington State. Unpublished master of arts thesis, University of Chicago, Chicago, IL.

Katz, Alfred H. (1961). *Parents of the Handicapped.* Springfield, IL: Thomas.

Kirk, Margaret L. (1939). *The Social Utility of the Curriculum in the Special Rooms of Tacoma, Washington.* Unpublished master of arts thesis. Seattle: University of Washington.

Kitsap (1938-40). *Minute Book.* Children's Benevolent League, Kitsap County Chapter, Bremerton, Washington.

Laing, James M. (1955). *A History of the Provision for Mentally Retarded Children in the State of Washington.* Unpublished doctoral dissertation. Seattle: University of Washington.

Lakin, K. Charlie (2001). Personal interview.

Lakin, K Charlie et al. (2008). "Twenty-Five Years of Medicaid and Home and Community Based Services (HCBS)," *Intellectual and Developmental Disabilities*, 46:325-28.

Landsburg, Leona (1975). Personal interview, Aberdeen, Washington.

Lash, Frederick M. (1934). *An Historical and Functional Study of Public Education in Seattle, Washington.* Unpublished doctoral dissertation. Seattle: University of Washington.

Lensink, Brian (1976). "ENCOR, Nebraska." Pp. 277-96. In Robert B. Kugel and Ann Shearer, eds., *Changing Patterns in Residential Services for the Mentally Retarded,* rev. ed. Washington, DC: President's Committee on Mental Retardation.

Lerner, Herbert J. (1972). *State Association for Retarded Children and New York State Government, 1948-1968.* New York: New York State Association for Retarded Children.

Levine, Erwin L. and Elizabeth M. Wexler (1981). *PL 94-142: An Act of Congress.* New York: Macmillan.

LeWarne, Charles P. (1975). *Utopias on Puget Sound, 1885-1915.* Seattle: University of Washington.

Lindley, James H. (1982). *This is Exceptional Foresters.* Shelton, WA: Exceptional Foresters.

Lindquist, Cecile (1991). *Model Rich and Revenue Poor.* Olympia: State of Washington Department of Social and Health Services.

Lippman, Leopold (1972). *Attitudes Toward the Handicapped.* Springfield, Ill.: Charles C. Thomas.

Lippman, Leopold (1976). "The public." Pp. 95-103 in Robert B. Kugel and Ann Shearer, eds. *Changing Patterns in Residential Services for the Mentally Retarded.* Washington, D.C.: President's Committee on Mental Retardation.

Magnuson, Anna (1985). Personal interview, Kirkland, Washington, August 12.

"Miss Goodhue bids farewell to school" (1929). *Seattle Educational Bulletin.* Volume 5, number 9. June.

Musso, Louis (1993). *'Less Children from the Unfit': Eugenic Sterilization in Washington State, 1909-1980.* M.A. thesis, Central Washington State University, 1993. Reviewed in *Seattle Times,* May 9, 1993

Nelson, Bryce E. (1981). *Good Schools: The Development of Public Schooling in Seattle, 1901-22.* Unpublished doctoral dissertation. Seattle: University of Washington.

The News. Newspaper published at Buckley, Washington; transcripts of articles on file at Rainier School in Buckley.

Niebuhr, Reinhold (1932). *Moral Man and Immoral Society.* New York: Scribner's.

Nirje, Bengt (1969). "A Scandinavian visitor looks at U. S. institutions." In Robert B. Kugel and Wolf Wolfensberger, eds., *Changing Patterns in Residential Services for the Mentally Retarded.* Washington, DC: President's Committee on Mental Retardation.

Noll, Steven & James W Trent, Jr, eds.(2004). *Mental Retardation in America. A Historical Reader.* New York: New York University Press.

Oakley, James A. (1935). Speech and correspondence, Seattle, Washington, 1935; in possession of The Arc of Washington, Olympia.

O'Connor, Harvey (1964). *Revolution in Seattle.* New York: Monthly Review.

Osborne, Harold F. (1955). "Regular schools are able to educate many handicapped children." *Seattle Times.* February 6.

Parker, Charles L. (1937). "State Custodial School." Pp. 158-63 in *Department of Finance, Budget, and Business, Biennial Report, 1934-36.* Olympia: State of Washington.

Parkinson, C. Northcote (1964). *Parkinson's Law.* New York: Ballantine.

Parsons, Talcott (1960). *Structure and Process in Modern*

Societies. New York: Free Press, 1960.

Pelka, Fred. (1975). *The ABC-CLIO Companion to the Disability Rights Movement.* Santa Barbara: ABC-CLIO.

Pierce (1935-36). *Minutes.* Children's Benevolent League, Pierce County Chapter, Tacoma, Washington; in possession of The Arc of Washington, Olympia.

President's Committee on Mental Retardation (1977). *MR 76. Mental Retardation: Past and Present.* Washington, D.C.: Government Printing Office.

Quigley, E. G. (1915). Letter of superintendent to the Seattle School Board, December 7. Seattle School District archives, Seattle, Washington.

Reilly, W. Newland (1941). "Suggestions for the Interim Committee, 1941-42." Spokane CBL: Spokane, Washington.

Reilly, W. Newland. (1941)."Let the Parent Live Again." *American Journal on Mental Deficiency* 46: 409-13.

Reilly, W. Newland (1945). *For the Happiness of Children. The Story of Children's Benevolent League of Washington.* Spokane, Washington.

Remmerde, Barbara (1966). *"Seattle's Epton Schools."* Unpublished bachelor of arts thesis. Seattle: University of Washington.

Rich, Chester L. (1921). *The Progress of Humane Legislation in Washington.* Doctoral dissertation. Seattle: University of Washington.

Robinson, June (1985). Personal correspondence, August 6.

Roos, Phillip (1978). "Parents of mentally retarded children—misunderstood and mistreated." Pp. 12-27 in Ann Turnbull and H. R. Turnbull, eds., *Parents Speak Out.* Columbus, OH: Merrill.

Rothman, David J. and Sheila M. Rothman (1984). *The Willowbrook Wars.* New York: Harper.

Sampson, Alan H. (1947). "Developing and maintaining good relations with parents of mentally deficient children." *American Journal of Mental Deficiency* 52: 187-94.

Sampson, Alan H. (1951). *Special Bulletin*, April 23. National Association of Parents and Friends of Mentally Retarded Children.

Sarason, Seymour B. and John Doris (1979*). Educational Handicap, Public Policy, and Social History.* New York: Free Press.

Scheerenberger, R. C. (1983). *A History of Mental Retardation.*

Baltimore: Brookes.

Schmidt, Sally Nowak (1970). *Out of the Shadows.* Cleveland: Council for the Retarded Child.

Schmidt, Sally Nowak (1976). *The Birth of the Ohio Association for Retarded Children.* Cleveland, Ohio: Council for the Retarded Child.

Schwartzenberg, Susan. (2005) *Becoming Citizens: Family Life and the Politics of Disability.* Seattle: University of Washington Press.

Scott, Naomi, K. Charlie Lakin, Sheryl A. Larson (2008). "The 40th Anniversary of Deinstitutionalization in the United States: Decreasing State Institutional Populations, 1967–2007." *Intellectual and Developmental Disabilities* 46: 402-05.

Seattle Times (1956). "Officials split on need for Fort Worden school for retarded." January 24.

"Seattle's Honored Mother" (1956). *Seattle Times*, May 6.

Segal, Robert M. (1970). *Mental Retardation and Social Action. A Study of the Associations for Retarded Children as a Force for Social Change.* Springfield, Illinois: Charles C. Thomas.

Shorter, Edward (2000). *The Kennedy Family and the History of Mental Retardation.* Philadelphia: Temple University Press.

Sills, David (1957). *The Volunteers.* Glencoe, IL: Free Press.

Simmel, Georg (1971). "The metropolis and the mental life." Pp. 324-39 in Donald Levine, ed., *George Simmel on Individuality and Social Forms.* Chicago: University of Chicago.

Sloan, William and Harvey A. Stevens (1976). *A Century of Concern.* Washington, D.C.: American Association on Mental Deficiency.

Smith, Stevenson (1912-21). *Miscellaneous correspondence.* Filed with the Charles R. Strother Papers, University of Washington Archives, Seattle.

Smith, Stevenson (1916). "Provision for feebleminded in Washington." *Addresses and Proceedings of the Thirtieth Annual Session.* Seattle: Washington Educational Association,.

Spokane Valley Herald (1954). "Mrs. Epton seeks post of state representative." June 8.

Stackhouse, Max L. (1966). "James Luther Adams: A biographical and intellectual sketch." Pp. 333-57 in D. B. Robertson, ed., *Voluntary Associations: A Study of Groups in Free Societies.* Richmond, VA: John Knox Press.

Stern, Edith M. (1942) *Mental Illness: A Guide for the Family.* New York: Commonwealth Fund.

Strayer, George D. (1946). *Public Education in Washington.* Olympia: State of Washington.

Strother, Charles.(1992) *Child Development and Mental Retardation Center.* Olympia: State of Washington, Department of Social and Health Services.

Subcommittee on Mental Retardation (1961). *Everybody's Child: The Mentally Retarded.* Olympia: State of Washington.

Swift, Helen (1937). *First Annual Report of Services to Crippled Children.* Washington Public Documents. Olympia: State of Washington.

Sykes, Gresham (1958). *The Society of Captives.* Princeton, N.J.: Princeton University Press.

Thomas, Joseph K. (1991) *Dedicated to Serving the Disabled.* Olympia: Washington State DSHS.

Thomas, Orlando (1986). Interview, Seattle, Washington, July 21.

Thompson, Lorelei and Larry A. Jones (1980), eds. *How to Make the Law and Justice System Work for the Retarded Citizens of Washington State.* Olympia: Washington Association for Retarded Citizens.

Thomson, Mildred (1963). *Prologue.* Minneapolis: Gilbert Publishing.

Trent, James W. (1994). *Inventing the Feeble Mind. A History of Mental Retardation in the United States.* Berkeley: University of California Press.

Tri-City Herald (1959). "Handicapped children may get assist in state bill." February 2, 1959. Newspaper published in Pasco,Washington.

Turnbull, Ann P. and H. Rutherford Turnbull, III (1982). "Parent involvement in the education of handicapped children: A critique." *Mental Retardation* 20: 115ff.

Walsted, Mary B. (1917). "Should diagnosis determine school training?" *Addresses and Proceedings of the Thirty-First Annual Session.* Seattle: Washington Educational Association.

Wanamaker, Pearl A. (1944). *Thirty-seventh Biennial Report of the Superintendent of Public Instruction.* Olympia: State of Washington.

Wanamaker, Pearl A. (1948). *Thirty-eighth Biennial Report of the Superintendent of Public Instruction.* Olympia: State of Washington.

Washington State Dept of Social and Health Services (1991), *Alan Hungate Sampson: Association for Retarded Children,* Olympia, 1991.

Weber, Max (1947). *The Theory of Social and Economic Organization.* New York: Free Press.

Weingold, Joseph (1985). Personal correspondence, New York, N.Y., August 7.

Williams, Mae F. (1943). "Together again," quoted by Lillian Hill, "News letter of the Pacific Coast Region, AAMD." *American Journal of Mental Deficiency.* 48:122.

Wolfensberger, Wolf (1972). *The Principle of Normalization in Human Services.* Toronto: National Institute of Mental Retardation.

Wolfensberger, Wolf (1973). *The Third Stage in the Evolution of Voluntary Associations for the Mentally Retarded.* Toronto, Canada: National Institute on Mental Retardation.

Wolfensberger, Wolf (1976). "The Origin and Nature of Our Institutional Models." Pp. 35-82 in Robert B. Kugel and Ann Shearer, eds. *Changing Patterns in Residential Services for the Mentally Retarded.* Revised edition. Washington, D.C.: President's Committee on Mental Retardation.

Wolfensberger, Wolf (1983). "Social role valorization." *Mental Retardation* 21: 234-39.

Wooden, Harley Z. (1980). "Founding of the Council." *Exceptional Children.* 47: 47-55.

Woodruff, Samuel C. (1910). Superintendent's Report on the State Institution for the Feeble-Minded. *Twentieth Biennial Report of the Superintendent of Public Instruction.* Olympia, Washington.

Woodruff, Samuel C. (1914). Superintendent's Report on the State Institution for the Feeble-Minded. *Twenty-second Biennial Report of the Superintendent of Public Instruction.* Olympia: State of Washington.

INDEX

322

On-the-Job Training Project, 181

Oregon, 7, 10, 50, 228, 246, 256, 306

P.L. 94-142, 125, 167, 233, 234, 235

PARC v. Pennsylvania, 166

parent pay, 139, 140, 141, 142, 143, 144, 169

Parent to Parent, 43, 226, 267

Parker, Charles, 8, 9

Parkland Lutheran Children's Home, 182

Pasco, 183, 305, 320

Pearl Harbor, 43, 47

Pennhurst State School & Hospital v. Halderman, 306

Pennsylvania, 89, 166, 216, 220, 301

Penry v. Lynaugh, 249

People First, 7, 230, 239, 246, 252, 271, 310

Percival, Monty, 9, 11

Perske, Bob, 235

phenylketonuria (PKU),, 196

Pierce county, 10, 27, 41, 109

Pierce, Narda, 254

Plymouth Congregational Church, 232

Port Angeles, 134, 186, 276, 278

Potter, Linda, 217, 220

pre-school, 90, 102, 116, 122, 155, 163, 166, 167, 218, 247

President's Committee on Mental Retardation, 232

prevention, 55, 88, 129, 133, 172, 174, 191, 192, 195, 241, 309

Program Analysis of Service Systems, 214

Program Options, 238, 239, 241

PTA, 18, 57, 66, 72, 73, 103, 114, 115, 141, 160

Purple Cross, 10, 114

Rainier, 252

Rainier State School, viii, 17, 61, 112, 126, 127, 129, 132, 157, 216, 252, 278, 297, 304

Rap House, 231

Ray, Dixy Lee, Gov., 190

Reagan, Ronald, 4, 269

recreational programs, 146, 198

Red Cross, 10, 27, 283, 312

Referendum 15, 137, 138

Referendum 29, 180

Referendum 37, 202

regional centers, 146

Reilly, Newland, 7, 23, 40, 42, 43, 45, 49, 52, 54, 102, 128, 130, 172, 201, 276, 281, 284, 285, 286, 287, 288

Reilly, Phil, 59, 61, 87

religious education, 198

Renton, 109, 224

Republican, 15, 54, 57, 144, 175, 311

Research Trust Fund, 192, 193, 241, 266, 303

Reser, Yancy, 118

Residential Habilitation Centers, 250

307, 315, 316, 317, 318, 319

Value Village, 244

Vancouver, 50, 109, 112, 115, 148, 231, 276, 278, 279, 313

Vineland, 24, 77, 94, 139, 193, 282, 297

Vocational Rehabilitation, 110, 176, 177, 178, 180, 181, 182, 186, 234, 313

Voorhees, Donald, 219

Walker, George, 253

Walla Walla, 13, 14, 62, 109, 158, 230, 276, 278

Wallgren, Mon, Gov., 48

Wanamaker, Pearl, 91, 158

WARC v. Thomas, 216, 220, 252, 310

WARC Walk-a-thon, 118

Washington Association of Prosecuting Attorneys, 231, 249

Washington Association of Sheriffs and Chiefs of Police, 231

Washington Educational Association, 29, 152, 283, 319, 320

Washington Protection and Advocacy, 252

Washington Spastic Children's Society, 115

Washington State Association of Group Homes, 217

Washington State Catholic Conference, 249

Washington Voters for Disability Issues, 248

Wastradowski, Frank, 189

Watkins, Harold, 76, 97

Weicker, Lowell, Sen., 235

Weingold, Joseph, viii

Wenatchee, 13, 15, 109, 114, 131, 158, 278

Western Washington State University, 199

Weyerhaeuser, George, 120

Whatcom, 195

Wilcox, Mary Jo, 245

Wilkins, Patricia, 120, 188

Will, Madeleine, 228

Williams, Mae, 9, 41

Willowbrook, 65

Winter, Boyd, 186

Wise, Mae, 99

Wolfensberger, Wolf, 12

Woodruff, Samuel C., supt., 150

Working Age Adult Policy, 257

Works Progress Administration, 281

Wyatt v. Stickney, 215

Yakima, 13, 109, 112, 123, 131, 132, 137, 160, 224, 229, 276, 278, 279, 281, 308, 315

Yakima Valley School, 132

Yepsen, Lloyd, 72

YMCA, 6

330